Hearts of Pine

HEARTS OF PINE

Songs in the Lives of Three Korean Survivors of the Japanese "Comfort Women"

Joshua D. Pilzer

OXFORD
UNIVERSITY PRESS

OXFORD
UNIVERSITY PRESS

Oxford University Press, Inc., publishes works that further
Oxford University's objective of excellence
in research, scholarship, and education.

Oxford   New York
Auckland   Cape Town   Dar es Salaam   Hong Kong   Karachi
Kuala Lumpur   Madrid   Melbourne   Mexico City   Nairobi
New Delhi   Shanghai   Taipei   Toronto

With offices in
Argentina   Austria   Brazil   Chile   Czech Republic   France   Greece
Guatemala   Hungary   Italy   Japan   Poland   Portugal   Singapore
South Korea   Switzerland   Thailand   Turkey   Ukraine   Vietnam

Copyright © 2012 by Oxford University Press

Published by Oxford University Press, Inc.
198 Madison Avenue, New York, New York 10016
www.oup.com

Oxford is a registered trademark of Oxford University Press

Library of Congress Cataloging-in-Publication Data
Pilzer, Joshua D.
    Hearts of pine : songs in the lives of three Korean survivors of the
Japanese "comfort women" / Joshua D. Pilzer.
        p. cm.
    Includes bibliographical references and index.
    ISBN 978-0-19-975956-9 (hardback) – ISBN 978-0-19-975957-6 (pbk.)
1. Songs, Korean–History and criticism. 2. Women singers–Korea.
3. Music–Social aspects–Korea. 4. Comfort women–Japan–History.
5. Comfort women–Korea–History. I. Title.
    ML3752.P55 2011
    782.42082'09519–dc22   2010050682

Publication of this book was supported by the AMS 75 PAYS Publication
Endowment Fund of the American Musicological Society.

1 3 5 7 9 8 6 4 2

Printed in the United States of America on acid-free paper

For the survivors of the Japanese military "comfort women,"
and for all other victims of sexual slavery and violence

CONTENTS

PREFACE

I began the research for this book in 2001 as my dissertation project in ethnomusicology, the study of the social and cultural life of music. I felt like an odd sort of person to write a dissertation about song in the lives of elderly Korean female survivors of the "comfort women," the organized system of sexual slavery that the Japanese military implemented during the Asia-Pacific War (1930–45). I was a relatively young, white man from the United States, studying at an elite American university. I seemed tailor-made to the worst possible subject position from which to take on the project, radically separated from these elderly Korean women survivors of sexual violence and war by gender, generation, culture, class, and experience. At the outset, with the possible exception of my love of Korean singing and the repertoire of Korean folk songs I knew through time I had spent in South Korea during my master's study, I could not think of a single reason why I was well suited for this project. Thinking such thoughts, after writing one essay on the subject I put the idea aside and wrote a dissertation proposal about something else.

But when I went to South Korea in the summer of 2002 to begin my doctoral research, I visited a small group of survivors, hoping that the project would somehow seem possible. I was surprised by the warmth with which many of them received me and the interest they showed in the project. I was also overwhelmed by the diversity of their personalities and singing styles. I took stock of my subject position and gave myself over to the project. This book tells something of the story of what happened after that: my eight years of intermittent fieldwork with the survivors of Japanese military sexual slavery, beginning with one year in 2002–3, three months in the fall of 2003, two months in 2004, and other trips of varying length since then, until the present.

Spending time with the women, I learned how they had carved out unique identities in the course of their lives, which were to varying degrees lives of song. I also learned how these identities had become overshadowed by the image of a generic, archetypal elderly victim of the "comfort women" system in South Korean public culture.[1] And I learned about how, as the "comfort women" become part of Korean national history, many in the South Korean public sphere have framed the women's experiences as national experiences to which all Koreans can relate, or (more rarely) as essentially female experiences which all women can understand. Dominick LaCapra, a literary scholar of the Holocaust, calls this the process by which empathy becomes identity (1999: 699).[2]

Traumatic experiences are by their very nature inscrutable even to those who suffer them, unless they are made sensible through long processes of reckoning. So to even begin to understand *someone else's* traumatic experience, and to understand that person, one must listen very carefully to her and become acquainted with the unfolding of traumatic experiences and the ways that she has come to understand them. When people prematurely claim to identify with or understand the survivors of the "comfort women" and their experiences, what they typically get are new versions of what they think they already know. In such cases the particularities of women's identities and experiences are easily eclipsed by prepared modes of understanding. Points of identification can of course be an advantage, allowing for special kinds of empathy, sharing, and intimacy that further understanding of people and their experiences, but these hazards need to be borne in mind.

In my case there were few points of identification through which I could lay claim to any aspect of the women's experience. Because of this, I began to feel that I had certain advantages as a researcher, in addition to my numerous limitations. The many differences and disjunctures of experience which separated us were compulsions for me to *listen*—to what the women were saying and singing, to how they were saying and singing it, to the sound of their voices, and to things that they listened to. My interest in music, of course, provided me with another such imperative to listen.

From such a perspective, the women were, and are, my teachers—of song, life, and experience. They have shown me, as a musician, something about the fundamental social power of music. They have taught me, as a man, something about women's experiences of sexual violence, which are so persistent in our modern world. They have shown me, as a Westerner, something of the traumatic aspects of East Asian modernity and something of the workings and consequences of imperialism. And they have taught me, as an economically privileged and relatively young person, something about hardship and the experience of aging. After eight years I am still at the beginning of these processes of learning, and regarding some of these subjects I suspect I always will be. I am aware of the nature of the disjunctures of experience that separate me from the different survivors, and of the boundaries of our relationships, the special intimacies and understandings that we share and those that we do not.

This book is stubbornly, agonistically, and happily based in these complicated and unequal human relationships. The relationship between researcher and subject is neither an inconvenience to be minimized nor something to fetishize and celebrate. Rather it is a very fraught and very hopeful thing. Fieldworkers struggle to understand and overcome the disparities of power inherent in this relationship not only out of ethical obligation, but also because such effort is the very condition of scholarly understanding.

This struggle features in the prose that follows. As part of it I have tried different ways of collaborating with the women themselves and others in Korean society to determine the project's direction and outcomes. We listened together to the recordings I made and discussed them, and I chose survivors' favorite songs and recordings to focus on in the book and to post on the book's website.[3] I made numerous choices about language, organization, and other aspects of form and content based on different women's preferences. For instance, I use the phrase "comfort woman" because the majority of Korean survivors are averse to being described by the more descriptive "sexual slave," which has become the generally preferred expression in contemporary English-language activist circles, although many survivors acknowledge the descriptiveness of the latter phrase, as do I.

The book does not spend much time on the intimate details of these women's experiences of sexual violence during the war, which many other books describe.[4] I do discuss some songs from the women's period of wartime captivity, but in the main I focus on pieces that the women cherished and sang often during the times we spent together, most of which were from other periods in the women's lives. Rather than focusing on the war, I wanted to study another, neglected aspect of the women's lives: their ongoing postwar work of survival, self-making, and performances of selfhood and sociality in song. I wanted to focus on the women as people—and singers—for whom the wartime experience of sexual slavery is but one aspect, however important, of their rich and complex lives.

As such the book is focused on the present. It is at times quite critical of the South Korean public-cultural framing of the survivors of Japanese military sexual slavery. These are not criticisms of the South Korean social movement on behalf of the women, which I support wholeheartedly, but efforts to understand the broader social context in which it has to operate.

In the interest of maintaining a focus on the three women and their expressive lives, I have also chosen not to make this a book of extended explorations of issues in the social sciences and the social study of music that bear upon the work. The book is about how people use song to "make do" (de Certeau 1988: xv), getting by in the course of everyday life, and as such is indebted to the domain of scholarship known as "practice theory," especially the work of Michel de Certeau (1988), Pierre Bourdieu (1977), and Tia DeNora (2000). It is about music's part in the shaping of human subjects in social environments, and hence is inspired by Louis Althusser's (1971) concept of interpellation, Judith Butler's work on gender, subjectivity, and subjection (1990, 1997), and other theories of subject formation and socialization. It is about how marginalized people use the opacities and the special expressive power of song to maneuver between public and private, and is in this way indebted to studies of expressive opacity (Quine 1960), studies of cultural intimacy and the public sphere (Herzfeld 1997; Berlant 2000; Warner 2005; Stokes 2010), and the investigation of "public secrecy" (Taussig 1999). It is a study of music and traumatic recovery, and draws on work in trauma studies, especially the remarkable work of Judith Herman (1992). But rather than delve into any of these issues at length in the abstract, I have tried to assimilate these ideas to a narrative about the women, whose voices and artistic achievements remain in the foreground. Likewise although the three chapters about particular survivors are based on different methods of analyzing music as a social and cultural phenomenon, I avoid extended discussions of Korean music in the abstract, and I have avoided musical transcriptions, preferring to direct readers' attention to the audio recordings of the women singing on the book's website. I have also limited these things in order to make the book more readable for people who are not music specialists, social scientists, or area specialists of Korea or East Asia. I will publish a number of focused theoretical essays in the years following the publication of this book.

But although I have limited abstract discussions, as the three women at the center of this book tell us about their songs, their lives, and themselves, they guide us toward discoveries about key issues in the study of music, social life, women's experiences, and East Asian modernity. They lead us, ultimately, to speculative terrains in which we attempt to understand the social life of music, processes of trauma and recovery, the relations between the sexes, and other facets of human life.

In a nutshell, the book replicates the fraught process of discovery, conversation, and transformation inherent in carefully listening to others. I believe that such practices of listening could not be more important today, amid the ceaseless shouting that characterizes so much of our present world. As a work about three women, their social worlds, and their singing, the book tells only the stories that they tell—and only some of those. It is not meant as a definitive statement on the musical lives of three individuals, but an exploration of song in the life of three women who are at times more and less (but never entirely) distinct from the various social formations that have shaped them and which they shape in their turn. Likewise, although it is largely concerned with a fractious and changeable community of survivors, it is not representative of that community, nor is it representative of the songs of the survivors of the "comfort women" system as a whole. There are countless other stories left to be discovered in the lives of the survivors—as singers, workers, cooks, craftswomen, family members, dancers, painters, philosophers and storytellers. Furthermore although the book provides a kind of introduction to the "comfort women" issue, it is not a comprehensive one by any means. For those interested in learning more about the "comfort women" system and its aftermath in the English language there are plentiful options in print.[5]

Even as an intentionally limited project of listening to a small number of people, the book is only a flawed beginning. It has already been criticized for being too intellectual and not intellectual enough. It has been reasonably criticized for long interpretive passages in which the women's voices seem to be replaced by my interpreting voice, and in multiple revisions I have done my utmost to change that. This has been particularly difficult in some cases; for instance, Pak Duri's hearing loss stopped her singing in 2002, and I had to reconstruct her artistry out of a rather limited amount of songs and conversations that I and other people had previously recorded. In such cases I made interpretive choices guided by my relationships with the women, our conversations, our shared experiences, and the advice of others who knew these women well.

All the same, in the course of its explorations this book is highly prone to problems of gendered, ethnic, and generational translation and to the general difficulties of writing about other people and about music. I bear all the responsibility for its flaws. I conducted all the fieldwork for the book, in Korean and Japanese. I transcribed all of the Korean and Japanese songs and conversations, with the exception of one song, transcribed by my friend Kim Dong-Won, and a few taken from documentary film transcripts. I translated all the songs and conversations.

There are a great many people without whose inspiration, input, assistance, friendship, and guidance this book would never have come to be. Most of all I thank the survivors whom I worked with for their interest, patience, kindness, and friendship. I am grateful for the many lessons they taught me about song and about being a person and a man. I thank them for helping me develop the ideas in this book and commenting on them as they took shape. I owe a special debt to Bae Chunhui, Mun Pilgi, and Pak Duri. Many thanks also to Pak Ongnyeon, Yi Yongsu, Kim Sundeok, Kim Gunja, Yi Okseon, Pak Okseon, Ji Dor-i, Kang Ilchul,

Yi Okkeum, Han Dosun, Kim Bunseon, Kim Sun-ak, Kim Sun-ok, Shim Dal-yeon, Jin Hwasun, and Yi Yongnyeo. For all the food, clothes, *jeong* (affection), cigarettes, alcohol, strength, and support you have given me, and for all the wisdom with which you have guided me, I thank you.

I am deeply grateful to the staff of the House of Sharing, the rest home where I conducted most of the fieldwork for the book (www.nanum.org). Ahn Shinkweon, Kim Jeongsuk, the nuns Neunggwang and Seungyeon, and the rest of the staff supported me in innumerable ways over the years in which this book was conceived, researched, and written. Numerous friends whom I made at the House have given valuable support, in particular Namba Koji, Byeon Sangcheol, Kim Eungyeong, and Yajima Tsukasa, who contributed many of his beautiful photographs to the book. I am also grateful to Choi Sang-il, Yi Bohyeong, Izumo Masashi, Kuroda Haruyuki, Kumito Fujiko, Kim Seong-nae, Kim Dong-Won, Roald Maliangkay, and a great many other scholars in Korea, Japan, and elsewhere who encouraged, inspired, and advised me in my work.

I would also like to express my gratitude to, respect for, and solidarity with Director Yun Mee-hyang and the other staff of the Korean Council for the Women Drafted for Military Sexual Slavery by Japan (www. womenandwar.net). In their concern for the women and tireless work on their behalf they have been inspirations to me. Their support made this book possible, and their criticisms have helped it beyond measure. As readers will find out in the coming pages, the Korean Council holds a demonstration on behalf of the women in front of the Japanese Embassy in Seoul every Wednesday at noon, and they welcome interested people to join them.[6]

I owe a lasting debt to each of the members of my dissertation committee for the advice, expertise, and imagination they contributed to this project: Martin Stokes, Philip Bohlman, Bruce Cumings, Martha Feldman, and Norma Field. I would like to thank Martin, my doctoral advisor, for giving me such an inspiring model of an honorable, compassionate, vigorous intellectual and human being. I owe similar thanks to Berthold Hoeckner. I am particularly grateful to the staff, faculty, and fellows of the University of Chicago Center for Gender Studies for believing in and encouraging this work. I would never have found my way to this project had I not been a part of a remarkable interdisciplinary atmosphere at the University of Chicago, and I am grateful to my many friends and colleagues who made those years what they were. Equally important were the inspiration and guidance of Byongwon Lee, Peter Manicas, Ricardo Trimillos, and Viren Murthy during my master's study at the University of Hawai'i and afterward, and Mark Levensky during my bachelor's study at the Evergreen State College. I would also like to thank my friends and colleagues from the University of

Hawai'i, the University of California, Santa Barbara, Columbia University, and the University of Toronto for all of their advice and encouragement. Students in my "Survivors' Music" seminars at UC Santa Barbara and Columbia University and in my "Sound, Music, and Everyday Life" seminar at the University of Toronto gave me valuable criticisms and suggestions for rewriting. I am thankful to the Mellon Foundation, the Korea Foundation, Fulbright IIE, the Korean-American Educational Commission, the University of Chicago Music Department, and the University of Chicago Center for Gender Studies for the scholarships and fellowships that supported this work, and to the University of Toronto Faculty of Music for allowing me to finish my postdoctoral award at Columbia University, during which I finished a draft of this book. In the last stages of the publication process Martha Feldman, Andrew Killick, Nathan Hesselink, Suzanne Ryan, Yoonhee Lee, and Judith Hoover have provided detailed and critical readings of this draft, and I am much obliged to them.

I also thank my family: Ethan, Jay, Bernice, Betty, Zeb, Simon, Woody, Yoji, Tomoko, Thomas, Hiroshi, Yoko, my nieces- and nephews-in-law, and my dear uncle Colin and aunt Robin for all of the patience, support, booze, advice, music, food, inspiration, encouragement, and love without which this book would never have come to be. Lastly, my wife, Yukiko Amano, inspired and challenged me to write this book, and she is present, in different ways, in all of its best moments.

A NOTE ON TRANSLITERATION

Although I have tried to use English expressions wherever possible for ease of reading, I have used transliterations, mainly of Korean and Japanese, where necessary. I use the system for transliterating Korean called the Revised Romanization of Korean, currently used by the South Korean government. The system has limitations, and conventionally academics use a different one, but I have chosen this one because non-Korean speakers, on journeying to Korea or visiting Korean English-language websites, will typically find place-names, people's names, and other words romanized as they are here in this book. I use "Pak" instead of "Bak" (which would be accurate under the Revised Romanization system) because it is a more familiar romanization of this common Korean family name, most commonly romanized as "Park." Personal names of authors and artists are written using the romanizations they conventionally use themselves. I transliterate Japanese using the Hepburn System. None of these systems is perfect; I encourage you to use the audio pronunciation guide for key terms on the book's website, and to listen to the recordings of songs on the website as you read the romanized song texts in the notes section of this book, which are also available on the website.

ABOUT THE COMPANION WEBSITE

www.oup.com/us/heartsofpine

Oxford University Press maintains a website of audio-visual materials for this book. The website has three main parts. First is a collection of audio recordings of the women who feature in this book. Second, there is a pronunciation guide for the women's names and for Korean and Japanese terms that appear often throughout the text. Finally, some of the photographs in the book were originally in color, but they are reproduced here in black-and-white; so the website includes a gallery of these photographs so that the reader may experience them in color.

This is a book about listening—to singing, to people's voices, and to what they have to say. It is not a book, therefore, that is composed solely of text, but one of which the audio recordings are an indispensible part, and a book which is meant to be read *and* listened to. Please listen to the sound recordings on the companion website as you read. The main text features translations of lyrics, and the notes at the end of the book included romanizations of song texts, which allow readers to follow along in real time.

Recorded examples available on the website are marked throughout the text with the symbol ◐.

Hearts of Pine

Introduction

On a warm, moonlit night in the summer of 2008 Mun Pilgi and I are sitting together in the courtyard of the rest home called the House of Sharing (Nanum ui jip).[1] The House lies around one hour southeast of Seoul, at the back of a valley that faces the Gyeongancheon, one of the Han River's many tributaries. From the courtyard we can see the surrounding rice paddies and fields, the earth-mound tombs dotting the hillsides of the valley, and a handful of its many homes. There are some traditional commoners' houses left over from the old village, made from mud and thatch and covered over with blue tin roofs. And there are new suburban houses, a riot of middle-class fantasies—contemporary cottages, slick neo-Victorians, even a log cabin—which are replacing the fields one by one with their own splendors. The frogs that live in the standing water of the remaining rice paddies are not singing, but a common cuckoo echoes ceaselessly down the valley.

We are talking about food. Mun Pilgi, who is eighty years old, begins to tell me about things she used to eat when she was little.

"There were times when I was young when my family was very poor, you know? We had such a big family and times were so hard. So there were times we couldn't afford rice or grain. So my father and I went to the mountain, and he cut down a pine tree. And he split it open and we scraped out the insides [the inner bark], and we mashed them and ate them instead of rice."

"How did you prepare it?"

"We'd boil it, and eat it just like that. . . . God, how we suffered," she answers, scrunching up her face. But her eyes shine. "But you know . . . it was *so* delicious."

Kung, kung.

We are in her apartment. She is talking about quiet, and loneliness, and about her radio-cassette player. "Don't you like the quiet?" I ask, stupidly.

> No, I don't like it.
> It's that I'm so lonely,
> so I turn on the TV, or turn on the radio,
> *kung, kung, kung . . .*
> Because I'm so lonely,
> I turn on the TV, or turn on the radio,
> *kung-jjak, kung-jjak . . .*
> That's how I live.
> Because I'm lonely. I'm bored, you know.[2] 1

Mun Pilgi raps out the basic pulse of a Korean pop ballad, and elaborates it, and thus tells the story of a progression, in her everyday life, from a fraught quiet to a space of music.

The basic pulse of a song is a sound produced by human action, a human ascription of rhythm and order to the sounds of life and the silences in between. It is a time scheme, and may have any number of relations to the world of time-keeping devices that organize social worlds: clocks and abstract time, the relatively even rhythms of walking, work, machines, radio, and television broadcasts. The pulse of song is also often compared to a heartbeat, one of the ways that songs and music can remind us of ourselves[3] or others, or of the bonds between us. "A song is like a person," Mun Pilgi tells me, "like a friend." She leaves the TV or the radio on when she sleeps.

As *kung, kung* becomes *kung-jjak kung-jjak,* a song takes shape, a song from the Korean pop genre *teuroteu*. Devotees of the genre use these rhythmic vocables to accompany each others' singing, and these onomato-poeias often feature in song texts as well. Which song this will be is as yet undetermined, because we stand on the threshold of song, on the threshold of Mun Pilgi's world of song. It is a world that she has assembled from available cultural objects to suit herself, as a forum in which she can fashion and sustain herself and her social world. In song she joins with others—the others in the songs, others out there listening and watching by themselves or in groups, and her fellow fans and friends with whom she sings socially. Mun Pilgi and her father had prized sustenance from a pine tree; now, through an ongoing process of listening, imagining, and singing, she forges a self, friends, and a social world from the noise of her life and the quiet of her room.

Pak Duri,[4] seventy-eight years old, is sitting in the living room of the House of Sharing, surrounded by half-liter bottles of beer and friends from across Korea and Japan who have come to visit her and the other women living at the rest home. We are at a song party, a common event at the House and elsewhere throughout the Korean peninsula. Everyone is sitting in a circle and singing in turn.

When inspiration strikes, Pak Duri doesn't wait her turn, but begins to sing suddenly, as is her custom. She sings her first song of the night in a genre of improvisatory folk singing borrowing from central Korean melodies, in her half-sung, half-declaimed, emphatic style:

> The paulownia tree's nuts are bum-bumpy . . .
> The young woman's milk jugs are plum-plumpy![5] 2

She explodes with laughter at this somewhat bawdy celebration of the female body in its fullness and fertility. She laughs too at the audaciousness of singing this song before all these people, and most of the Korean speakers laugh as well. The uncomprehending foreign guests laugh despite not knowing the meaning of the words, feeding off of her infectious exuberance and joy. A second wave of laughter spreads across the room as interpreters explain the lyrics in Japanese.

At Pak Duri's side, Kim Sundeok, her "big sister" at the rest home, is trying her best, through a wry smile, to give her a disapproving look. She laughs, stifles her laughter, and laughs again.

Pak Duri ignores her big sister's look of mild censure. She has found her space of song, where taboos relax and intimate things are faced frankly. In many other spheres of her life, such directness about sex is not possible. During the Asia-Pacific War she, like Mun Pilgi, had been made an object for the purpose of sex, but now she deals masterfully with the subject of sex and with the human body. She has made them her own over many decades of struggle and serious play.

Pak Duri continues, striking a more somber note in the wake of her outrageous first verse:

> You're that kind of cruel-hearted man—
> Getting mixed up with you was my mistake.
> Things being as they were
> I certainly knew you'd throw me away.
> But knowing, or not knowing, I'd have been fooled just the same.[6]

Singing this wistful rumination Pak Duri laughs—at the cruelty of men and at a woman's foolishness—with both gravity and a hard-won lightness of heart. The others join in her laughter, some comprehending and commiserating, some just feeding on her energy and her delight.

In a sense, laughter and its togetherness are a life raft on a sea of hardship and sorrow. As Pak Duri sings the laughter swells, until it becomes a place in which to stand, to live, and to sing again.

It is the early summer of 2010, and I am going back to the House of Sharing after a year. I walk into the living room, where Bae Chunhui, having heard of my arrival from the House staff several weeks before, is sitting by herself, watching television and waiting.

She asks a few basic questions about my last year. Then quickly, as is her custom, she shifts the conversation to music. She has been channel surfing, and has found among the fifty-odd channels a broadcast of a recent Seoul concert of the Irish and Norwegian new instrumental music duo Secret Garden. They are playing "Lotus," a piece inspired by East Asian music. Bae Chunhui praises the music and lingers in its swooping glissandos and pentatonic feel, which are references to Chinese music. The melody, she says, raises a scene before her eyes of a distant inner Asian plain. "I can see it, like it's right in front of my eyes," she tells me. These remind her of other, much older songs she knows from Japanese-occupied Shanghai and elsewhere that make such references to China.

Her ears catch a fragment of melody that reminds her of yet another song: "This melody, you know, uses a scale similar to that one, you know. 'Scarborough.'" She begins talking about Simon and Garfunkel's version of the English ballad "Scarborough Fair." She tells me about hearing the song when she saw *The Graduate* while she was living in Japan after the war. She begins to sing a Korean version, which the folk duet Ddua e Mua (Toi et moi) sang on an album in 1970 as "Memories of Scarborough" ("Seukabeuro ui chueok").[8]

> Scarborough, in my treasured memory
> When shall I meet you again?
> The place where my love resides,
> My beautiful hometown.[9] 🔊 3

We sit together comparing the English and Korean texts. Both reminisce about a lost love, but in the Korean version Scarborough becomes the singer's longed-for hometown (*gohyang*), an omnipresent trope of midcentury South Korean popular music.

Bae Chunhui turns back to the scene that rises before her eyes as she listens to "Lotus"—the wide, alpine plain—and a bird flies into the picture.

She recalls another song, also made world-famous by Simon and Garfunkel, which this scene reminds her of: "El Cóndor Pasa" (The condor passes). The same Korean folk duo had released a Korean version, "Like a Flying Bird" ("Nareuneun sae cheoreom"), in the year following their "Memories of Scarborough." But Bae Chunhui sings the song with me in English, although this is not one of the many languages she speaks. In her mind's eye, she tells me, the condor ranges wide, majestic, and free over a high mountain valley.

Bae Chunhui also floats through the world, gathering its wonder together in associative chains of song and story. She stores that wonder in her memory, filled with thousands of songs that she has picked up over the course of a life of wandering and hardship. She unpacks these songs when the opportunity arises. Today she has brought out two songs to greet me, the returning American; on other occasions I have heard her do this for visitors from across Asia, the Middle East, Africa, Europe, and elsewhere. She encounters the world and answers with song. In so doing she harmonizes her tastes and experiences with those of others and brings people together in singular combinations. And she extracts from her life experience a soundtrack that demonstrates the promise of the world.

Inside hard and bitter things and experiences there is nourishment and warmth—heartbeats, joy, contentment, and quiet. And in those small nooks there may yet again be darkness, which may contain yet other, smaller places of sustenance, and so on, and so on, cavernous things living in tiny spaces. For many this splitting and finding is the very work of survival, and that very same work, with all of its twists, turns, and contradictions, is one of the origins of music. Music is one part of a larger process by which people and societies make sense of the world, create and express themselves, and feel connected to others. It can be a particularly useful tool for people who have been hurt, who have had themselves or their social relationships damaged or destroyed.

Many people cannot speak or write of things that happen to them, because states, societies, families, or friends will reject, condemn, or harm them if they do, or because their traumatic memories are too terrifying or too elusive to approach in language alone. The women featured in this book were among the 50,000 to 200,000 girls and women from across Asia and the Pacific who were tricked, coerced, or abducted by the Japanese military and affiliated private business into sexual slavery during the Asia-Pacific War (1930–45).[10] The Japanese military euphemistically called them "comfort women" (*ianfu*) and called the places where they were imprisoned and made to have sex with soldiers and affiliated civilians "comfort stations."

The experiences of the girls and young women varied, as the system of "comfort women" existed at every rank of the military: some were private sexual slaves of officers; others lived in tiny rooms and were forced to serve many soldiers a day, in some cases more than fifty. They sustained physical and psychological traumas of different kinds and degrees of intensity. A large percentage of these sexual slaves, of whom many were Korean, were killed by warfare, ill health, and mass execution. Many committed suicide. Of those who did survive the war, many were unable to return to their home country.

The Korean survivors who managed to return to South Korea feared to reveal their secrets for many, many years and did not come forward to speak publicly about their experiences. For the most part, therefore, they lived in isolation from one another. They were afraid to disclose their past for fear of being disowned or further ostracized; and they feared to speak because during the long decades of postwar South Korean authoritarianism, governments discouraged people from critically reexamining the era of the Japanese colonial domination of Korea (1910–45). The various regimes were afraid such frank appraisals would remind the public that many contemporary politicians, military personnel, and businessmen had participated in Japanese imperial domination and profiteering in colonial Korea. They were also concerned that critical thinking about the colonial era would inevitably draw attention to similar acts of exploitation, atrocity, and other violations of human rights perpetrated by postwar South Korean military governments, the occupying U.S. military, and the postwar sex industry.

In this atmosphere the survivors of Japanese military sexual slavery sang, like so many others in our sorrowful modern world who are afraid or reluctant to speak. Why might this be?

The women in this book sang not because doing so gave them more direct access to "authentic" emotions and selves, but because singing opened up a space in which they could confront taboo subjects, cull resources for living from the world around them, and craft a sense of self and of the world. In short the women sang because it was an activity that allowed them to become themselves, in the deepest sense. But why did song make all these things possible?

Like writing and speaking, songs and singing are, for the most part, performances for others. They are usually public in some respect, but at the same time they are capable of being very intimate. One reason for this is the seemingly paradoxical way that songs can be both precise and unclear at the same time; for instance, they can be exceedingly clear about content but vague about authorship, or vice versa. A song can be commonly held to express the essence of something, such as love, but not be specific about who loves whom. What such a song expresses most clearly is the feeling and the social relation of love (or any other relationship) and the abstract subject positions associated with it (the lover and the loved, or whatever applies in a given cultural scenario). A song also allows people to slot themselves into these positions at will and modify them. People are changed as they adopt these social roles; they learn how to love, or how to be a friend, a citizen, a parent, or a woman or a man.

However, people can also distance themselves from the subject positions of song. It is often unclear who wrote a folk song; conversely the author or original singer of a popular song is often well-known. In either case, as the women in this book sang folk and popular songs, they had a way of disclaiming responsibility for a song's content by attributing it to the ether of folk tradition or to a particular songwriter. There is an opacity in the relationship between the singer and the song, which serves as an exit strategy when one feels the need to distance oneself from it. This was so even for survivors who composed texts themselves, who could still claim to be singing about someone else even when they sang "I." There is a deep and pervasive opacity as to what songs refer to, an "opacity of reference" (Quine 1960: 141–45),[11] which survivors have made use of as they have needed or wanted to. In song they could forget, remember, express their experiences, and form identities and solidarities without giving themselves away.

For these same reasons song allowed survivors to wrestle with aspects of their experiences that others assumed to be "unspeakable," a fraught concept that often represses more than it explains.[12] They could sing about taboo feelings and experiences without fear of reprisal, and they could sing of those aspects of experience that others didn't understand, or didn't want to understand, and would therefore call unspeakable or ineffable. And, yes, they could sing beyond the margins of language and understanding, where things lay that actually deserve those names.

The women sang to survive, to contain or to keep memories alive, and to rebuild themselves and their social relationships in the wake of what had happened. They sang for themselves, but also for others, and in their public performances they were protected from full disclosure by the veils of opacity surrounding song. In this way women and other underprivileged classes have long forged solidarities and strength in the teeth of power, and they have written the pages of their history in song and other veiled forms.[13]

By such means also the secrets that bind nations together have long circulated publicly, if discretely—public secrets in which almost everyone partakes but that are rarely spoken of (Taussig 1999). The past of American slavery, the decimation of native populations throughout the world, the ritualized domination of women—all are such public secrets. In postcolonial South Korea the experiences of the "comfort women" were another. They were a spectral presence, a murmur of the tragedy of the colonial era and the victimization of Korea by Japan that circulated in song and other veiled cultural forms and became a vital part of South Korean national identity in the wake of Japanese domination. They had a similar spectral presence in postimperial Japan, where one of the women in this book lived for thirty years.

In the 1990s, the era of the gradual democratization of South Korea, the women began to speak. They became part of a political movement to win justice for themselves from the Japanese government and to rid the world of sexual violence, exploitation, and slavery. But even in this era of openness they are still singing, learning songs, and making songs to console themselves and enjoy themselves, to forge relationships with each other and feel part of a broader social world. After years of isolation and being ostracized they sing to bind themselves in the community of survivors that has coalesced since the movement began. They sing as part of their effort to come to terms with their past and to become full-fledged members of South Korean society. They sing as they assume prominent roles in the movement, as they stand before the media and South Korean public, trying to remain themselves while assuming the weight of the powerful symbolic roles given to them. They sing against the single, rarified mask of the victim that threatens to subsume them all, despite the efforts of activists and others, as they are assimilated into the pantheon of postwar victim archetypes that feed South Korean nationalism. They cling to songs as though they were talismans of their identity and experience. In the face of governments and others that would pretend that Japanese military sexual slavery is a fabrication or a bygone "historical" issue, they sing to remind people that they are alive.

Over the length of the twentieth century each of the three survivors featured in this book became a certain kind of composer and singer, using song for her own ends. Some of these uses are unique to each woman and her situation; others are decidedly familiar as common social uses of music. But even these conventional uses had a special significance for these marginalized women, as a kind of normal participation in social life. The women sang to relate unwritten histories; they sang as part of their struggles to remember and to overcome; they sang to be part of society and culture and to be with others. They also sang to show others the beautiful things they have made and the selves capable of making them. They created worlds out of song and worlds within song. They built places where they felt at home.

The survivors sang because song escaped certain kinds of surveillance and therefore allowed them a relative freedom when compared with speech and other kinds of expression. But they were nonetheless performing, singing for an audience, asking that audience to listen. When they sang for me, when they sing for us, they invite us into a public yet intimate sphere of alternative understanding. They invite us to enter their worlds of song.

It is surprisingly difficult to listen, however. Despite the outpouring of books, films, and art related to the "comfort women" issue,[14] South Korean public culture and international social movements have found it easy to pass over the voices of the survivors of Japanese military sexual slavery. To give just one telling example: since the breaking of the "comfort women" issue in the early 1990s, art therapists have encouraged a number of survivors to paint, and these paintings have received considerable domestic and international attention. Meanwhile their singing, through which they have done similar work of self-construction and recovery for their entire postwar lives, goes largely unnoticed. Voices do not stay still, nor do they stay quiet. They talk back, and most of us have been unwilling to listen, preferring instead the silence of still images, which we can more easily invest with our own thoughts and agendas. We can ignore the survivors altogether and focus our outrage around the historical injustices, or we can use them as symbols to help us do so. Or we can comfortably continue to ask, with somewhat paternalistic good nature, what we as individuals or as different kinds of social group (nations, students, genders) can *do for* the survivors, rather than what they have done, and what they can teach us.

It is difficult to listen because most of us are the products of cultures, masculinities, and modernities—East and West, Korean, North American, European, Japanese—that value assertion over comprehension, language and meaning over voices and sounds, and sound-making over listening. We desperately need, in our various ways, to cultivate what the philosopher Gemma Fiumara (1990: 97) calls "listening silences": silences in which we hear others and the world around us rather than waiting for our next opportunity to assert ourselves.

To do so we need to first understand the myriad forms of social and cultural nonlistening that we have learned throughout our lives. Then, instead of asking ourselves what we can do for these survivors, instead of seeking to explain their experiences in terms of preformed ideologies, or stopping once we have acquired statistical knowledge of the "comfort women" system, we will learn something new.

First we will learn something about the many obstacles and difficulties of listening, and we will struggle, not always with success, to understand and overcome these. That process is recorded in the following pages. Through this effort we will gain a glimpse into how, through song, these women have designed themselves and their social worlds in the wake of traumatic experiences of sexual violence; we will see the tactics of recovery and nourishment that have sustained them, and which, in their singing, they make available to others who may also need them.

By examining these techniques of recovery and self-making we will gain a richer appreciation of what these women's traumatic experiences were and what their enduring consequences have been. We will thereby grasp something of the histories of women's experience that often live in ephemeral forms such as song, and in the ambiguous spaces between song and speech, and that are so often written out of history. As a part of this we will find in the rich fabric of these women's songs and stories their wisdom about the nature of things—not only about war and sexual violence and song but also about human relationships, cross-cultural encounters, living in foreign lands, returning, aging, the nature of "home," fairness, justice, happiness, sorrow, suffering, and many other things.

We will get to know the survivors of Japanese military sexual slavery not only as victims, but as creators—of music and visions of the world. We will get to know them as women, active in projects of self-reclamation and artistic creation and expression, entangled in complex relationships of mutual influence and expectation with their society, public culture, and political institutions.

At length (but not too soon) this will lead us to reflect on our own lives and on the uses of music in the pursuit of survival, happiness, identity, everyday life, and social and political projects. And through this whole, arduous process we will learn about how to listen.

This book is the product of my years of listening to the "comfort women" survivors, and so it is about many things that they shared with me. It is about complex social processes of song and self-making. It is about sexual violence and healing, women's cultures, and Korean modern life. It is a rewriting of Korean twentieth-century music history as a history of music in Korean people's lives, set against the dehumanized compendia of songs, pieces, genres, and customs that abound in Korean music scholarship. Because the experiences of the women in this book have involved Japan and other places in circuits of human and cultural circulation, it is a transnational revision of the reductive categories of "Korean music" and "Korean experience," and it is a similar revision of ideas of "Japanese music" and Japanese cultural history. It is a story of the social utility and the social poetics of traditional Korean folk songs, mass-mediated Korean pop, and cosmopolitan East Asian song repertoires. But all of this is because it is really only about three women, three singers, who have put songs to work in their efforts of self-making in the course of their both extraordinary and remarkably familiar lives.

Beginnings

It was the winter of 2001, and I had been studying Korean music and its place in modern life for about five years. Drifting through the University of Chicago's imposing graduate library I browsed various books about Korea for the familiar signs—italics, insets, quotations—that announced the beginning of a song.

I had just returned from a trip to Eastern Europe, where I had visited the remnants of several Nazi concentration camps. I had been to Theresienstadt, the famous camp where the Nazis had collected Jewish artists, musicians, and others to present to the world as a model Jewish settlement. I had also been to Auschwitz and Birkenau, where members of my extended family had died. I was reading Gila Flam's *Singing for Survival* (1992), about the songs of the survivors of the Jewish ghetto in Łodz, Poland, and Szymon Laks's *Music of Another World* (1979), about music in Auschwitz. Through these books I was learning about how music could participate in traumatic experiences, document them, and serve as an expressive response to them.

I had heard of a book through friends in Korean studies called *True Stories of the Korean Comfort Women*, an English translation of testimonies of South Korean survivors of Japanese military sexual slavery (Howard 1995). I found it and began to read, experiencing the shock that so many people receive on first encountering the stories of the survivors of the "comfort women" system and putting faces to this immense project of sexual violence. And as I read, inset italics—those visual intimations of song—leapt off the page. Survivor after survivor sang during testimony or made reference to singing in the sex camps where they had been enslaved. Why? I wondered. That question would preoccupy me for the next decade.

A year and a half later, in July 2002, I traveled to South Korea intending to study song with the many government-registered and supported survivors who live throughout the country.[1] On July 17 I went to my first "Wednesday demonstration," the protest held every Wednesday at noon in front of Seoul's Japanese Embassy by the Korean Council for Women Drafted for Military Sexual Slavery by Japan.[2] The protests, which are attended faithfully by many survivors, have gone on since January 1992, all year long, regardless of Seoul's humid summer heat, the deluge of the rainy season, and the frigid winter months.[3]

The Korean Council, founded in 1990 by a consortium of women's organizations, is the central organization in the "comfort women movement" or "comfort women grandmothers movement," as the protest movement is often called.[4] The group pursues national and international activism on behalf of the women and coordinates the welfare of registered survivors in conjunction with different support organizations throughout South Korea. The Council, together with these other organizations, fought successfully for the system of national stipends that now supports registered survivors and for other social welfare measures. The Wednesday demonstration is the organization's core event, and the core event of the movement.

On one of my previous visits to the Korean Council's offices, one of the staff had told me that a van brought a number of the women to the protest from the House of Sharing, a rest home and center of activism for survivors of Japanese military sexual slavery, where a changing group of around ten women live. At the protest I wanted to introduce myself to these women and to others who came from elsewhere, and I hoped to arrange a visit to the House, although I imagined that might be difficult.

To get to the demonstration by Seoul subway, you walk out of exit 2 of subway line 5's Gwanghwamun station and head north toward the great gate of Gyeongbok Palace and the mountains. Passing the American Embassy, you turn right just beyond the adjacent Ministry of Culture and Tourism building and walk straight for five minutes more, until you reach the tall black steel gates and red brick of the Japanese Embassy.

When I arrived the gates were already fronted by two of the green-and-white armored police buses that have long been a staple of life in downtown Seoul, and a small police brigade stood watch. A small crowd of activists and participants was already assembled on the sidewalk, and reporters, photographers, and camera operators were checking their machines. One survivor was sitting on a plastic stool, dressed in an elegant *hanbok* Korean traditional dress, surrounded by young people. A staff member of the Korean Council introduced me to her. She told me her name was Hwang Geumju and that she lived in Seoul. She had come by subway, she said, and was taking a rest after the trek.

Soon the House of Sharing's deep evergreen van arrived, carrying seven survivors and a few activists. The driver parked in the narrow street pressed in upon by the forest of office buildings and embassies.

The women stepped out of the van one by one, surrounded by volunteers and activists and students, all offering to give them a hand. "Halmeoni, halmeoni!," they cried, "Grandmother, grandmother!," calling them by the name Koreans bestow on all elderly women. Volunteers and Council staff grasped hands and ushered each woman to one of about ten blue plastic chairs arranged in a row on the edge of the sidewalk. Some women refused help and walked alone to their seats, looking across the street and coolly eyeing the row of riot police stationed in front of the gates of the embassy and the photographers and film crews setting up to shoot the protest.

After the women sat down the Council activists fitted each one with a yellow protest jersey that proclaimed the name of the Council and laid a banner over the laps of the ten or so survivors, which they would hold throughout the protest. The banner also displayed the name of the Council and slogans demanding apology and reparations from the Japanese government.

At twelve sharp the protest began with the Council's song, "Like a Rock" ("Bawi cheoreom"), blasting through the portable PA system. "Like a Rock" is an upbeat, poppy protest piece written by Yu Inhyeok in the 1990s in the heat of the "people's movement" (*minjung undong*) that helped bring about the end of decades of authoritarian rule in South Korea. It remains popular among former participants in the huge student movement from that time, some of whom now work for the Korean Council, and it bears the imprint of that era's earnestness and optimism: "Let's be like a rock that will become the foundation of the coming free world!" The music pushed the small PA beyond the distortion threshold. An activist sang into the microphone, leading everyone in a sing-along. Some of the survivors at the protest sang along, others did not. The protest song style wasn't well-known or popular among people of their generation, but many sang to participate in the demonstration.

Mun Pilgi, a diminutive survivor in a pink windbreaker, sang in her soft voice and stared defiantly at the brick walls of the embassy. Bae Chunhui, a colorfully dressed and rather youthful-looking woman, sat on the end of the row of benches and mimed the words perfectly beneath her breath. I don't think Pak Duri was there that day, but I would subsequently go with her to the protests and watch as she alternately participated and sat to the side, grumbling and smoking chocolate-flavored cigarettes.

The emcee from the Korean Council greeted the survivors in their row. She gave a rallying speech, discussing current developments in the political struggle for reparations and apology from the Japanese government and other aspects of the movement. She then introduced the participants in the day's demonstration: Japanese visitors, school groups, religious organizations, and others. Representatives of each group took the microphone in turn and greeted the women, explaining why they had come. In between the speeches and introductions, the emcee invited everyone to participate in a group cheer, a common practice in South Korean protest movements. She led the group in chanting slogans one by one, touching on some of the Korean Council's core demands: that the Japanese government acknowledge the crime of the military "comfort women" system, make a formal and accurate investigation of it, make a formal resolution of apology, give reparations to survivors, record the system in history textbooks, build a memorial and establish a museum, and punish the perpetrators. As of 2010 all of these demands are still pending. The closest the Japanese government has come to acknowledging the sex slave system and Japanese military culpability for it came in 1993, when Chief Cabinet Secretary Kôno Yôhei made a vague statement of apology, which minimized Japanese government culpability, omitted discussions of slavery and sexual violence, and never said what a "comfort woman" was.[6]

So the protestors restated these demands on my first visit to the Wednesday demonstration and every other time across the nine years that I have visited the protest. Depending on the occasion, the emcee may include other injunctions, responding to world politics and South Korea's changeable political scene: for the fickle South Korean government to lend the movement its support, for an the end to world sexual slavery, the prosecution of sex criminals among U.S. troops in South Korea, and the end of government toleration and encouragement of South Korea's immense modern sex industry.

For each demand, the emcee shouted a sentence and then repeated the last line with the group three times, throwing a fist in the air.

> Leader: *We demand the Japanese government give reparations and apologize to the victims!*
> Others: *Apologize!*
> *Apologize!*
> *Apologize!*

Some of the survivors participated in the group cheers. Some threw their fists in the air but did not chant; others chanted but did not gesture; others did nothing. Some moved their mouth, but no sound came out.

Figure 1.1.
Left to right: Survivors Kil Won-ok, Pak Okseon, Kim Sundeok, Yi Yongsu, Mun Pilgi, and Bae Chunhui (in the mask) at the 600th Wednesday demonstration, March 17, 2004.
Photo by Yajima Tsukasa.

Others looked around with amused expressions, people-watching. I didn't know how to read this variety of responses, although I would soon begin to learn.

The Korean Council's director, Yun Mee-Hyang, came forward for her weekly address. She spoke about the goals of the movement in her sharp and humorous style, addressing the women directly. They yelled back spirited replies to her many questions. Mrs. Yun also spoke of upcoming events—meetings, related protests, and some summer trips that the Council was planning for the women, including a September outing to Jeju Island in the South.

Next, one of the survivors called for the microphone, and three or four women gave short statements in turn. The photographers and camera operators swarmed in on each woman as she spoke, moving around with their machines and clicking like scuttling beetles at any display of emotion. Hwang Geumju took the microphone and railed at the Japanese government: "I'm old, and I've waited so long! I don't need any money! Please, just apologize to us!" Finally she was overwhelmed: "Get outta here! You sons of bitches [*gae saekki*]!!!" She yelled in her deep, raspy voice, her traditional Korean dress billowing, as she was alternately restrained and supported by the activists, all in their yellow smocks—looking like a female soul singer and her entourage, a bursting rock-and-roll soul railing against a line of riot cops and the embassy walls.[7]

Some of the police, who were all young men doing their duty in lieu of mandatory military service, had trouble suppressing their smiles and admiration. This delicate-looking elderly woman was expressing herself frankly in the face of a power for which they had no overabundance of respect. They themselves were defending the Japanese Embassy against a handful of Korean grandmothers, and a few of them were visibly embarrassed.

Eventually the activists gathered around Hwang Geumju and took the microphone; one of them led her back to her seat and gave her consoling pats. As she caught her breath, the emcee read the weekly closing statement off the back of the program. The protest was over. People crowded in to greet the survivors and to walk with them to the *galbi tang* (beef rib stew) restaurant where they ate lunch after each Wednesday demonstration.

In the flurry of activity one of the activists introduced me to the Buddhist nun Neunggwang, the director of the House of Sharing. She invited me to visit the House that afternoon, and I accepted.

I had been wrong to think it would be difficult to arrange a visit. This South Korean social movement bore the imprint of the country's "speed personality" society, shaped by decades of rapid industrialization and development. It was armed with cellular phones, name cards, and networks that made it run fast and made results easy to obtain. I had stepped into one of its well-established currents. But although such impromptu visits to the House of Sharing were quite clearly normal practice, I felt far from relaxed. As I ate the beef rib stew, I swallowed the lump that formed in my throat and nerved myself for my first trip to the House of Sharing.

After lunch I found myself in the van with the group of survivors and social workers heading into the foothills east of Seoul, toward Gyeonggi Province's Gwangju City and the House of Sharing. I was sitting in front, next to the driver, who was the House's administrator. Behind me were six survivors and a number of Japanese volunteers coming to visit the House and its adjacent museum.

From west to east, central Korea slopes gently upward, from rolling hills to low mountains to the vast mountain ranges of Gangweon Province, culminating in the sprawling peaks of Mount Seorak and Mount Geumgang. As the House of Sharing's transportation van drove east out of Seoul along the Han River, we entered the low mountainous region. Here the Han split, a large extension winding away northward, the Han continuing to the east and a broad tributary, the Gyeongancheon, heading directly south. We took a two-lane highway that followed the Gyeongancheon south through the center of Toechon village, past fried chicken shops, beer houses, and super-markets. These gave way to wetlands and farmland again. We watched herons, storks, and egrets fishing in the river and in the rice fields. We saw farmers stooping to weed or talking on their cell phones and smoking in between stints of working. The bus driver had me sing a few Korean folk songs that I knew, and the women laughed.

A few minutes later we turned left onto a valley road and drove about a kilometer up through a tiny hamlet toward the back of the valley. We passed old post-and-stucco thatched houses (*jogakjip*) and a riot of villagers' newly constructed houses and suburban dream homes—Western-style log cabins, "farmhouses," ranch houses, and other postmodern confabulations—peppered among the rice fields and greenhouses. Some time later, on our many daily walks along this road, Kim Gunja and Yi Okseon would lament about this viral explosion of suburban housing. They spoke and sang in associative chains of the disappeared fields, the vanishing world, fleeting youth, and their own lost or departed loved ones.

At the back of the valley road was the complex of buildings that made up the House of Sharing and its neighboring museum. The hills ringed in the House on three sides and cooled the area on this summer day, casting shade and sending soft winds down into the river valley. The occasional water bird swept over the densely wooded hillsides and the homes and rice paddies of the village below, cruising for frogs and other small animals that lived in the paddies, fields, and forests.

When we arrived one of the staff gave me a tour and told me something of the history of the place. The House was founded in 1992 by socially conscious monks and followers of the Jogye Order of Korean Buddhism, one year after the first survivor in South Korea to come forward, Kim Haksun, had made a public testimony. The House came into being in the early energy and outcry at the revelation of the "comfort women" system, before the South Korean government had established much in the way of a support network for the women; the House was designed to fill that gap, supporting financially needy survivors and offering support for those who risked being ostracized or disowned by coming forward. It was a modest operation, however, unable to provide for the hundreds of women who came forward and registered as survivors. It began in a rented home in Seoul and moved three times as it slowly grew in size.

In 1995 the Jogye Order received a large donation of land for an expanded suburban site, and the House relocated to its present location in the coun-try. It soon became an officially recognized social welfare organization, although it continued to rely on private donations as well. In 1998 the House opened a historical museum, which hosts educational programs, testimonial events, and a slowly evolving series of exhibits contributed by artists and researchers. Sangcheol, the staff member who was giving me the tour of the House, worked in the museum.

Sangcheol told me that the House was much more than a rest home; it was a center of activism and education as well, with the women living at the center of it. The survivors were constantly surrounded by Korean, Japanese, and international guests and volunteers and by activists and members of the media—television, radio, and newspaper reporters, photographers, and videographers. This was a very special sort of everyday life, one that was cosmopolitan, intergenerational, and pervasively mass-mediated. This contradicted many of my preformed images of the survivors' lives in the countryside, images that the media itself was busy producing.

Next Sangcheol took me around the grounds. He showed me the wood-paneled administrative building and the red-brick living quarters, which contained the bedrooms, living room, and dining room. Next was the shrine building, a round structure that housed a Buddhist shrine on the second floor and a first-floor room where educational programs, meetings, testimonial events, and parties were held. The room was equipped with a PA system and an enormous television. Several months after I arrived it acquired a

Figure 1.2.
Front to back: Pak Ongnyeon, Pak Okseon, Mun Pilgi, and Kang Ilchul (with cameramen) take a photo-op stroll in the field behind the House of Sharing, winter 2004.
Photo by the author. A color version of this and other photographs are available on this book's website.

Figure 1.3.
The statue of *Unblossomed Flower* in the courtyard of the House of Sharing, in front of the living quarters.
Photo by the author.

"song room machine" (*noraebanggi*), a Korean karaoke machine, which had been donated to the House for the women's amusement. This room, along with the living room of the dormitory, was one location of the many song parties at the House.

In front of the dormitory and the shrine building stood the museum, an imposing gray brick and concrete structure with two sharp and jutting wings separated by an open courtyard in the middle. The wings were connected by an underground passage so as not to obstruct the women's view down the valley.

In the midst of the four buildings was a large gravel courtyard, framed by four young gingko trees and peppered with picnic tables and chairs and two tables with large Hite Beer umbrellas covering them. The courtyard was also set with flowerbeds and small garden plots, many of which integrated memorials and sculptures. At the center of the courtyard stood a bronze statue, *Unblossomed Flower* (*Motdapin kkot*), made by Yun Yeongseok in the image of survivor Kim Sundeok's painting of the same name. It shows a young girl in traditional Korean clothing standing amid unopened lotus flowers. I was to find out later that this statue commemorating lost innocence was a symbol of the House, reproduced on the cover of its monthly newsletter, on the museum's informational pamphlets, on books, and on other memorabilia such as shirts and postcards sold at the museum gift stand.

The statue focused an ideology of stolen youth and innocence that had become the popular lens through which the survivors were seen in South Korean public culture. It was symbolic of the women's experiences of sexual slavery, but through it the survivors and the dead whom they represented became symbols of the Japanese colonial exploitation of Korea more generally.

Behind *Unblossomed Flower* was the aged bronze statue *Woman of the Earth*, a naked torso of an elderly woman rising up out of the ground, created by Im Oksang without reference to the issue of Japanese military sexual slavery. It had been bought and installed by a former director who felt a resonance between the sturdiness and inevitability of the statue and the strength of the survivors themselves. This rather philosophical statement, however, would be misread by many visitors to the house, especially because the statue was just steps from the monuments and gravestones dedicated to survivors who had died in their term at the House of Sharing.

The two figures of the maiden and the grandmother dominated the iconography of the House and of the "comfort women" issue in Korean popular culture.[8] Rarely did one see a picture of a survivor in middle age; the women seemed to have no lives between their stolen youth and the

Figure 1.4.
Photo of Pak Ongnyeon in front of *Woman of the Earth*, on the wall in the House of Sharing education room.
Photo by the author.

wrinkled old age and death of the "comfort woman grandmother," as the women were often called. It was as if the survivors were, though courageous and resilient, also irreparably wounded, as if they lived to share this unhealable wound with the public, to give fuel to the political struggle for historical justice from Japan and to the ongoing postcolonial struggle for national flourishing.

During South Korea's long authoritarian dawn, even as so many violations of human dignity perpetrated by the Japanese colonial regime in Korea remained buried, the wounds of the colonial era and the war had become a source of moral authority for South Korean dictatorships that otherwise found legitimacy in short supply. The authoritarian South Korean state could not draw its legitimacy from the notion that it was elected by the people, especially after the military coup d'état of 1961. Unlike North Korea, whose leader Kim Il-sung stood on the solid foundation of his anti-Japanese guerrilla activity during the colonial era, the South was run by many men who had collaborated with Japanese colonial authority and business. But the government forgot and remembered this according to its convenience, and the historical reality of the national wound became an important source of moral authority for the government and a focal point of South Korean national identity—a "wounded attachment," to borrow a phrase from the political theorist Wendy Brown (1995). The resulting nationalism could be called a "wounded nationalism," which is how Hongkoo Han (1999) describes a similar phenomenon in North Korea.

So when the "comfort women" issue broke in the late 1980s and early 1990s, it was into a prepared ideological landscape. As it became assimilated into national history, the colonial suffering of the "comfort women" became a kind of ultimate example of the violation of a meta-phorically female national body. As happens so very often in postcolonial nationalisms the world over, women victims of colonial sexual violence became symbols of national violation rather than people, or women, with problems unique to their experiences (Chatterjee 1993). Consequently the women's wounds were *shared*, which is one of the senses of the name "The House of Sharing."

The name House of Sharing (Nanum ui jip) was chosen by the Buddhist leadership of the committee for the House's establishment in 1992. It was based on Korean ideas of *nanum* (sharing), a keyword in Korean culture that does a tremendous amount of identity work in South Korean society. Korean life is built around many different kinds of intimate sharing—people eat from the same soup bowl and share drinking cups, for example—and this sort of sharing harmonizes with ideologies of shared national identity, seamlessly uniting private and national life.

Day-to-day practices of sharing have grown to their present strength during an arduous twentieth century of colonialism, war, and post–Korean War authoritarian capitalism, during which people banded together in small groups and struggled together for livelihood and survival. Similarly a national identity based on sharing resources and racial and cultural identity has reached maturity in a late twentieth century of national division, class struggle, and political factionalism, all of which it helps to assuage. References to sharing have figured largely in the public cultural reception of the "comfort women" issue ever since it became an open conversation in the 1990s. The designers of the House of Sharing had intended it to be a place for sharing the wounds of the past, a common political goal, and identity, labor, life, sorrow, and joy.

The House was most of all a place for the sharing of the "comfort women" experience and its legacy. For visitors this sharing could result in increased understanding of what military sexual slavery was and what it was like; it could also result in a sense of transference of the "comfort women's" experience, to a sense that the visitor, the citizen, was himself or herself an indirect victim of the "comfort women" system. The House's adjacent museum had an "experience chamber," a mock-up of a room in a generic "comfort station," which was perhaps the most potent example of this fraught process of sharing. This was an important process of empathy and understanding. But here, and elsewhere in South Korean society, as the "comfort women" issue was assimilated to national history, some people came to feel ownership of the "comfort women" legacy. Some even took this as an excuse to stop listening to the women and begin speaking, presumably on their behalf.

One thing the House of Sharing was built to encourage survivors and others to share was *han*, a rich and flexible Sino-Korean emotional complex that involves pent-up sorrow, anger, pain, resentment, and frustration at the conditions of one's life and the impossibility of revenge. There are as many definitions of *han* as there are people defining it, but one compelling definition is that of the literary scholar Chungmoo Choi, for whom *han* is an emotion felt by those who are powerless to decry or stop their suffering at the hands of others.[9] The concept rose to prominence as a central marker of Korean identity in the postcolonial era, when the ideology of national victimization became so important to the South Korean state and its citizens.[10]

This notion of unity in *han* assumes that similar emotions accumulate in the experience of different kinds of suffering: Korea's victimization by foreign powers, humanity's suffering in war, women's suffering at the hands of men, and the difficulties of everyday subsistence. The flexibility of the concept makes this possible. It is the ideology of shared *han* that above all has made it possible for some ordinary Koreans to assume that they are capable of understanding and laying claim to the survivors' experiences of sexual violence. The festival brochure for the 2003 Nanum ui chukje (Festival of Sharing) expressed this pithily: "the wound" of the survivors of sexual slavery was "*our* wound, it belongs to all of us."

All of this means that South Koreans who hear the survivors sing are already deeply socialized to listen for *han*, and its anger, sorrow, trauma, bitterness, and cynicism, at the expense of the other kinds of feeling (overcoming, hope, joy, love, humor) that the women so often express in song. One listener put it to me directly: "These are not songs—they are the sounds of crying."[11] In the women's song worlds, however, these two emotional hemispheres are complementary, joined in patterned transformations of feeling that they make use of in the course of everyday life to deal with sorrow and to make intelligible stories of traumatic experience. But this other side is often bracketed out in representations of the women in the South Korean public sphere—in media reports, photographs, works of fiction, plays, artworks, and other media that circulate "woundedness ideology."

In this ideology of the unhealed wound, survivors found a tremendous moral authority that caused others to listen to them and a powerful acknowledgment of their suffering. This recognition became a crucial part of many survivors' ongoing processes of posttraumatic recovery and integration into society. At the same time the women faced pressure to reawaken or perform their woundedness, after half a century of trying to heal and reimagine themselves as whole. For many this meant uncovering long-repressed memories and wounds, an act of discovery that often brought with it catharsis. But the utility of the perpetual wound in South Korean public culture meant that many were not particularly interested in the women's efforts at self-reconstruction. While the long and hard work of survivors and activists created a place in South Korean public culture for the "comfort women" and encouraged the economic and psychological well-being of survivors, most instances of acknowledgment in public culture were practical applications of the women's suffering to the causes of national solidarity and moral authority. It was hard to generate sustained interest in the issue at all, much less in the survivors as women, or as people, bringing their strength, cleverness, and hard-won philosophies of life to bear on the pursuit of selfhood, social life, and happiness. As a consequence of this, as has so often happened with other historical figures in postcolonial Korea,[12] the "comfort-woman victim" has been reduced to a composite of the expectations of public culture and prominent characteristics of high-profile survivors—the changeable archetype of the "comfort woman grandmother."

Activists, social workers, and most of all the women themselves have long struggled in the shadow of South Korean wounded nationalism. Korean Council Director Yun Mee-hyang described to me the importance and the difficulty, in the case of the "comfort women" issue, of creating an alternative to such a patriarchal nationalism, which is uninterested in issues of sexual exploitation, and to universalist feminism, which has often been insufficiently interested in issues of race and colonialism. What is needed, she told me, to understand the "comfort women" issue is a way of understanding the victimization of the "comfort women" as a composite of colonial, sexual, and other sorts of exploitation. But the proponents of the various ideologies make this kind of acknowledgment difficult to propagate.

Activists and survivors have also long had difficulty cultivating sustained interest in the women's well-being and the "comfort women" issue at all, since the press and public culture generally lose interest once they have restocked their moral coffers with the righteousness of the national wound, which they do ritualistically on Independence Day (August 15) and according to the requirements of the moment. Also activists and the women themselves have long been at pains to show the South Korean public the many different faces of the "comfort woman grandmother" beyond the archetypal images at large in the mass media and public culture, and to show glimpses of the endurance, ingenuity, healing, and self-making by which the women have survived.

Song has had an important role to play in this atmosphere, as a reservoir of particularity and personality and a simultaneously popular and personal expressive form that harmonizes the social and the personal. Many of the women have continued to make use of song to find ways of relating their own wants, needs, and sense of the uniqueness of their selves and experiences to the expectations of public culture. The women at the House of Sharing sang at home, alone in their rooms, in the car on the way to the Wednesday demonstration, at song parties, at events where they met with other survivors, and in testimony and interviews. As they have struggled to make themselves heard in song and in speech, and as woundedness ideology has gradually loosened its grip on South Korean popular consciousness, more and more members of South Korean society have begun to listen.

This was the complicated scene that I was about to become immersed in at the House of Sharing. After my brief tour of the grounds on my first day, and a late afternoon rest while the residents waited for the heat of the day to break, the six-o'clock dinner bell rang. My guide took me to the dormitory's kitchen area. At the dinner table he and the nun Neunggwang introduced me to the group of seated women, explaining that I was an American student interested in their songs. Everybody nodded and was friendly and polite, greeting me with warmth and a practiced reserve. Han Dosun joked about my appearance; Yi Okseon and Kim Sundeok related things we had sung and talked about in the car; Kim Gunja tried out some of her English phrases on me. Then most of them encouraged, begrudged, cajoled, joked, or insisted: "*Aigo* [good grief] . . . you've come all the way from America, you must be hungry. Go get yourself something to eat!"

Pak Duri

Water, water, load it up
Bring it to the house on fire
Load up a truck full of widowers
And spread them around Pak Duri's room! 🔊 4
　　　　　　　——Pak Duri, "Ballad of the Traveling Entertainer"

I ate my first dinner of rice, vegetable side dishes (*panchan*), and grilled fish at the dining room table, sitting and talking with the House staff and the survivors and looking down the table from face to face. Nine survivors lived at the House, but there were only seven at the table. I could see Bae Chunhui in the adjacent living room eating alone on the couch. She was alternately watching and pretending to watch the television, while keeping one ear on the conversations in the dining room. Occasionally she grumbled with disapproval or interjected an opinion. A funnel of cigarette smoke poured out of a cracked door right next to the sofa, signaling the presence of another.

After we finished eating, some of the survivors and I moved to the living room to watch television. The door to the smoke-filled room swung wide and Pak Duri came out among us. She sat on the couch looking around; her eyes settled on me with what I took for hostility. I went over to her and tried to introduce myself, but she just leered, grabbed a rag from her room, and held it up. Pointing to the kitchen, she spoke, her voice raspy and loud: "Wash the dishes!!!"

On my second visit I sat down in the courtyard near Pak Duri and tried again to engage her. She looked at me severely and said, "Hey, American, what'd ya come here for? Get outta here! Get out!" After a few seconds of

Figure 2.1.
Pak Duri in Seoul, summer 2002.
Photo by the author.

watching me squirm she turned to a staff member, Kim Jeongsuk, whom she called "Office Girl" (*samusil agassi*), and laughed.

This rather stringent comment took me off guard. Jeongsuk told me not to worry, that Pak Duri took pleasure in needling strangers and seeing how they reacted. So on my third visit I got up my courage and sat down next to her again in the yard, about a half hour before I was to leave for Seoul. I asked her where her hometown was, and she asked me if I knew anything about Korean geography. She told me her home was in Chungcheong Province, in the midwestern part of the peninsula, and she laughed again, and I didn't know why.

After a little while I had to leave for the city and I said goodbye. She looked at me with the same severe expression as before and bellowed a new order: "Hey, American, what're ya leaving for? Sleep here!" She looked at me and laughed, sharing the joke of the past few weeks with me, and showing what I hoped was a measure of budding affection.

Pak Duri had many reasons for this protracted, testing joke. Although she had been at the House of Sharing from its founding in Seoul in 1992, and though she felt a great sense of propriety, she had little control over who came and went. A constant stream of visitors flowed through the House.

Korean students from high schools and colleges, Japanese college students, leftists and "conscience tourists" came to learn about the "comfort women" system and to hear survivors give testimony in the education room. Volunteer teams from Korean religious organizations and community groups came to the House to clean, work in the garden, tour the museum, and give performances for the women's entertainment. Like these other visitors, I had been invited to the House of Sharing without her permission. In her game she asserted an authority over the place through sheer force of will, through the magnitude of her persona and her voice.

Many visitors to the House of Sharing promised to return and then failed to, inadvertently reinforcing a long pattern in Pak Duri's life of being left behind. So she watched people's actions and had fun at their expense, as she had done with me, to see if they would last and could be trusted. She grew deeply fond of those friends she decided she could respect and trust. Meanwhile she defended the borders of her inner world; she had long grown used to doing so.

Pak Duri had laughed when she told me about her hometown because she was playing another trick. She had not grown up in Chungcheong Province, but near Miryang, in the Southeast.[1] She was born in 1924, the eldest of eleven children in a relatively prosperous construction worker's family. Her father and her uncle womanized and squandered the family's estate, and the family grew destitute.

As a young girl Pak Duri was already strong-willed and selective, and she refrained from marrying, waiting to meet the right man. But she worried about burdening her large family, and so she wanted to work and contribute to the household. In 1940, when a group of Japanese and Koreans came to her village recruiting young girls to work in factories in Japan, she seized the opportunity.

She was taken to the southeastern port city of Busan and put on a boat. She had no idea where she was going. She struggled with seasickness during the long trip and eventually arrived not in Japan but in the Taiwanese port city of Changhua. Taiwan, like Korea, was controlled by the Japanese, and so Pak Duri remembered Changhua as Shôka, the Japanese pronunciation of the Chinese name.

She was taken into the foothills and dropped off with a number of other girls at what appeared to be a private home. It was a large, one-storey home with latticework on the windows and a sign out front. She was led into the main corridor of the house, which had small rooms lining either side, and placed in one of the rooms. She waited to be taken to the factory, but no one came to take her. Instead soldiers began coming, demanding sex. She lost her virginity this way.

This was a "comfort station," the Japanese euphemism for a military sex camp. The Japanese who had recruited her was the camp's proprietor. The proprietor and staff kept Pak Duri imprisoned and for the next five years forced her to have sex with soldiers. She received no salary, although men who stayed overnight would sometimes leave tips. She was unable to leave without a military escort, and she was beaten for any violation of camp rules, including refusing to have sex. These beatings left her with severe head trauma, among other things, and would contribute to her deafness in her old age.

When the war ended in 1945 the proprietor left Pak Duri and the other women alone in the "comfort station." Soon Taiwan was occupied by the Allies, and Pak Duri met her first Americans. She told me, "I like Americans, because they leave some money," and I wondered what that meant. I had fantastic visions of people who looked like me liberating Pak Duri and giving her some money for the trip home. But that was not what she meant. When the Allied troops arrived they had assumed the sex camp to be a brothel and kept operating it for about three months before sending the women home. Pak Duri had meant that American soldiers were better tippers than the Japanese had been.

Returning to Korea she became the second wife of a polygamous farmer, who, despite being less than prosperous, later took a young concubine as well. Pak Duri gave birth to one son and three daughters. Two of her daughters died while still children. She told no one about her experience of Japanese military sexual slavery.

She was not fond of her husband, and she said that when he died in 1975 she didn't cry for him. When the concubine managed to win inheritance rights for her branch of the family, Pak Duri and her children were cut out of the family registry and deprived of the inheritance rights it had granted them. She was left with no income and no assets. So she moved to Busan, where she sold vegetables and fruit in an open-air market. In the marketplace she cultivated her enormous voice, which lent itself well to her pungent songs.

Six years after her husband's death Pak Duri's thirty-year-old son suffocated to death on coal fumes, then commonly used to heat the houses of the rural and urban poor. She was left with only her youngest daughter. She said, "That was when I started smoking and drinking. What else could I have done?" At the House of Sharing years later she and other women would gossip, more and less fondly and scandalously, about her alcohol consumption. "*Takju* [unfiltered rice wine], *maekju* [beer], *soju* [spirits]— I drank them all!" she told me. Other women at the House reminisced about the long rows of bottles that she would set outside her room after a long night of drinking with friends. The alcohol and cigarettes left their traces in the grain of her singing voice.

In the late 1980s an impassioned South Korean democratization movement brought the long darkness of the country's postwar military governments to a gradual end. Many of the atrocities and injustices of the Japanese colonial era in Korea (1910–45) and its aftermath began to surface. After more than four decades of domestic and international suppression of the issue of Japanese military sexual slavery, activists and historians in Korea and Japan began to gather evidence and seek survivors.

In 1991, in response to both Korean and Japanese pressure on the Japanese government, the Japanese Embassy in Seoul issued a statement denying the existence of an official system of military sexual slavery. Survivor Kim Haksun, enraged by the embassy's statement, responded by becoming the first woman in South Korea to testify about her experience of Japanese military sexual slavery.

One year later, unable to survive on her earnings from the market, Pak Duri registered with the South Korean government as a victim of the "comfort women" system. She moved from Busan to Seoul and became one of the first residents of the House of Sharing, founded that year. In 1995 she moved to the House's new rural location.

When I first met Pak Duri in 2002 her relationship with her surviving daughter was strained, and it was the principal source of worry in her life. Her daughter had two children, a girl in middle school and a boy of elementary school age. Pak Duri waited desperately for them to visit her at the House of Sharing. But her daughter typically brought them only during the Harvest Festival and New Year, traditional occasions when elders give money to their offspring, or on other occasions when she needed money. When I met Pak Duri in 2002 she spent much of her time sitting in her room smoking Rose (*jangmi*) 100s and worrying about her grandchildren and her relationship with her daughter.

Pak Duri had recurrent nightmares in which the souls of her dead children and husband would visit her. She often spent large sums of her pension on shaman rites to appease them; when she couldn't afford that, she agonized and grew increasingly afraid. At such times her good friend and big sister (*hyeongnim*), Kim Sundeok, would burn dried hot peppers in Pak Duri's room and perform other small rites to drive away the ghosts.

In my early days at the House of Sharing I stumbled across a disproportionate number of television spots, documentaries, newspaper articles, essays, and books on the "comfort women" issue that focused on Pak Duri.

For many years she had been one of the movement's most ardent and recognized participants. She was consistent in the content of her testimonies and eloquent in speeches at rallies, media interviews, and testimonial events. She was passionate, extreme in her emotions, and quick of wit, and she channeled all of this into her virtuosic expressions of pain and suffering in public, where she balanced the pain of an unhealed wound with the competence necessary to express it in public. For all these reasons she had quickly become a major figurehead in the movement on behalf of the women and a central image that popped to mind in the national imaginary when someone said the key words of the movement: "comfort woman" or "comfort woman grandmother."

In 1998 Pak Duri and several other women brought an action against the Japanese government in the southwestern Japanese prefecture of Yamaguchi. The prefectural court ruled that the Japanese government should give each of the plaintiffs 300,000 yen (about $2,500 at the time) as compensation for the experience of wartime sexual slavery. She was not happy with the tiny monetary compensation, which was not enough to give the women security in old age or to allow them to leave something to their families. Both sides appealed, and in 2002 the case was thrown out of court, to her dismay.

Pak Duri's participation in the movement waned after this, partly due to the gradual weakening of her physical condition, but also as a result of this disappointment. Her experience in the movement became a part of the large store of evidence she had amassed of the cruelty of men, states, and life in general. Over the course of her life she had been lied to, betrayed, abused, and abandoned by the men in her family, by the staff of the "comfort station" and the hordes of soldiers, by her husband, her daughter, and others. Now she had the fresh example of the Japanese government, which continued to shirk responsibility for its wartime crimes and

Figure 2.2.
Pak Duri on the Korean Council's website (www.womenandwar.net), 2005. The text reads, "Tears had not yet dried. . . ." Original photo by Ahn Hae Ryong.
Used by permission of the Korean Council.

compensate its victims. When I told her on Wednesdays that I was off to the protest, she would tell me, "Don't go. I protested for years and years, and still there's no money."

When I met Pak Duri in 2002 she was at the peak of her practical cynicism. She took what she could get in the moment, planned ahead, and defended herself, her friends, and her family with shocking intensity. She was extremely cautious about depending on others. So she made jokes at my expense and put me through a battery of tests to see if I could take it, and if I could be trusted. But when she committed, she did so with a passion and an intensity that was the opposite of the stony reserve with which she had first greeted me. Over the four years that we knew each other, as we watched her TV together, smoked Rose 100s, drank and talked, our relationship grew.

Because Pak Duri's room at the House of Sharing was right by the main entranceway and its door opened onto the living room, she enjoyed a kind of lookout position. She kept careful watch on the comings and goings of the many staff, volunteers, and visitors that frequented the House. She looked out for gifts brought by visitors, volunteers, and friends, and together with the other House residents oversaw the theoretically equal division of gifts among them. In her crow's nest at the center of the House's busy social life, she waited for friends to come from near and far.

On my third visit to the House a group of around ten Japanese activists and lawyers came for a visit. They were old friends of Pak Duri, having helped in her lawsuit in Yamaguchi in 1998. She was elated to see them; she said that despite the unhappy outcome of the court case, they had caused her to rethink her prejudice against Japanese people and refocus her anger at the government.

The group brought snacks and beer, and in the early evening we gathered in the living room outside of Pak Duri's room to drink and talk and sing. Two other survivors were there. Kim Sundeok, Pak Duri's elder and close friend, held court in her fluent Japanese, surrounded by admirers and constantly rotating her head left and right, taking in the scene. Yi Okseon, who had returned from northeastern China to South Korea and moved into the House in 2000, was welcoming the guests and practicing her Japanese, which she was studying in her free time.

Pak Duri's hearing was failing, but with the help of her hearing aid she was able to carry on conversations. She sat on the couch near the entrance to her room, smiling and smoking, occasionally talking to staff and guests, her hearing aid feeding back and filling the room with its almost supersonic whine.

In time the guests began to take turns making brief spoken introductions and singing a song, in accordance with the common Korean custom of introducing oneself by singing. This was one kind of song party that was commonplace at the House of Sharing. If anyone talked too long Pak Duri would shout out "A song, a song!" and laugh.

The singing moved clockwise around the room. When each survivor's turn came, she sang her "number eighteen" (*sipbalbeon*),[3] her showpiece song. People use showpiece songs to tell listeners something about their tastes, skills, and self all at the same time. "Number eighteen" songs are generally rather well-known, so they reach out to others, variously invoking, creating, and sustaining communities of shared knowledge and understanding. A person may sing her showpiece song at work and play, at home and in public, thereby weaving a thread of coherence and identity through her daily life.[4] For the women at the House of Sharing singing showpiece songs to a group was a display of this coherence and the self that displayed it and a way to blend personal history into a realm of shared experience.

When Kim Sundeok's turn arrived, she sang the famous Korean pop song "Tears of Mokpo" ("Mokpo ui nunmul"), a piece from 1935, at the height of the Japanese colonial domination of Korea, when Japanese military ambition and violence in Asia was on the rise. The song tells of a painful parting at Mokpo Harbor in the Southwest, which Kim Sundeok related to her ferry ride from Busan to mainland China when she was taken away. Yi Okseon sang the colonial "Tear-Soaked Duman River" ("Nunmeul jeojeun Duman-gang"), a song from 1938 in which a woman sits on the banks of the river and remembers her lost beloved, who, according to a popular story about the song, has been killed in the anticolonial struggle in Manchuria. Grandmother Yi described how she herself had been taken away across that very river into Manchuria, not to return for fifty-eight years. She hadn't known the name of the river at the time, but once she found out, she said, the song became burned into her memory. "Even if I die, I won't forget it," she told us.

Following this she began to sing the early twentieth-century Japanese elementary school song "Spring Has Come" ("Haruga kita") to lighten the mood.[5] Most of the Japanese guests and several of the survivors sang with her.

In the midst of the orderly procession around the circle, Pak Duri's moment of inspiration suddenly arrived, and she cut into the order of the group singing with her strident voice, surrounded by beer bottles and friends. She related those few verses of her own compilation and composition, about the young, full-figured girl, about the cold-hearted man who deceives, and the foolish woman who believes him and is left behind, which we heard in the introduction.

The moment was a prime example of Pak Duri's compositional and performative style. She had selected various texts from across the broad swath of Korean folklore; she drew the text about the shapely maiden from the southwestern folk song "Jindo Arirang," where it also appears, or from somewhere else across the landscape of Korean folk life. She combined these with other texts of her own making and rendered the whole in her half-sung, half-spoken declamation, based in the primary melodic mode of central Korean folk song. ◉ 2

The strength and wry wit of Pak Duri's reflections echoed around the room in whispered translations and appreciative laughter. Spurred on, she continued with the early twentieth-century Japanese folk song "Kusatsu bushi" (Ballad of Kusatsu), which she sang to amuse and welcome her Japanese friends. To switch between such a Korean song and one so familiar to Japanese was striking and outrageous, as she often endeavored to be, and the sudden transition provoked another wave of laughter, this time joined with group singing.

"Ballad of Kusatsu" praises the baths at this famous Gumma Prefecture spa (*onsen*). It describes flowers blooming in the hot waters, which can "cure everything but heartache." I never did find out whether she learned this song during the war, on one of her recent trips to Japan, or in some other way; the final vestiges of her hearing disappeared soon after this night, and I was unable to ask her this, along with many other questions. ◉ 5

The nun Neunggwang and the other staff members encouraged other people to sing, because otherwise Pak Duri would keep going. The nun asked me to sing, and I began tapping out a rhythmic pattern on the hourglass drum (*janggo*) that she had set before me. I sang a few words of a folk song from the north that I had learned five years before, during my first extended stay in South Korea.

I had just begun the refrain when Pak Duri, inspired by the drum, began to sing again. She matched the twelve-beat rhythmic pattern perfectly, singing a verse she had set to the central Korean folk ballad "Changbu taryeong" (Ballad of the traveling entertainer):

Water, water, load it up
Bring it to the house on fire
Load up a truck full of widowers
And spread them around Pak Duri's room! [6] ◉ 4

The room erupted in laughter at Pak Duri's outrageous joke, which cut like a knife into popular images of the "comfort woman grandmother" as someone terminally deprived of her sexuality. Some laughed for the same reason that some of her colleagues excused themselves before she began to sing: because Pak Duri was so flagrantly breaking the unspoken rules and defying overwrought public expectations. More than half of those in the room didn't understand Korean, so these folks laughed as they fed off of her vitality, revisiting in their minds other times when they saw their old friend sing, and laughing along with those who got the joke. Their laughter came in two waves, an initial one and a renewal upon hearing her lyric translated into Japanese by the translators who had come with them. Many of us were feeling the differences of experience and power separating us, and we were trying to laugh away the awkwardness, which the song party tempered through the laughter and sharing of song.

Following the custom of the song circle, which would carry on long after introductions were over, Pak Duri created a kind of intimacy by exposing her emotions and experiences and showing herself off in performance. Even those who didn't understand Korean (such as many of the Japanese guests) or her thick southeastern dialect (such as myself, at that time a product of Seoul-based education in standard Korean) grasped her effort and the fondness it expressed. And we noticed the pleasure she took in her admirers' fond attentiveness, laughter, and applause. Over the years, I would come to learn just how much we were missing.

Pak Duri was a gifted entertainer, and she was giving her all to entertain her guests and herself. She was playing, in the strictest sense of the word *nolda* (to play), which all Koreans, regardless of age, use to signify having a good time. The Korean word for "song" grows out of this one; *nolda* (to play) becomes *nor-ae* (a prototype of the word for "song") and finally *no-rae,* "song," in a common verb-noun transformative operation (see Kim Ji-pyeong 1987: 23). Song and play are thus affectively related in the Korean language.

It seems very right, then, to call Pak Duri's singing "song play." That did not mean it was entirely spontaneous; it was a kind of play, like so many other kinds of social and musical improvisation, that was made possible through long preparation. Over the decades Pak Duri, like many other elderly Koreans, used the remarkable plasticity of the folk song medium to compose her own pieces, tailoring them to her experiences, thoughts, and feelings. She devised her own unique versions of melodies. She gathered lyrics from a variety of sources—folk songs, proverbs, jokes, verses she made up herself—into her own versions of a small number of well-known folk songs. As a composer she was both a creator of verses herself and a patchworker, piecing together these inventions with her vast collections of verses from across the spectrum of modern folklore.

I spent many evenings with Pak Duri over the next several years. One evening after Pak Duri's hearing had mostly gone, and after I had learned my way around her dialect, I put an imaginary microphone up to my lips and pretended to sing. Then I asked her if she was fond of singing. She replied enthusiastically, "Song!" She told me she sang what she couldn't say. "If I sing I get a cooooooooooool feeling,"[7] she told me, running her forefinger along her breastbone, mimicking how accumulated, stifled sentiments flowed out of her body as she sang. "I feel so suffocated, and so when I sing it feels good." Listening to her many songs, I began to understand that song was in part a means of addressing subjects—her experience of Japanese military sexual slavery, her lifetime of domestic suffering and abuse—that propriety had long pressured her to keep quiet about. She partook of a veiled tradition of Korean women's song that had long made it possible, by use of metaphor and other techniques of layering, displacing, and concealing meaning, and also by private singing practices, for women to sing of what they couldn't speak. No one, in the last instance, could really hold Pak Duri accountable for the songs' contents; she could say they were old songs that she had picked up somewhere and strung together, although this was only partly true. Wrapped in this opaque aura she could pour her heart out in song without fear of unmanageable repercussions. And she not only expressed herself; she also laid claim to sorrowful experiences and transformed them. Her patchwork folk songs were tools of emotional transformation, passing from pent-up to free, sad to joyful, and back again. In the verse about the house on fire and the truckload of widowers, she inverted the conditions of a long life of suffering at the hands of men, mastering them with her powerful sexuality. In her song play and in her life Pak Duri transformed the violent forces arrayed against her into the very strength of her survival.

The central Korean folk song "Ballad of the Traveling Entertainer" ("Changbu taryeong"), which Pak Duri had sung last at the party, was her favorite song. She didn't use this title, however, and called it "my song" and "the song I sing every day." She performed it often, both alone and for others; it was a thread of consistency and identity in her daily life and a forum for her continual project of self-making. In the song she encouraged herself, gathered meanings unto herself, reckoned with experience, forged an identity, and invited others to join with her in a community of understanding and enjoyment. It was the center of her world of song play.

Figure 2.3.
Pak Duri singing in the House courtyard, Parents' Day celebration, May 2001.
Photo courtesy of the House of Sharing/Museum of Sexual Slavery by the Japanese Military.

Appropriately enough to the "song play" idea, the song is itself about playing. The iconic refrain of the piece, "*a-ni nojineun mot harira*," an archaic and poetic phrase typical of folk songs, refers to the evanescence of life and exhorts people to have fun while they still can. It thus serves as both a moment for celebration and a meditation on the transient nature of life, an idea derived from Korean Buddhism and shamanism.

The song has shamanist origins, as do most songs in the well-known folk song genre *taryeong* (interview with Yi Bohyeong 2003). Shaman rituals of central and northern Korea are typically organized into sections (*geori*), during which a shaman, who is usually female and called *mansin* or *mudang*,[8] summons different spirits. In their original forms *taryeong* are songs associated with particular spirits; a shaman sings the song to bring the spirit or the spirit sings once it has entered the shaman's body, for its own entertainment and that of the ritual participants. If the song makes the spirit happy, the spirit will grant good fortune to the worshippers.

The "Ballad of the Traveling Entertainer" was originally sung by shamans during the "Traveling Entertainer's Section" (*Changbu-geori*) of central Korean shaman rites (interview with Yi Bohyeong 2003).[9] The Traveling Entertainer Spirit (*gwangdaesin* or *changbusin*) is a deified version of the *gwangdae*, itinerant outcaste entertainers who traveled throughout the Korean peninsula singing, dancing, playing instruments, and performing acrobatics and other entertainments throughout the Joseon Dynasty (1392–1910).

The song summoned the Entertainer Spirit, male or female,[10] into the body of the shaman. Then the spirit sang it together with the participants as he or she blessed them with good fortune. The shaman/spirit would sing most of the verses. Participants would join in on the refrain, and occasionally sing verses for the amusement of the god. Much as when shamans from this part of Korea dance on sharp knives while possessed by a mighty warrior spirit, the shaman's virtuosity in singing the "Ballad of the Traveling Entertainer" was also a means of proving that the Entertainer Spirit had in fact entered the shaman's body. However, the song was first and foremost about play, in all of its philosophical richness: about the association of play and good fortune and about connecting the mortal coil with the realm of spirit, thus becoming a simultaneous celebration of life in its context and an apprehension of death—all elements that would eventually make this song important to Pak Duri.

Like many Korean folk songs that had origins in shaman ceremony, the "Ballad of the Traveling Entertainer" was a popular folk song in its region by the late nineteenth century. It was circulated in the ceremonies themselves as shamans taught the refrains to participants, and it was circulated by at least two types of professional singers, *gwangdae* (itinerant male entertainers) and *gisaeng* (professional female entertainers). Both of these groups often had family relations in the shaman world; *gwangdae* often had shaman wives and played instruments in large shaman ceremonies.

Throughout the Joseon Dynasty (1392–1910) professional male entertainers traveled all over the peninsula. In the late nineteenth century central province entertainers were popular in the Southeast, Pak Duri's home region, because of the political, economic, and cultural ties between the two regions. The folk songs of central Korea were popular there, and as a result the prevalent musical scales and modes of central and southeastern Korea grew quite similar, while remaining dramatically different from those of other parts of the peninsula (particularly the Northwest and the Southwest).

Central province folk tunes such as the "Ballad of the Traveling Entertainer," "Song-tune" ("Norae garak"), and "Song of Youth" ("Cheongchun-ga") were popular in the Southeast in the decades prior to Pak Duri's birth there. Their popularity increased with the construction of a national railroad system during the Japanese colonial period (1910–45), which increased the flow of entertainers and listeners between the central area and the Southeast. Perhaps most important, the advent of Seoul- and Tokyo-based sound recording in the early decades of the twentieth century and the advent of colonial state-supervised radio in Seoul in the 1920s increased the popularity of central Korean musical culture in southeastern Korea. Famous Seoul-area female professional entertainers and *sorikkun* (itinerant male entertainers who were professional folksingers) could be heard singing central province folk songs on radios and record players throughout the region. When Pak Duri was growing up in the Southeast the "Ballad of the Traveling Entertainer" was wildly popular there, as we know from the large number of versions of this song that persist among members of her generation in the region.

Although the song was circulated in the colonial period on records and radio, the industrialization of folk songs as popular music did not have quite the standardizing effect that it would develop in later years. The tendency of mass-media circulation to homogenize, to establish certain versions of songs as canonical, existed side by side with its capacity to diversify. Popular folk songs circulated in many versions, much in the manner of jazz standards, and singers and versions vied for popularity.

In this way the practices of variation, improvisation, and personal stylistic development that had characterized Korean vernacular music for centuries survived the colonial era. In this cultural aesthetic, both professional and amateur folk singers, like other types of traditional musicians, were deemed quality performers based on the uniqueness of their personal style and the particular interest of their versions of songs. Singers distinguished themselves with recognizable vocal timbres, signature ornamentations, and the ability to tailor their repertoire to suit different performance occasions, audiences, and changing times (Seo 2002: 17). Professionals often studied with multiple teachers in the interest of developing personal style, and amateurs learned in even more diverse ways: listening to records, singing in amateur clubs, and studying with teachers. Performers, whether amateur or professional, developed personal styles as they adapted and transformed songs in the learning process.

In postcolonial, late twentieth-century South Korea, however, standardization would carry the day in the mass media and the halls of national culture. New genres of mass-mediated music, such as colonial and postwar popular songs, and performance, such as *noraebang* ("song rooms," the Korean adaptation of Japanese *karaoke*), emerged that valued relative obedience to the form and content of originals. Inspired by late twentieth-century anxieties about losing traditional cultural forms, the state selected musical genres to be codified and fixed to represent Korean tradition. In doing so the state was influenced by educational and scholarly paradigms in Western classical music, which prioritized written literacy and fixity.[11]

Within the music industry and the halls of national culture this had a drastic impact on the "Ballad of the Traveling Entertainer" and other folk songs. Certain popular versions of famous folk songs—those of performers acknowledged as masters—became canonical. In the interests of cultural preservation, institutes of national culture such as the National Center for Korean Traditional Performing Arts and the Office of Cultural Treasures have encouraged the codification of folk song style and form.[12] In the most extreme cases a song is standardized to the extent that personal style is distinguished only by the timbre of the singer's voice.

However, if we step away from the highly institutionalized field of national cultural music-making, we find many elderly South Koreans continuing to shape folk song form and content to suit their personal styles, experiences, and occasions for performance. Throughout the twentieth century such singers have often appropriated the "Ballad of the Traveling Entertainer" as a song of celebration, and as a result there are many "liberation songs" (haebang-ga) about the end of Japanese colonialism set to variants of this melody. But as the joy of liberation was quashed by national division and the Korean War (1950–53), and as other moments of happiness have been eclipsed during Korea's arduous twentieth century, the evanescence of life that the song traditionally describes has remained a central focus of the piece.

As twentieth-century history and the aesthetic priorities of Korean folk music have kept alive the practice of "versioning" folk songs such as the "Ballad of the Traveling Entertainer," we also find that the valuation of personal singing style has anything but disappeared in the twentieth century. The aesthetic prioritization of personal style that characterized early twentieth-century singing was only reinforced by the subsequent tragedies of war, poverty, national division, development, and authoritarianism, as people have continued to use music to express personal memories, feelings, and aspirations. Although canonical versions disseminated by mass media exert a strong influence, for many, Korean folk song performance remains an ongoing process of developing voice and style as a performer accommodates changing social contexts.

The folk music scholar Kim Hyejeong has shown that this is particularly true for elderly Korean women. She found that elderly women in southwestern Korea, unlike their male counterparts, are rarely concerned with conveying the "correct rendition" of a learned song melody or text (2002: 150). With some important exceptions, elderly Korean women prioritize self-expression in song. They transform received musical materials with this in mind, composing and improvising new melodies and lyrics and patchworking together different musical materials to create effective templates for self-expression.

Across the world we find that women and other subordinated social groups create special liminal realms away from public morality,[13] where they are freer to express themselves than social order and its morality would lead us to believe. Flexible song genres are almost always a mainstay of these special social spaces. Pak Duri, who endured a lifetime of suffering at the hands of men and had more than the average store of experiences and emotions to express, pushed this practice to the breaking point.

Accordingly Pak Duri's "Ballad of the Traveling Entertainer" bore little resemblance to the most famous version of the song, the *gisaeng* (female professional entertainer) version that was disseminated by touring performers, radio broadcasts, and sound recordings during the colonial era. She sang one of her rather unusual versions of the song at a song party in Byun Young-joo's 1995 documentary *Najeun moksori* (The murmuring), the first of an exceptional three-part trilogy about Korean "comfort women" survivors.[14] The scene was shot at the House of Sharing, then located in Seoul's Hyehwa district, in the winter of 1994–95.

About ten activists and survivors have gathered for a year's-end party. A few people are exhorting Pak Duri to sing "that song," meaning the "Ballad of the Traveling Entertainer," although no one speaks of it by its generic name. Most of the young people present don't know the name, although some have heard the song title before and most know the tune. The other survivors, who are more familiar with the song, ask Pak Duri to sing "that one" because many elderly Koreans put little stock in titles, often calling songs by their first lines. In so doing they draw attention to the act of singing and the particular details of someone's version rather than the generic title.

Pak Duri half-resists the cries of encouragement for a matter of seconds, not bothering to hide her delight at being asked to sing. Under the barrage of requests she complains, "My head hurts so I've forgotten everything."

At this her housemate Kang Deokgyeong joins in the exhortations: "Of course it'd be so great, big sister . . . if you sang one." And suddenly, in the space between the beginning and the end of her short request, Pak Duri has begun singing. Her song explodes out of the hubbub of conversation, cutting into the rhythm of speech and social interaction and transforming it, focusing the moment even more thoroughly on her.

Let's play, let's play, we're young so play,	*No-se, nolja, jeolmeoseo nora,*
You get old, you get sick, and you can't	*Neulgeoseo byeong deul ma*
play any more.	*mot nonira.*
Life is one night's dream of spring;	*Insaeng iljang chunmong inde*

So we've got to play while we can.	*A-ni nojineun mot harira.*
Anybody who can't play to this beat	*I jangdan-e mot noneun sarameun*
Is a total eunuch!	*Wanjeon gorae ui goja roda!* 🔊 6

As in the introduction, Pak Duri uses song as a platform for her rather unbridled expression of joy, fear, and her philosophy of life. The song is also a compelling example of her style, and a little explication will help us understand the technique and content of her expression.

The first striking thing about this piece is the unusual way Pak Duri begins. In contrast to the low pitch most sing at the beginning of their versions of this song, which typically begins with the refrain, she opens with a high outburst. Her music seems to explode out of the scene, suddenly expanding its boundaries and possibilities. The energy with which she begins the song propels her through veils of repression. That first note is like the sound of a striking match that starts a fire.

The first four lines of this version of Pak Duri's "Entertainer" are her rendition of a traditional opening text to the song that dates back at least to the colonial period and most likely well before.[15] The first couplet became quite well known in amateur song circles over the course of the twentieth century, and some people, young and old, now call the tune by the canonical first line ("Let's Play, Let's Play, We're Young So Let's Play!").

But whereas the canonical version of this text begins "no-se, no-se, jeolmeoseo no-se" (let's play, let's play, we're young so let's play), Pak Duri sings only the first *no-se* (let's play), which is a special propositive conjugation of the verb "to play" in the poetic language of folk song, uncommon in everyday speech.[16] After this first *no-se* she returns to common spoken forms: the propositive *nolja* and the imperative *nora*. In this way she gives a hint of the special poetic language of song, but in the ensuing words she switches back quickly to common speech and the everyday. In the second line she follows this with a similarly ordinary sentence: "You get old, you get sick, and you can't play any more."

In the next line she expresses a similar meaning in an elevated language form, making use of the Buddhist philosophical expression *iljang chunmong* (one night's spring dream), imported to Korea from China many centuries ago. "Life," she sings, "is one night's dream of spring": even the brief flowering of the world is but a passing illusion. Her songs involve transformations back and forth from common to extraordinary language and expression, at times like these becoming classically philosophical.

At the fourth line we make a rather striking discovery. Pak Duri has folded the canonical refrain "ani nojineun mot harira" (we've got to play while we can) into her verse, rather than giving it a separate statement.

The line expresses the meaning of the first two lines about play in the special language of song, and in the well-known form of the canonical song refrain. So in the space of these four lines Pak Duri seamlessly moves her listeners from the realm of ordinary language into the exalted language realm of song, expressing the same feeling from different perspectives, as if examining the facets of a diamond. And in her reference to the widely known and appreciated refrain, she transforms language from a medium for solitary declaration into a medium for collective singing and empathy.

In more canonical refrains of the "Ballad of the Traveling Entertainer," the melisma of the conventional refrain line's two syllables *a-ni* plays out over an entire rhythmic cycle of twelve eighth-notes.[17] This prolonged phrase allows a singer to mark the boundary between the preceding speech and her song; the archaic poetry of the refrain signals a shift away from spoken language toward a different space of expression, as does the extreme prolongation of a single word. The refrain is also an opportunity for a singer to display the timbre of her voice, to display the trademark ornaments and variations of her style, and to consolidate the participation of the audience with the most familiar part of the song.

But Pak Duri skips the initial refrain and all of its opportunities, and when she does sing it, she integrates it into a verse. She does this melodically as well as textually, lines 3 and 4 becoming a question and an answer, respectively.[18] She bypasses the refrain because her song erupts from the midst of conversation, transforming everyday talk rather than breaking with it. Her style is not based on a stylized presentation of her voice or of a melody in variation, but in her virtuosic manipulation and transformation of language and in her presentation of text, especially jokes. She does not linger on the finery of her singerly voice or on the particular musical stamp of an initial refrain. She gets right down to business—to what she wants to say.

In this way Pak Duri "locate[s] the roots of song in the textures, grammars, and concerns of everyday talk," in a manner similar to the working-class Texan practices that Aaron Fox (2004: 248) describes in his book on music and language among country music practitioners. She uses the special lexical expressions of folk song sparingly, and so her texts are more understandable than those of many other singers.

But as we have seen, if Pak Duri's song was rooted in everyday talk, it was also a transformation of it. Song is a kind of magnification of the possibilities of speech, much in the same way that dance is an expansion of the possibilities of everyday movement (Roseman 1996: 233). When people sing, their voices are often louder and project further than in speech; they prolong words, enunciate differently, use uncommon words and nonlexical sounds, address taboo subjects, and do countless other things that expand the possibilities of everyday speech. Pak Duri's "Entertainer" signals a transition to such a space of enhanced expressive possibility, characterized by lack of propriety, unflinching honesty, and a stylized roughness nicely characterized by the musician and educator Kim Dong-Won as *golbangmi* (rough beauty).[19] Her song contains a number of explosions that put pressure on the veils of propriety, from her first explosive note. The last couplet of the song, a bawdy joke expressing the importance of play and laughing at decrepitude, bursts through the final veil of propriety and enters even more fully into the enhanced space of the expressiveness of song. It brought the listeners together in laughter, a laughter that cast out, for a moment, the fear of infirmity that is the preoccupation of many in their old age. As the laughter faded and the women began to speak, the ensuing conversations were of a frankness made possible by Pak Duri's challenge to propriety and the unspoken fears that live behind it. She thus imparted the energy of her song world to everyday speech; put differently, she brought speech into the realm of unmasked reality. Pak Duri and her cohort were now free to brush up against the unadulterated truths they had apprehended throughout their lives.

In the Buddhist expression "Life is one night's dream of spring" Pak Duri confronted and explained life's transience and cruelty. The Buddhist language of transience in Korea relates the evanescence of life and the immanence of death—its inevitability and omnipresence as life's constant companion. When people and societies reject the presence of death and cling helplessly to the impermanent things of the world, the result is suffering.[20] For Pak Duri the fear of death enfolded a lifetime of suffering and domination at the hands of men and imperial Others, and the fact of her own age and inevitable passing. In this way she found a place for herself in Korean folk Buddhist and shamanist thought. As she explained evanescence as fact, and accepted it, she laid claim to it as a subject and not as its object. She gained both selfhood and a measure of peace, and she joined a fickle community of acceptance, which her singing and back-porch philosophizing helped to bring into being. Her bawdy joke about decrepitude took the self back from the fear of death and united the community in a sexualized laughter that temporarily overcame the fetish of death and its fear.

In the verse quoted above, as in other songs, Pak Duri worked through these issues of life's cruelty, the body, and mortality in a three-part pattern. First, she expressed vitality—in her text about play, in the explosion of song out of language, and in her dance, as she clapped and swayed through the lines. Second, she commented on the impermanence of that life, or the nature of human cruelty, or the various sorrows of her life.

Third, she turned impermanence and suffering into a wistful joke. The fetish character of suffering and death evaporated in the ensuing laughter and its togetherness.

This three-part transformational structure—the expression of vitality, the rumination on life's transience, and the joke—was the gentle, dialectical means by which, left to her own devices in the wake of her traumatic experiences, Pak Duri brushed up against memories and fears in the pursuit of understanding and acceptance. It was a means of interrogating trauma and experience and rendering them gradually intelligible without letting them overwhelm her.

In 1995, during a small drinking party with the young film crew and a staff member at the House of Sharing's new rural location, Pak Duri sang a three-verse version of the "Ballad of the Traveling Entertainer." The party is one of the showpiece scenes in Byun Young-joo's second documentary about the women, *Habitual Sadness* (*Najeun moksori 2*, 1997). She sits with the others in a forest of *makgeolli* (unfiltered rice wine) bottles and sings each verse, pausing after each to comment. She begins with a variant of her familiar joke about the truckload of men:

> *Water, water, load it up*
> *Bring it to the house on fire*
> *Load up a truck full of widowers*
> *And spread them around the House of Sharing*

Pak Duri: If one truck is too much, we'll share them around, OK?
Byun Yeong-joo: Yeah.

> *Oh time and tide, you go on by,*
> *You've got to go back alone.*
> *Why did you take with you*
> *The regretful, pitiful spring of Pak Duri's youth?*

Pak Duri: My heart is still fifteen years old . . . but somehow I'm seventy-four—what happened!?!
Byun Yeong-joo: You say your heart's still fifteen?
Pak Duri: My heart, here inside of me, is still as it was at fifteen, so how have I ever come to be seventy-four? Why did I grow old like this? Why did my age keep rising?

> *Hey dog, dog, you black dog,*
> *You blurry, fuzzy, shaggy dog*
> *When I scraped that leftover rice for you* [21]
> *Do you think I gave it to you because I was full?*
> *In the midnight, my extra lover is coming, so I fed you to shut you up.*

Pak Duri: Isn't that right?

Byun Yeong-joo: That's right.

Pak Duri: I've gotta give the dog some *nurunbap*. . . . My old man's here, my husband's here, but another guy is coming, you know. I can't help feeding the dog, or else the other guy won't come around. Here where my husband is, someone else's husband is coming. But if the dog up and barks, he [the other man] can't come, you know. So "Do you think I gave it to you because I was full? In the midnight my extra lover's coming, so stay put and don't bark! I gave you *nurunbap*, so why are you barking to let my husband know?" The meaning is deep, that one! (group laughter)

(Refrain) *Whoopee, it's wonderful, it's truly wonderful*
We've got to have fun while we can.[22] 🔊 7

Pak Duri is at the height of her humor and pathos, railing against the unfairness of the world, and seizing, in the winter of her life, that share she was never granted. She approaches the painful issue of aging, but cushions this confrontation by bookending it with jokes, creating another instance of her three-part pattern of vitality, death, and laughter. Verse 1 is the familiar joke about life and sexual union. Verse 2 is another woeful meditation on life's transience, a confrontation of life's inner cruelty. And in the final verse, her resetting of a famous verse from the southeastern folk song "Ballad of the Dog" ("Gaetaryeong"), she tells another, more elaborate joke on the theme of sexual union. Returning here to the lighter note, Pak Duri transforms the sorrowful contemplation of aging back into vitality and laughter, but a laughter permeated by a new understanding. After each verse, she calls on her audience to acknowledge its truth, making these truths speakable, inviting her discoveries into the ordinary realm of language and life.

Her joke about the dog is radically different in tone from the canonical text of "Ballad of the Dog" in circulation in contemporary South Korean traditional music circles, although it relates essentially the same story. In that text a genderless person beseeches a dog to be quiet, saying, "My beloved is coming,"[23] using the floral "beloved" (*nim* or *im*) and honorific verbs to signify respect and adoration. Pak Duri's verse is, as ever, considerably more direct. There are no honorific verbs. The obsequious references to the beloved so prevalent in folk and popular song are absent. The protagonist waits for a *gunseobang*, literally a "spare husband." Pak Duri towers over men, ordering them as she might order food delivered to her home, and not bothering with romantic gestures. Flaunting her powerful sexuality in the social space of song play, she reverses the relations of power that have dominated her life and becomes, for a moment, master of her own fortune.

The themes of sexual union and sexual play are perhaps the most striking aspect of Pak Duri's song play. For many of us it is somewhat surprising to hear elderly women or men, whom we assume to have been desexualized by age, speaking frankly about sex. On the other hand, many of us are familiar with characters such as the "dirty old man" and the "bawdy grandma." In Korea and elsewhere the status one inherits with age, combined with the freedom that many elderly people enjoy from the sexual policing by which cultures regulate human reproduction, allow elderly people to be more freely expressive about the subject of sex.

But the theme of sex is surprising in Pak Duri's case for another reason. As the "comfort women" survivors have become symbols of the national wound, the public expression of sexuality has become incompatible with the image of the archetypal "comfort woman grandmother." The sexuality of that archetype is assumed to have been irreversibly destroyed by Japanese colonialist sexual violence. The women's agency, where it is granted, is thought to be a sexless one, often identified with a transpersonal Korean Spirit that purports to have no sexuality.

In this light Pak Duri's racy musings are scandalous, destabilizing the archetypal victim and throwing South Korean popular consciousness into confusion. But she and many other survivors have not let the subject of sex alone for very good reasons. Trauma specialists and other scholars agree that for survivors of sexual violence the articulation of sexuality is a critical part of the process of recovering from traumatic experience.[24] The body and sexuality are the loci of the women's trauma, and hence they are a ground on which trauma must be overcome. In the experience of sexual violence, a person's body is rendered an object for the purposes of others' sexual use; reckoning with the subject of sex, a survivor of sexual violence lays claim to her body and makes it a part of herself as a subject.

Pak Duri's singing about sex was in this very basic sense a process of subjectivization, the process of "making 'one's own' something that was formerly alien" (Fink 1995: xii). This meant that she laid claim to her experiences of domination at the hands of men, the undigested and com-partmentalized traumatic memories that only cease to be traumatic when given a place in the story of one's life. The trauma specialist Judith Herman (1992) calls this process of integrating traumatic experience to a life story "narrativization." This was a moment of ownership in which Pak Duri became the subject of her own fate (Fink 1995: xiii), one of several essential steps in traumatic recovery, as described by Herman in her landmark *Trauma and Recovery* (1992: 175).[25]

Pak Duri gave a pithy characterization of this inseparability of sexuality and self in a song-joke she told to us at that song party soon after I first went to the House of Sharing:

Can't live on food alone

Can't live on booze alone

You and me, in the long, long night . . . ahahahaha![26]

Pak Duri's frank discussion of sexuality in song also helped her to participate in and feel part of society, another crucial stage of traumatic recovery outlined by Herman (1992: 196). As she inverted her life's pattern of suffering at the hands of men, she transformed that suffering into a community of laughter. This community shared a liminal freedom of expression, a range of emotions, and a special understanding about the nature of things. She transmitted her pain to her listenership and then turned it into laughter; the result was a temporary exorcism of fear and the birth of a new solidarity.

This community was changeable, depending on whom Pak Duri was singing for: a community of female listenership, or of elderly female listenership, or of survivors, or sometimes, in the last years before deafness stole her songs from her, a cross-generational and transnational community, including even those masses who watched and appreciated her performances on film. These communities coalesced around her, in part as social groups of her own design, and were thus a measure of her social power and a source of her confidence.

In her daily life Pak Duri stood balanced on a fulcrum between despair and isolation, and laughter and togetherness. In song her gallows humor and sexual jokes tipped the balance, not by shedding the presence of death, pain, and cruelty, but by entering more fully into them, interrogating them, seeking reconciliation and laughter. In so doing she edged closer to a freedom that was already "within the zone of death" (Adorno 1992: 153). In the frankness and expressivity of song, she opened up a space in which suffering was transformed into a kind of serious play, where victimization became the competence of a coherent self, where the male violence that objectifies women was transformed into an embodied female subjectivity, and where loneliness became the joy of companionship.

We might want to end with this discussion of Pak Duri's semicloistered social sphere of singing, with its wisdom and its humorous transformations of experience and the relations of power that governed her life. This wish to linger forever in the refined universe of art is a natural temptation in the study of the expressive life, of ritual, religious practice, and other alternative social arenas that exist within dreadful social realities. But these practices and their social spaces are variously dependent on, derived from, and responsive to the rest of social life, and so if we wish to edge closer to an understanding of Pak Duri's song world and its significance we cannot stop now. This is especially so because of the intense publicity of her later life, after she joined the movement and became one of a handful of star survivors. She lived only a small part of her life in the haven of song, and that haven was already in many ways a mirror image of the changing world that surrounded it.

Although Pak Duri's ribald song world turned the relations of sexual domination upside down, in some respects it left them intact, changing only the positions of the players. This is a common survivor response in the wake of traumatic experience. In *The Body in Pain* Elaine Scarry (1987) describes how, in the wake of torture, victims seek the very kinds of power that their torturers had denied them. In this way their reformed selves become mirror images of the torturer's desire.

Pak Duri's inversion in song of the power relations between men and women seems eerily like a reflection of the social patterns of sexual domination that bore so much of the responsibility for her traumatic experiences of captivity and sexual violence. Like other inversion rituals, her fantasies of power ratified those structures by embracing them even as she challenged her place in them. But in so doing she was able to reconstitute herself as a person, to grasp a measure of social power, and to reclaim her body and experiences from a history that had rendered her an object for male pleasure and an inert vessel of traumatic experience. And her inversions and parodies destabilized the categories of power, opening up on unknown possibilities (Butler 1990), if only for moments at a time.

Pak Duri knew she was generally not supposed to speak of certain things, and song became a place where she could express them. In this way, much as the song world mirrored structures of domination, it also was an inverse image of public speech. At the borders of her song world she encountered propriety, repression, and a learned deafness. These conditions created the need for the song world, gave it its shape, and quarantined certain kinds of taboo expression within it. Although such social forces from her distant wartime past and her postwar life influenced her song world, the conditions of her current life at the House of Sharing and in the "comfort women grandmothers movement" did so just as much. As she was called upon to speak publicly in the era of the movement, her song world maintained its status as an arena of a certain freedom to which other arenas of social life would edge closer but never fully accept.

In these ways her song world reflected the rest of her social life. But the opposite was also true: the self and world she designed in song shaped and transformed other arenas of her life. The song world was the greenhouse of an agency that, unleashed in the era of the movement, would loom large in the history of 1990s Korea: the figure of the thunderous, defiant "comfort woman grandmother," Pak Duri, who produced an archtype stamped with her image. The patterned expressiveness of song manifested in her everyday speech and testimony (*jeung-eon*). The more obvious characteristics of music, such as outright melody, would disappear, but many formal traits, such as rhythm and motives, remained.

In October 1994, during the filming of the first film in Byun Young-joo's trilogy of documentaries about Korean survivors of Japanese military slavery, Byun interviewed Pak Duri in her room at the House of Sharing in its final Seoul location before it was moved to the countryside. Byun asked her about her late husband:

> Byun Young-joo: Don't you ever want to see your husband?
>
> Pak Duri: Ugh, that leper, I hate seeing him even in my sleep. 'Cause he gave me so much grief. 'Cause he'd get drunk and give me grief. When he died I didn't cry—no tears, no water from my nose—nothing. Not even a drop.
>
> Byun Young-joo: Have you suffered a lot?
>
> Pak Duri: I've got no heart left. Cause I suffered so much. My daughter, and at that time I had a son, you know, I had a son, and when his father died he didn't cry a single teardrop. He suffered a lot, had so many troubles, that he didn't even look up. If his mother, his own father died, he wouldn't cry.
>
> Byun Young-joo: Grandma, in that case, as you've lived, was there no time when you didn't suffer?
>
> Pak Duri: *Ahyu* . . . when haven't I suffered? My whole life I've suffered. When I was growing up I suffered. In my parent's home we couldn't survive and so I begged for food. Then I went to Japan and suffered too.[27] Then I went to the countryside and suffered too. Then I had to go to Busan and buy and sell produce and what not and apples and that kind of stuff and eat and live like that. And paying rent, and water, and electricity, I suffered.[28] 🔊 8

Although she speaks, Pak Duri's answers flow like songs, or raps, speckled with motives, rhythmic devices, and melodic formulas. Her speech and song are formally interconnected by these shared traits. Her answer to the last question quoted above (which starts at 40 seconds on the online recording) is divided into phrases of increasing length, all of which she begins in a relatively high-pitched voice before gradually descending to the final expression, "I suffered" (*gosaeng haetji*).[29] In the first two phrases we can hear Pak Duri establish "I suffered" as a short refrain, a cadential formula like the amen at the end of chains of Judeo-Christian prayer. Although her riffs get progressively longer, they always end in the same way: "I suffered." Her last two sentences make up one long continuous blast, linked and punctuated with the percussive *go* (and). "Then I was living in Busan *and* buying *and* selling produce *and* what not *and* apples *and* that kind of stuff *and* eating *and* living like that. *And* paying rent, *and* water, *and* electricity, I suffered."

The final rapid-fire articulation of her various trials slides down gradually into her closing refrain, "I suffered."

If we compare this slice of Pak Duri's interview with her versions of the "Ballad of the Traveling Entertainer" we can find closing motifs in both: "I suffered" and "We've got to have fun while we can." Both of these refrains are arrived at via a descending pitch contour, which is crystallized as melody in the song but is no less present in speech. The difference between her use of pitch, form, rhythm, timbre, and other musical parameters in speech and song lies only in the degree of formalization.

I am not trying to claim a one-way relationship by which song provided the generative patterns for Pak Duri's speech. Rather it seems more likely that her different verbal virtuosities were mutually sustaining, and there was a good deal of crossover in both directions. But the song world had been a special space of expression during Pak Duri's long decades of secrecy about her experiences as a "comfort woman," so in the face of these many musical features of her speech it seems reasonable to assume that when she finally stepped forward onto the national stage and began to recount her experiences in testimony, she drew on expressive techniques that she had long cultivated in her song world.

She borrowed from song a technique of controlling emotion through structured expression. She also made use of the highly individualized style and voice that she had cultivated in her world of song in her public speech. In the 1990s, in the era of the movement, South Korean society would look to her to testify on behalf of thousands and would take her stories as representative ones. But Pak Duri would speak resolutely about herself, striving continually to make people acknowledge the particularity of her self and her experiences in addition to their generic qualities—a sense of particularity that she cultivated in song. She brought to bear the self that she cultivated in song and its resources—expressive talent, humor, wisdom, and confidence—on her public testimonies.

So just as Pak Duri's song lingered on the threshold of speech, her talk traversed the continuum between speech and song, allowing her to draw on the expressive resources of singing in the course of interviews and public speech. She cultivated this position on the threshold of talk and song in the Korean folk genre called "Ballad of Life's Trials" ("Sinsae taryeong"), a rumination in song-like speech on life's sorrows especially popular among elderly women. In "Ballad of Life's Trials" vocalization singers pour their hearts out in an improvised recitative in which a varying percentage of the text syllables have clear pitches, and which may or may not have a regular pulse or metric pattern. The genre is a kind of heightened speech in which intense emotion is formalized into musical elements such as vibrato ornaments, voice-breaking sounds, and long, downward glissandos.[30]

Figure 2.4.
Pak Duri, November 1998.
Photo courtesy of the House of Sharing/Museum of Sexual Slavery by the Japanese Military.

In the late 1990s, some years after Pak Duri joined the "comfort women movement," a television crew filmed her speak-singing a "Ballad of Life's Trials" on the couch outside her room at the House of Sharing. It was night, and Pak Duri was talking with the monk Hyejin, who directed the House at the time and with whom she had a close relationship. At the end of a long argument with Hyejin she began to half-sing a melody loosely related to the central Korean folk song "Norae garak" (Song-tune), which provided a melodic framework for her song-speech. She oscillated between set and free rhythm, and between pitched and nonpitched vocalization:

> *Because my fate turned out rotten like this,*
> *I went off to Japan to suffer for six years.*

I came back to Korea and suffered for many years.
I couldn't speak of it in public . . .
To whom shall I say something?
Even when Grandma Pak Duri dies,
She'll have so many regrets.[31] 9

Pak Duri sang her "Ballad of Life's Trials" at times of particular emotional strain, when she needed the thread of melody and the structure of music to help discipline her emotions. In this case it also gave weight to her words, through which she intended to explain to the monk the emotions that had fueled her end of their argument. The disciplining of emotions through the structuring elements of music was therefore a means of expression, self-consolidation, and restoring social harmony.

I heard her use this style of vocalization once during my tenure at the House of Sharing, late one night in 2002. She lay in her room worrying about her grandchildren and admonishing her daughter, who had not called for some time. Her hearing was almost gone, so I was not able to identify the tune that served as the melodic framework for the piece, if there was one. But the musical gestures—glissandos, rough melodic sequences, and rhythm—were unmistakable. She lay on her side singing toward the doorway, as if hoping that her words might reach through the ether to her daughter.

In this moment I sensed the importance of the spaces between speech and song for Pak Duri and thought about the means by which the expressive resources of song, and the self that she cultivated in song, found their way into speech. Her public persona as an articulate speaker was the site where the expressive competence and the coherence of self and world that she developed in song took up residence in the realm of the movement.

Paradoxically, however, public culture expected her and other survivors to be competent speakers precisely in order to give voice to brokenness. Pak Duri thus lived a double life, pulled between poles of an intimate sphere of tears, laughter, and ongoing healing, and a public sphere of the competent performance of brokenness. Her spoken expressions of suffering in the context of the movement contrasted dramatically with the humorous and ribald transformations of suffering found in her song play. After years of repression she wanted to express her lifetime of suffering publicly, and this is precisely what South Korean society wanted to hear.

The public sphere of performing woundedness was therapeutic because it gave Pak Duri a receptive audience that acknowledged and validated her experiences, making her into a national martyr. She and other survivors derived a sense of validation from their mass mediation, from the dissemination and amplification of their voices. But as she moved in the sphere of the movement she became subject to the expectations of public culture. She became assimilated into an archetypal, if changeable, image of the "comfort woman grandmother," although it bore her stamp. Wounded nationalism insisted on the persistence and the preservation of the wound and asked for infinite encores of the performance of suffering. The song world persisted as a social space in which healing was a possible goal, which the pressures of public cultural life continued to inspire.

In the heyday of her participation in the movement in the mid-1990s, Pak Duri appears to have gone to some lengths to keep her song play within her intimate sphere of friends, perhaps suspecting that it was not appropriate to the media spotlight. Maybe she felt that the often happy face of her songs and the imperfect healing it implied contradicted the image of the victim of Japanese military sexual slavery that was growing in South Korean public culture as the women and their supporters struggled for public recognition and support. She had much vested in her public image as a victim and had no wish to harm the cause of the movement. Perhaps she contained her song world because it was essentially intimate, and so its freedom was based on its relative distance from public culture.

One example of Pak Duri's and her peers' efforts to contain her song world appears in *The Murmuring* (1995), the first film of Byun Young-joo's documentary trilogy, which takes place in the early years of the movement. Son Panim, a fellow survivor, is trying to get Pak Duri to go to the capitol building to talk with government officials about the "comfort women" issue. Pak Duri says she won't go if she doesn't have to, because she is not confident in her speaking ability. Son Panim tries to cajole her into going by quoting her familiar verse from the "Ballad of the Traveling Entertainer":

> Son Panim: Big sister, you go there and then do something like this.
>
> (half singing) "Water, water, load up some water / Take it to Pak Duri's room." What was that ... "Take it to a place that's caught on fire...."
>
> Pak Duri: What're you telling me to do? Over there ...
>
> Son Panim: Hahaha.
>
> Pak Duri: What, over there ... you tellin' me to go there?
>
> Son Panim: "Load up a truck of widowers and / Bring them to Pak Duri's room!" That, that's what I mean.
>
> Kim Sundeok: All these things you're saying come out here [in the movie], they all go into it. They all come out, these things you're saying....
>
> Son Panim: So what if I say that? 🔊 10

Son suggests that Pak Duri should go to the capitol because she has a sung eloquence that will transfer to speech. The comment is an example of how much many elderly Koreans associate social competence with song. But Pak Duri ignores the comment, seeming slightly embarrassed at the exposure of her intimate song world. Finally Kim Sundeok steps in to put a stop to Son's transgression of the unwritten rule—that Pak Duri's sexualized, tragicomic expression stay out of the public-cultural face of the "comfort women" movement. Son resists, but lapses into silence.

Pak Duri and her small community of survivors were not alone in this work of containment. The movement was in the difficult position of wanting to acknowledge the women's strength, courage, and selfhood, while preventing reactionary misreadings of their songs, stories, speeches, and other expressive forms. In 2003, as I planned an exhibition of the songs of survivors, a male activist advised that it might be best not to exhibit Pak Duri's "Ballad of the Traveling Entertainer" because people—Koreans, perhaps even the Japanese right wing—would hear in it the voice of a prostitute who became a "comfort woman" by choice. Although I ignored the advice, I knew that his concerns were legitimate and made a point of mentioning the vast significance of the song and its sexual content in the exhibition literature.

The English subtitles of the exchange from Byun Young-joo's *The Murmuring* provide a fascinating example of the containment of Pak Duri's song play. Below I give my translation (left) alongside the film's English subtitles:

Son Panim:	Big sister, you go there and then do something like this. "Water, water, load up some water Take it to Pak Duri's room" . . . What was that . . . Take it to a place that's caught on fire. . . ."	I want you to go. Get the compensation money. You take the money back to your room . . . "take it somewhere or share with the needy.
Pak Duri:	What're you telling me to do? Over there . . .	What for?
Son Panim:	Hahahaha.	
Pak Duri:	What, over there . . . you tellin' me to go there?	
Son Panim:	"Load up a truck of widowers and Bring them to Pak Duri's room!" That, that's what I mean.	Load the money in a car and take it back.
Kim Sundeok:	All these things you're saying come out here [in the movie]. They all come out, these things you're saying . . .	Stop the nonsense. This is filmed.
Son Panim:	So what if I say that?	I don't care.

In the English subtitles Pak Duri's musical realm is rendered as a series of political statements by one woman encouraging another to participate in the movement. The translation staff, not knowing the context of Son Panim's quotation, misinterpret Pak Duri's song, "normal forming" the text as a political message (Cicourel 1973: 86; Mehan and Wood 1975). Her terms are not translated verbatim or decoded, but are simply replaced with the conventional expressive forms of the movement. This may have been intentional or just a telling instance of sloppy work, although that is unlikely, as the published Korean-language transcript of the movie is quite accurate (Girok yeonghwa jejakso Boim 1998: 71–72). In either case the consequences are the same: Pak Duri's expressive life is normalized to meet social expectations, and another layer is added to the membrane of propriety that surrounds her song world.

The sociologist of knowledge Harold Garfinkel (1967: 53) claimed that common understanding is based on "the enforceable character of actions in compliance with the expectancies of everyday life as a morality." The mistranslation of Pak Duri's lyric about bringing a truckload of men to her room to quench her sexual desire and relieve her loneliness demonstrates the incomprehensibility of that lyric in the terms of the national imaginary of woundedness, which is an example of the kind of morality that Garfinkel is talking about. The verse hints at an agency that is incompatible with the desexualized victim. Pak Duri's voice is transformed, here and elsewhere, through a complex, multilayered process of editing and assimilation. Her sexualized song play, her taboo means of overcoming, was filtered; her sense of self as whole, the taboo result of that overcoming, was refined and re-presented to the public as Pak Duri, the competent yet broken fighter-victim.

So there were many reasons why Pak Duri's song world would never fully appear in South Korean public culture. Although the majority of activists and others who came into contact with her were compelled by her bawdy, humorous song world, some were concerned about the confusion her songs could bring to the movement if they were misunderstood. Her songs were only one province of the world of women's song that had spent thousands of years being ignored, perfecting the technique of being ignored, and relishing the freedom that came with being ignored.

For all of these reasons a vast amount of Pak Duri's expressive life was never recorded, and is lost to history. But as she spent time in the movement, some activists, filmmakers, and journalists, almost all women, were drawn to her song world and began to listen to her carefully and document her song world. As the movement went on Pak Duri increasingly cooperated with such projects to record and broadcast her expressive life. Beginning to feel secure in the world of the movement and the House of Sharing, she began to admit growing numbers of people, including artists and media people, to her inner circle and her song world.

Byun Young-joo, whose films record several of Pak Duri's performances that we have discussed in this chapter, produced the first substantial record of her song world of which I am aware. Byun was struck by the radical aspects of Pak Duri's song world and of other women's arts of survival in the course of making her first film, *The Murmuring* (1995). Her project for the second film, *Habitual Sadness* (1997), allowed the women to showcase their favorite things: farmwork, songs, jokes. Pak Duri and her songs, such as the long three-verse "Ballad of the Traveling Entertainer" that culminates with the joke about the dog and the "spare husband," became a kind of centerpiece of the film.

With this film Byun provided a decidedly new framing of Pak Duri and her songs. Confronted with Pak Duri's transformations of suffering and death into laughter and togetherness, she created a straightforward, cinema verité–style film that allowed others to experience this confrontation and its revelations. Viewer-listeners had an opportunity to experience the way her song world grated, in its expressions of healing, sexuality, and transformation, against the normative expectations of the ideologies of national woundedness. They could also learn about this healing, sexuality, and transformation as contexts for understanding Pak Duri's experience of Japanese military sexual slavery and its aftermath, and rethink their received understandings of the "comfort women" issue and the survivors. They also had an opportunity to learn about the part that play may have in the process of healing and to admire the strength of a survivor who had found her way through the maze of traumatic recovery with only modern folk culture to guide her.

All the same, when Byun chose her Korean and English titles for the documentary she chose the Korean title *Najeun moksori 2* (The murmuring 2, a sequel title) and the English title *Habitual Sadness*, thereby remaining squarely within the language of national woundedness.[32] We see here the persistence of the boundary between what could be represented in film and what could be expressed in language. But the close attentiveness of the film to the women's voices and expressive practices, irrespective of their overt political usefulness, was new and part of a growing trend. In this way Byun's representations of Pak Duri's songs in her second film forecast changes in discourse and other aspects of the social life, which sometimes lag behind music, film, and other expressive forms.[33]

The film's gesture beyond ideologies of perpetual national woundedness did not go unnoticed. The *Hanguk Ilbo* (Korea daily news) printed a review of the film by the arts reporter Yi Yunjeong on Independence Day, August 15, 1997, titled "Songs of Hope—Sung by the Comfort Women

Grandmothers." As Pak Duri's songs became "songs of hope" (*huimang ui norae*), one might suspect that they were made subservient to the political struggle for official apology and reparations from Japan, which is at the forefront of most Koreans' minds when the words "comfort women" are spoken. But Yi Yunjeong makes no mention of this in her article, suggesting instead that the movie depicts women who have found the hope and the will to "live in the world" again. Yi suggests that the women had avoided the camera when Byun made her first film, but in the second one they "stood squarely in front of the camera to show their will and hope."

These survivors, who had hidden and been hidden from the public view for so long, had now seemingly found the strength to claim a place for themselves in the social world, to find their relation to the symbolic order, which was Lacan's (1977: 48, Fink 1995: 13) famous conception of the subject. The title of Yi's article suggests that song is a source of such strength. It grasps the basic mechanism of Pak Duri's songs, by which she transforms suffering into pleasure, crying into laughter, and victimization into power.

The film *Habitual Sadness* and its reception signaled the beginning of a new way of apprehending the women and their experience. Some South Koreans were less interested in the survivors' symbolic capital as victims than in appreciating them—as women, as Koreans, as elders—and in learning from them about survival, recovery, and life in general. The film portrayed the struggle for reparations and apology as one aspect of the women's lives, as opposed to portraying the women exclusively as victims (or at worst as mere resources in a political struggle), the more common treatment of the women in the mass media.

But despite the progressively intense mass-mediation and exposure of Pak Duri's songs, a number of factors ensured that they remained intimate, if public. One factor was the songs' opacity, the way their significance and import to her (and to other women who shared in women's folk culture) were strategically not audible in surface listening. This privacy was aided by the persistent social tendency to ignore the singing and stories of old women. And it was aided by the way that filmmakers and viewers represented and understood Pak Duri's song world as an intimate one, taking place in intimate spaces, concerned with intimate subjects, and addressed to intimate groups. So while the songs became a mass-mediated means of circulating sentiment and of giving the "comfort women" an explicit place in South Korean public sentimentality, they remained a means by which Pak Duri united people in a changeable, intimate community of young and old that shared sorrow, truth, and a partial overcoming. Many young people who sought her out had been inspired to do so after seeing her films, and so her community stretched beyond the boundaries of the small rooms in which it seemed to take place. The video camera and the newspaper helped to spread her secret joke and its dialectic in code—the ribald prattling of an old woman.

So a number of forces mediated between Pak Duri's social space of healing and the social space of competent brokenness: her expressive competence, which persisted in testimony, speech, and song; the coded circulation of her song play in the public sphere via various media; and the young people and others who came from the space of the national wound into her song world and its space of reckoning and healing. All of this traffic in and out of her song world destabilized the dichotomy between the social spaces of woundedness and song play, but the boundary remained.

Perhaps the lingering public cultural disinterestedness in Pak Duri's efforts of healing was one thing that stifled her work of recovery; certainly the frustrations of the political struggle were another, as were numerous other obstacles in her personal life. The work of healing and self-making are, by their nature, ongoing and never complete, but the processual nature of selfhood seems to me to at least have the potential to break away from those social forces that conspire to break us and keep us broken.

One day in the fall of 2003 Pak Duri set out for Kim Sundeok's room on the other side of the House of Sharing. The two women had long had a special relationship, having both moved into the House back in 1992. For years Pak Duri jokingly saluted Kim Sundeok, who was five years her elder, and she often sought her out for advice and assistance. With some difficulty Pak Duri climbed the stairs and knocked on her door, opening it without waiting for a reply. As she poked her head through the door she told her friend that during the night the ghosts of her dead husband and children had visited her. In desperation she asked Kim Sundeok, who had experience in getting rid of ghosts, to help.

As Pak Duri and I watched, Kim Sundeok gathered a bunch of dry red peppers and mixed them together with torn-up strips of newspaper in a pot. Then she set them on fire, and we all left the room, chased out by the acrid smoke, which I could have sworn was red.

Sitting with Pak Duri, who really looked as though she had just seen a ghost, I wondered why those phantoms were visiting her. There were many reasons, among which I learned only a few. There was the experience of Japanese military sexual slavery and everything that followed: a life of constant trial and privation, a herculean effort to rebuild herself and her life under postwar conditions of public secrecy, and an unresolved political struggle. There were the souls of her children, wandering restlessly in the wake of their untimely deaths. And I suspect that the national ideology of woundedness also bore some of the responsibility, wedging open the door that let in the ghosts. Pak Duri's singing, in all its pungency, was like fire and pepper smoke against all these malign forces, and this swirl of ghosts and smoke, sorrow and strength, tears and laughter was the dynamic of her split social world.

In the documentary *The Murmuring* she had made an eloquent statement of her fervent wish for death. In the summer of 2003 she told me the exact same story as a bottomless joke: "I know all these grandmas who want to live forever, and they just drop dead. But I, who have been thinking for so long 'I wanna die, I wanna die, I wanna die,' I just keeeeeeeeeep on living! Ahahahahahahahahaha!" In her alchemical songs and jokes, perched on the threshold of despair and hope, Pak Duri found the self, the strength, and the tools to convert adversity and despair into laughter and to transform the cruelty of the world into a hearth of human intimacy.

Pak Duri died at the age of eighty-one, in the early evening of February 19, 2006, at Metro Hospital in Anyang, up against the mountains south of Seoul. After a two-year hospitalization that began in 2004, she finally succumbed to cancer.

A few days after she died her body passed in grim procession through the streets of suburban Seoul. Mourner-demonstrators dressed in black carried black banners through the streets in front of the hearse (which was black), emblazoned with slogans calling for the Japanese government to issue an official apology and give reparations to the women. There were a number of tributes and memorials to Pak Duri over the next few weeks; a few mentioned her songs. She and the larger share of her unwritten history passed from the world with a quiet, ceremonial, and particularly official quality.

How shall we remember Pak Duri? Victim, survivor, activist, singer, mother, grandmother, philosopher—there are many words we will need. I want to remember, and I want others to remember, the history that she wrote into her world of song: a life story of pain, persistence, wisdom, and laughter. I want to remember Pak Duri's fantastically loud voice, a product of her life and her exuberance, with its timbre of striking and blazing matches. I want to remember how, when that voice collapsed into the black holes of her suffering or the maelstroms of her representation, Pak Duri pulled it back out again and remade it in the image of her toil, sorrow, and joy.

Hooray, it's wonderful, it's really wonderful—
We've got to have fun while we can.

Figure 2.5.
Pak Duri singing at the House of Sharing, late 1990s. Bae Chunhui plays *janggo* (hourglass drum)
accompaniment.
Photo courtesy of the House of Sharing/Museum of Sexual Slavery by the Japanese Military.

Mun Pilgi

In a strange, foreign land, that night, that young woman,
Somehow it won't let me, let me forget.
A love strung along a guitar's string, a wanderer's love—
Cry, oh guitar, oh my guitar.

　　　　　　　　　　—Mun Pilgi, "Cry, Guitar String" 🌑 11

I n September 2002 the Korean Council invited me to accompany about forty survivors on a trip to Jeju Island, a popular vacation and honey-moon destination about seventy-five kilometers south of the Korean peninsula. Council Director Yun Mee-hyang told me that this and other excursions that the Council organized were designed to give survivors, many of whom lived alone, opportunities to share memories and develop friendships. Together with other young volunteers, I was to accompany the women in their sightseeing, helping them with their luggage and other things.

On arriving at the island's small airport, I boarded my assigned bus. In the middle of the seats on the right side of the bus I saw Mun Pilgi, whom I had met at the Wednesday demonstration and who three years later would tell me the story of finding, preparing, and eating the inner bark of a pine tree.

As we toured the island, the Council activists passed a microphone and encouraged each of the women to sing. Singing like this on buses is yet another kind of "song party" quite common in South Korea; if you drive the speed limit and keep your eyes open on the highway, you are bound to see buses fly past you, aisles packed with middle-aged pop song enthusiasts dancing and singing beneath twirling disco balls. The survivors' version of this was somewhat more sedentary; they eschewed the disco balls and the ubiquitous *noraebang* (karaoke) machine for the reverberant sound of one amplified singer, supported by the clapping, interjections, and intermittent group singing of her peers and companions.

Mun Pilgi was sitting next to her close friend Kim Yushim, who was a few years younger than she and accordingly called her "big sister," as Pak Duri had called her friend and spiritual advisor, Kim Sundeok. The mic came to the pair, and Mun Pilgi's eyes lit up at the emcee's request for a song. Together the two women sang a long string of Korean pop songs from the genre popularly called *teuroteu* (a Koreanized abbreviation of "foxtrot"),[1] an assimilation of Japanese popular music to Korea during the colonial period. Not knowing any better at the time, I assumed that their songs were all quite old; later I was to discover that they spanned the whole of Mun Pilgi's life, from the colonial era to the turn of the twenty-first century.

The bus driver stopped for a quick break, and about half the women filed out for a stretch, a trip to the restroom, or a long-anticipated smoke. I approached Mun Pilgi and Kim Yushim, who were standing beside the road taking a breath of fresh air. Mun Pilgi was wearing a pink windbreaker, which softly reflected the bright island sun. As I would find out later, her favorite colors (and most of her clothes) were shades of pink, orange, red, and purple.

I asked her about the songs she had been singing. She stared back at me for a second in silence; then, with a grin, she began to sing and dance. "Hey, dance," she said.

When I told her I couldn't, she scolded me with a smile. "Are you sure you're an American?" Her image of Americans was shaped by the classic Hollywood films that had been brought to South Korea along with so much else of American popular culture in the post-1945 era, beginning with the American occupation of South Korea. She was thinking of a cinematic world where all American men could ballroom dance, and of a time when many off-screen Americans knew how as well. I answered that I was pretty sure I was American, and she shrugged. She taught me some basic ballroom steps, taking the male part and leading me through. She hummed one of her favorite pop songs, giving me instructions all the while.

A few days later, after a whirlwind tour of the island, we returned to Seoul's Gimpo Airport by plane. I escorted Mun Pilgi home in a taxi to her apartment in West Seoul, close to the airport, but she didn't invite me in for tea. She had a keen mistrust of people, especially men, and took her time getting to know them. At times in the past her survival had depended on such shrewdness.

Mun Pilgi was born in 1925 in the Jisu district of southeastern Korea, now part of Jinju city.[2] Her parents kept a small shop where they sold fish,

Figure 3.1.
Mun Pilgi at the House of Sharing, 2005.
Photo by the author.

persimmons, and sweet potatoes; her mother ran the store and her father went back and forth between the shop and the marketplace. They also owned some small plots for farming. Her family was poor, so she worked in the fields and at the spinning wheel and the loom from the age of eight.

The formal primary and secondary education of girls had begun in Korea in the late nineteenth century in metropolitan areas and grew throughout the peninsula in the early years of the twentieth century. But although the Japanese colonial government had proclaimed a universal education policy for the Korean peninsula, schools were in short supply, especially in rural areas, and societal codes discouraging female education persisted. So few rural girls had the chance to get an education. Mun Pilgi wanted to go to school, but her conservative father forbade it. Girls shouldn't study, he said, because they become too crafty and fox-like. But she persisted in wanting to study, and so her mother raised some money from the store and snuck her off to regular school one day when she was a teenager.

Her father found out within just a few days. He rushed into the classroom, dragged her back to their home, burned her books, beat her, and threw her out of the house. She came back home some nights later and said no more to her parents about wanting to study. But she continued to dream about learning to read, studying, expanding her mind, and gaining the skills she thought would better her life.

One day in 1943, when she was seventeen, a Korean man from her village who worked under the local Japanese police approached her. He said he would find her a position in which she could both earn a living and study. She agreed, boarding a truck bound for Busan. From there she traveled by train under Japanese military escort past Keijo (colonial Seoul) and Pyeongyang to Changchun, Manchuria.

Mun Pilgi had been tricked. She was taken not to a factory but to a Japanese military base. She worked for a short time as a nurse, but soon after a doctor at an army hospital raped her. He kept her for a while as his private sexual slave but soon put her to work in the "comfort station" located next to the military base. She had to serve around ten soldiers a day on weekdays and between forty and fifty a day some weekends. She was beaten and tortured when she resisted. One drunken soldier branded her with a hot iron, and another cut her with a knife.

The place was run by Koreans; one of them beat Mun Pilgi for the slightest infraction of "comfort station" policy. The staff made sure that she and the other young women didn't escape. In her three years there she left the camp only a few times, when the doctor took her to the movies.

Mun Pilgi found out the war had ended when soldiers stopped coming to visit the "comfort station." The Japanese military fled, leaving her and the other sexual slaves behind. After an interval of a few days the station was stormed by Soviet troops, who, rifles drawn, tried to rape her and the others. Everyone scattered; she escaped with the manager, his wife, and a friend through the back door. They jumped a train and took it as far as the Yalu River, on the Chinese-Korean border. She said farewell to her companions there. She began to walk, day and night, through the mountains and the plains of northern Korea. She walked for hundreds of miles without proper food or rest, eventually reaching Seoul.

At Seoul Station Mun Pilgi caught a train to her hometown in the Southeast. When she got home everyone greeted her like someone returned from the grave. She discovered that her father had died not long before her return. She told me that her mother said, "He died because of you." Her mother soon set to work to find her a husband, but, she said, "I couldn't bear the thought of being someone's wife, not with my past as a comfort woman to haunt me" (Hanguk jeongsindae munje daechaek hyobuihoe and Jeongsindae yeonguhoe 1993: 118). Not wishing to marry or to tell her mother what had happened to her, she left without a word and wandered from town to town in the countryside working in *suljip*, drinking houses where women pour drinks, make conversation, and sing and dance with male customers. Here as well she was tormented by clients' advances, so she kept moving from job to job. She eventually ran a drinking house of her own, with a motel attached.

At thirty-five years old she met a railway worker and they moved to Seoul to live together. Later she found out that he was already married and had children. He drank daily and died soon after they arrived in Seoul. She lived alone again for some years until she brought her sister's grandchild home to raise as her own. In the mid-1990s, after registering as a survivor of Japanese military sexual slavery, she moved into an apartment with support from the South Korean government fund for survivors.

In the late 1990s her adopted grandson moved away to do his military service, and she was alone again. Her neighbors looked in on her, and she was visited by occasional reporters, activists, and researchers. Volunteers and staff from the Korean Council visited her every so often. She went out to the weekly Wednesday demonstration in front of Seoul's Japanese Embassy, traveling by subway or taxi, and she went to the doctor and ran errands, but she spent much of her time at home alone. She was an enthusiastic participant in the many sightseeing trips organized by the Korean Council and gained a reputation as an enthusiastic singer.

Mun Pilgi had long been haunted by recurring nightmares of her wartime experiences, and they began to gradually return once she was alone again. In the fall of 2003, after a particularly intense spell of nightmares, she gave up her apartment in Seoul and moved into the House of Sharing. She took the bedroom adjacent to the kitchen, across the living room from Pak Duri, whom she had known for years through their mutual participation in the "comfort women" movement. On March 5, 2008, at the age of eighty-two, she died as the result of chronic illnesses of the lungs and kidneys in a geriatric hospital in nearby Yangpyeong.

I knew Mun Pilgi for a little more than a year before she moved into the House. I often met her at the Wednesday demonstration in front of the Japanese Embassy, and one day I asked her if I could come to see her at her apartment. On a cold day in February 2003 I visited her apartment for the first time. I went with some friends whom Mun Pilgi also knew: the museum director from the House of Sharing, an old friend of hers; Tsukasa, a Japanese activist photographer also working at the House of Sharing; and Amy, a young Fulbright student writing a critical report on

Figure 3.2.
Mun Pilgi outside her apartment, February 2003.
Photo by Yajima Tsukasa.

activist organizations involved in the "comfort women grandmothers movement."

Mun Pilgi's apartment was an upper-floor studio in a giant complex of identical high-rise buildings with huge numbers on the sides, of the type common in Seoul and throughout South Korea. Her door was flanked by *onggi* pots that stored *kimchi*, soybean paste, soy sauce, and other cooking essentials.

I knocked tentatively and shouted a greeting through the door. Mun Pilgi opened the door. "Ah, you came? Come on in," she said, gesturing. The four of us squeezed through the door, Tsukasa with his camera bag, me with my recorder and a gift box of juices, and settled on the warm *ondol* radiant-heat floor of her one-room apartment. It was a moment not unfamiliar to Mun Pilgi, as a participant in the "comfort women grandmothers move-ment," a moment when her solitude was suddenly interrupted by an inter-national group of researchers, or well-wishers, or activists. We tried unsuccessfully to make ourselves smaller than we were.

After the initial greetings Mun Pilgi began to talk quietly about her apart-ment and her life there. As she did so she laboriously put a tape into a small portable radio-cassette player. The tape was of Tae Jina, a Korean pop singer who debuted in the 1970s and had recently scored a hit with the ballad "Sarangeun amuna hana" (Can everyone love?), which she had been listening to and memorizing. A prior visitor had put a large green sticker on the play button of the boom box and a red one on the stop button to give her visual cues about how to operate it. We listened through to the end of one side; she turned the tape over and pressed play.

Mun Pilgi began to talk about her parents—her mother, whom she longed for, and her father, for whom she had long borne a profound resentment. Engrossed, she neglected to turn the tape over when it ended. Instead she began speaking about loneliness. Then we all fell together into silence; the only prominent sound was the low hum of the refrigerator. She began to speak again, her voice breaking through the veil of quiet, unfolding the story of the origins of song that begins this book.

> Mun Pilgi: I'm ... every day ...
> a lonely soul, a lonely soul.
>
> (pause)
>
> It's so quiet here! It's quiet, right?
> (*Amy and I laugh awkwardly, responding to her smile.*)
> Cause I've got nowhere to go.
> (*Mun Pilgi points to the radio-cassette player.*)
>
> Josh: Don't you like the quiet?
> Mun Pilgi: No, I *don't* like it.
> it's that I'm so lonely,
> so I turn on the TV, or turn on the radio,
> *kung, kung, kung* ...
> Because I'm so lonely,
> I turn on the TV, or turn on the radio,
> *kung-jjak, kung-jjak* ...
> That's how I live.
> Because I'm lonely. I'm bored, you know. 12

As Mun Pilgi told us about her loneliness, she described the ongoing process by which she created, out of popular media, a social world to set against her isolation. Although I touched on this process in the introduction, much of its texture and technique remains to be discovered. "So I turn on the TV, or I put on the radio, *kung, kung....* I'm so lonely, so I turn on the TV, put on the radio, *kung-jjak, kung-jjak.*" She repeated herself, and each time she mimicked the sound of rhythmic music issuing from the radio, but she elaborated the rhythm. A simple *kung, kung, kung* became *kung-jjak, kung-jjak*, an onomatopoeic expression similar to the alternate name of her favorite song genre, *teuroteu*. The name is *bbong-jjak*, an onomatopoeia generated out of these practices of singing the core rhythmic patterns of the genre.

These rhythmic mnemonics are a popular means by which *teuroteu* devotees vocalize instrumental accompaniment while singing or listening to others. They are a major feature of the soundscape of song-party picnics in Korean public parks, of the *noraebang* (karaoke) clubs of the Korean peninsula, and of the accompaniment to singing on tour buses and elsewhere. These vocalizations often appear formalized in recorded song, as in 1993's "Chan chan chan," or the plethora of songs that include the phrase *cha-cha-cha*.[3]

The vocalizations provide a means of participation for all fans of the genre. They shatter the hard divisions between singer and audience, those between recording and live performance, and those between language and sound. Perhaps these various alchemical gestures are one reason why Song Daegwan, in his 1999 hit "Nebakja" (Four-beat rhythm), could claim:

> *The laughing and crying history of our lives,*
> *which contains our life stories*
> *The novelesque history of the world*
> *The entire history of the world, a four-beat rhythm, kung-jjak.*[4]

Such onomatopoeic devices in *teuroteu* sit at the threshold of language, sound, and song, and hence are very useful for singers who wish to move among these different expressive realms. A mention of the genre name can trigger song; on the other hand, one can go from singing to speaking of *teuroteu* or *bbong-jjak* and still remain squarely within its aesthetic universe by way of rhythmic vocalization, which never quite ceases to be music.

In addition, as they occupy the threshold between sound and song, *teuroteu* onomatopoeias allow socially marginalized fans such as Mun Pilgi to make music out of the particular kinds of quiet surrounding them, the quiet of social repression and traumatic experience. At first Mun Pilgi had told me that the quiet was the sound of loneliness, but over the years she told me that it worried her because it made space for traumatic memories and nightmares. For years she had suffered from recurring dreams of being sexually attacked, beaten, and tortured by Japanese soldiers. Sometimes she would dream that she was back in the "comfort station"; at other times she would dream that the soldiers were in her present-day room. The dreams would subside when she was with others, but when she was alone again they would return.

So sometimes when Mun Pilgi turned on the radio-cassette player or the television she was trying to replace traumatic memories with the sociality of sound and music. No wonder she had told me, "A song is like a person" and "like a friend." Songs were her companions. When she turned on the cassette player, the radio, or the television, she opened doors into the social world. She let her selected companions pass through those doors, bringing her version of the social world with them. She grasped them and made them her own, a family to stand with her against her dreams.

There is something deeply asocial about the nature of traumatic memory, although we cannot say the same thing about the violence that produces trauma, which is usually quite social indeed. Scholars of trauma often characterize traumatic memory as a vivid sensation, lacking narrative or context and resisting integration into such a narrative or context (Herman 1992: 38). This quality of incoherence is one thing that marks traumatic memories as antisocial and explains their persistence. They exist beyond the narrative of the self, and hence beyond its power, and they recur involuntarily, unsettling or even paralyzing the self.

According to Herman (1992), recovery from trauma requires an integration of memories of traumatic experience into a coherence that corresponds to the rebirth of a person as a capable subject and social actor. As such, many medical professionals and scholars of trauma have focused on processes of testimony and storytelling through which traumatic experiences are rendered in the coherence of language and narrative. But the sensory nature of traumatic memory suggests that other expressive practices, such as song, may be more common tactics of recovery, as they live closer to the human sensory apparatus and the sensory nature of traumatic experience. In his semi-autobiographical *The Things They Carried*, Tim O'Brien, a Vietnam veteran, describes in graphic detail the death of a fellow soldier: "The gore was horrible, and stays with me. But what wakes me up twenty years later is Dave Jensen singing 'Lemon Tree' as we threw down the parts" (1990: 89, quoted in Herman 1992: 38).

Music appears often in the testimonies of survivors of Japanese military sexual slavery for a whole host of reasons, some of which this book explores. One reason is that a large percentage of "comfort women" were expected to sing with and for soldiers in addition to performing their sexual labors. Mun Pilgi told me that during the war she sang Japanese film songs and other popular tunes with soldiers. Some women were made to sing Korean folk and popular songs as well. Some had to perform on stage before assembled companies, and in this way perform their femininity, their colonial Otherness, and their manifold subordination. For many, song was part of a practice of domination and submission that made it a constitutive part of traumatic experience. The cognitive resonance between music and the sensory nature of traumatic experience was reinforced by their coexistence in the "comfort stations" as in O'Brien's story.

But if music can be a part of or reminiscent of the disassociated sense-substance of traumatic memory, if it can reach into the realm of raw, nonsignifying sound, this is but the far end of a continuum. It exists at a threshold: it is a kind of bridge that connects sounds with no attributed meaning to different kinds of sonic coherence. This is particularly true for song, which joins sound and language. Because song and music represent the structuring of sound and sensation into coherent social forms, they are capable, as are other art forms that unfold in time, of bridging the realms of inchoate sense experience and memory and the social world, with its coherences of language, narrative, biography, and social hierarchy. This is one reason why many trauma survivors make use of vocalization, song, and music as means of reckoning with traumatic experience.

We have already seen Pak Duri do so; many of her songs are, from one perspective, documents of her long work of self-reconstruction in the wake of her wartime and postwar traumatic experiences. But as we shall see, Mun Pilgi was engaged in her own work of posttraumatic recovery. Left to make due on her own over the long years of the postcolonial period, she turned to popular song and created a vast, imperfect system of self-defense, sustenance, and self-and-world creation. She used music as a tool of sublimation, a locus for the integration of traumatic memory into a coherent vision of her life history and the world, and as a tool of repression and substitution, a shield against traumatic memory.

The making of coherence in traumatic recovery is decidedly social, not a matter of the personal psychology of autonomous individuals. Like other survivors of traumatic experience, Mun Pilgi made coherence out of materials that were already mediated and social, imbued with ideologies of nation, gender, and self. She heard songs on the radio, on television, on cassettes; she learned songs from friends. These artifacts and practices of the social provided ways out of the windowless isolation of traumatic experience and toward an inextricably social and personal coherence.

Perhaps now we can begin to sense the weight of Mun Pilgi's statement "A song is like a person." The basic *teuroteu* pulse had an elemental social character, the character of time, of another person's heartbeat. Song developed this social character even further and structured experience into the figure of a full-blown social life. As she elaborated the rhythmic vocable *kung*, it became a long, extemporized rhythmic accompaniment to song, which she provided for herself in between the lines as she sang, or for others.

Or *kung* became a formalized part of song, such as the *kung-jjak kung-jjak, kung jja-jja kung-jjak* of the chorus of the song "Four-Beat Rhythm." In these ways, in song, she could participate in her social world and form and perform a whole array of social relationships.

I had seen her put the rhythmic vocalizations of *teuroteu* to such elaborate social ends once already, on the bus tour of Jeju Island. As we cruised around the island on the bus, as the women passed the microphone and sang songs in turn, Mun Pilgi clapped and vocalized. Survivor Yi Yongsu stepped to the mic and energetically sang a verse of her version of Kim Gukhwan's 1998 "A Person Like the Wind" ("Baram gateun saram"):

> Even though when you came, you came at will
> When you go, you can't just up and leave
> That terribly brief moment, that short meeting
> Left me so frustrated.[5] 🔊 13

Together with the other women, Mun Pilgi clapped along and called out rhythmic vocalizations. Yi Yongsu arrived at her final line:

> That thing called love, that thing called love . . .
> You can't trust it, you can't trust it, you can't trust it
> You, who dropped me and left, idiotic man.[6]

The whole bus erupted in a chaos of laughter and applause. Yi Yongsu had changed the last phrase of the final line from "you person like the wind," to "idiotic man." Korean elderly women are more and less free about changing the words of popular songs, however canonical, to suit themselves, as they are with folk songs.

Through rhythmic vocalization and clapping, Mun Pilgi and the other women took part in the song's transformation of sorrowful rumination and complaint to laughter. They were able to access and mold a number of different social solidarities: the fandom of Korean balladry, a community of women, and a community of survivors reckoning together with similar aspects of their experiences.

Mun Pilgi became part of a social world in this way, as she did while listening to the radio at home and elsewhere. She became subject to it, as it began to influence her hopes, her dreams, and her sense of self. And it became subject to her, for she, together with many others, sustained it and gave it life. This mutual influence characterized her life as a singer and her struggles away from the quiet of her lonely apartment and toward the social, musical life to which she aspired. I saw her shout out her approval to Yi Yongsu: "*Jalhanda* [bravo]!" Her voice was a little too quiet to be heard, though; it blended into the general tumult and rowdiness of the bus.

The *teuroteu* genre, the popular music of midcentury Korea and of Mun Pilgi's generation, provided the primary tools by which she participated in and molded her social world in song. Some background about Korean popular music history, then, is necessary in order to understand her work as a singer and creator.

In the late nineteenth century, the folk songs that traveling entertainers popularized across the peninsula, the circulation of Christian hymns by missionaries, and nascent Western-style music education laid the groundwork for the category of popular music.[7] But mass-mediated popular music came into being in the early twentieth century via radio and recordings of *yuhaeng changga*, popular songs derived from Western hymns, folk songs, and popular tunes brought to Korea by Western missionaries (Lee 2000: 37). In the ensuing decades more and more were imported from Japan, as Japan's cultural influence grew during its colonization of Korea (1910–45).

According to the pop music scholar Lee Young Mee (2000: 38), as Korean music came under the spell of foreign modernities and the heel of colonial power the origins of Korean popular music became inseparable from the rupture (*danjeol*) of the colonial encounter. Preexisting Korean genres had only sporadic parts to play in the evolution of Korean popular music, although the new genres assimilated different characteristics of these genres, such as timbral preferences and content. Korean folk song, for the most part, would continue in its separate stream, despite faltering attempts during the colonial era to create popular music out of folk songs by fusing folk and Western orchestral elements, as had been attempted in Japan (see Hughes 1990; Finchum-Sung 2006). The Japanese-influenced form of popular music that would rise to ascendancy throughout the colonial period is the genre today known by a host of names: *yuhaengga* (famous or popular song), *daejung gayo* (mass song, often simply *gayo*), *bbong-jjak*, its onomatopoeic name, or, most commonly, *teuroteu*, from the English "foxtrot."

Teuroteu was derived from Japanese *enka*, a form of popular song that developed as the modernizing late nineteenth-century Japanese state attempted to fuse Japanese traditional melodic patterns and sentiments with the conventions and instrumentation of Western pop music styles.[8] *Enka* became hegemonic in Japan as an East-West synthetic genre through its promotion in the new system of universal education and in its circulation via the modern technologies of recording and radio, and as such it lay at the heart of the modern nationalist project. Not surprisingly, in the era of Japan's most intense industrial transformation *enka* became increasingly preoccupied with loss, particularly of the rural home, rural lifeways, family relations, and love. *Enka* was increasingly identified with "the expression of modernity as despair" (Yano 1998: 260).

As Japanese imperial fervor intensified in the 1930s with the invasion of Manchuria and the onset of the Asia-Pacific War (1931–45), *enka*'s themes of lost love, friendship, family, and longing for one's hometown increasingly came to mediate relations between self, family, and empire. *Enka* provided means for the bereaved to memorialize loved ones lost in war or gone off to the frontiers, for urbanites and colonists to reminisce about their rural homes, and for people in general to express emerging modern notions of Japaneseness. *Enka* became a principal locus for reflecting on the tragic nobility of sacrifice for the benefit of the nation; this reached a peak in the months before the defeat of the empire in 1945.

Enka was transplanted to Korea through the initiative of the Japanese colonial government and private industry during the colonial domination of the peninsula. The colonial era in Korea began with fifteen years of harsh Japanese military policy (*budan seiji*). In the wake of the resultant independence revolts of 1919, commonly referred to as the March First Movement, the colonial government turned to a new cultural policy (*bunka seiji*) that aimed to "tutor . . . Koreans for a distant day of independence" (Cumings 1997: 156). The importation of Japanese traditional and popular culture intensified, and the number of Korean intellectuals and artists studying at Japanese universities grew. The first radio stations, controlled by the state, were established in 1926. Together with the nascent recording industry, which had come to Korea earlier, radio sped the proliferation of Japanese popular music.[9] All of this was encouraged by the rapid industrialization of parts of northwestern and central Korea and the creation of large industrial metropolises, which saw the rise of the entertainment industry and brought many Koreans within range of radio signals.

It was from this time forward that the Korean *enka*-style balladry that came to be known as *teuroteu* in the postcolonial era supplanted popular songs of Western derivation as the hegemonic form of Korean popular music.[10] As *enka* was transplanted to Korea, its themes were selected and reinterpreted to suit the colonial landscape. The lost hometown or the lost love of *enka* would be flavored with the air of lost national sovereignty or forced relocation. These tropes proved particularly useful for the covert, opaque expression of taboo political sentiments and experiences, which otherwise would have been censored by colonial authorities.

With the onset of the Asia-Pacific War the Japanese colonial government of Korea entered its third and most repressive phase, aimed at total assimilation of the peninsula to the Japanese empire and mobilization of Koreans for the war effort. Koreans were forced to adopt Japanese names, worship the Japanese emperor, and observe Shinto rites. Campaigns of forced labor and military conscription, including the conscription of sexual slaves, removed greater and greater numbers of Koreans from their hometowns.

During this time the *teuroteu* genre became increasingly important as a resource for expressing the traumas of the colonial experience. At the same time songs were subject to more and more surveillance and censorship. Musicians continued to develop the genre's extensive techniques of metaphor and opacity to evade censors, assimilating political sentiments into love songs and other seemingly innocuous contexts. The genre thus came to express the experiences of colonialism, up to and including the colonial repression of the expressive life; songs had the character of repression burned into them as a defining trait. In this way *teuroteu* songs became a clearinghouse for the fragmentary formation of a colonized national subjectivity, a fractured and repressed way of being Korean. And singing became an already repressed, intimate yet public sphere for the articulation of other taboo sentiments and experiences as well. These are a few of the reasons why *teuroteu* would become, much later, such an important expressive resource for Mun Pilgi and other survivors of the "comfort women" system.

After the end of the Japanese domination of Korea in 1945, *teuroteu* persisted, flourishing as a means of remembering and memorializing the sufferings and losses of the colonial period, at the same time as the wounds of the past became an important part of South Korean national identity and state ideology. Colonial-era *teuroteu* hits, stamped with the aura of the period, became the canon of South Korean popular song. Through the 1950s and 1960s songs such as Yi Nan-yeong's 1935 "Tears of Mokpo" and Kim Jeonggu's 1936 "The Tear-Soaked Duman River,"[11] which hinted at forced migration, lost sovereignty, and other aspects of the colonial experience, became the most popular and well-known songs in South Korea.

The Korean War (1950–53), the long decades of postwar authoritarian government, and the frantic race to reindustrialize the devastated country throughout the 1950s, 1960s, and 1970s created conditions that ensured the sustained popularity of the genre. As a practice of lamentation and memorialization, *teuroteu* produced new hits addressed to new crises and experiences and added layers of contemporary significance to old songs. Although *teuroteu* gradually fell out of favor with younger generations,[12] it remains deeply popular among those generations of Koreans for whom it is the musical language of youth. For these people it remains a resource for personal identity, a means of being social, and a practice of collectively remembering, memorializing, and making sentimental sense of the often traumatic past.

But the personal uses of *teuroteu* songs are in perpetual tension with the formalized traumas that constitute national identity and are enshrined in the genre. As we shall see, as fans such as Mun Pilgi try to make the genre suitable to their own projects of selfhood and remembering, these personal projects are all the while constituted and normalized by popular music's circulation of national traumas and subjectivities.

At her apartment and later at the House of Sharing, Mun Pilgi and I sang and talked together over six years about her favorite *teuroteu* pieces. She told me about the different contexts in which she had learned and performed songs and the different songs that had been her favorites over the course of her life. From this we pieced together a history of her relationship to *teuroteu*, a picture of her style as a *teuroteu* singer, and a compendium of her uses of song in the work of creating and sustaining a sense of self and a social world.

Mun Pilgi began learning *teuroteu* songs in her childhood, from friends, family, radio, and records. One of her favorites from this part of her life was "Bulhyoja-neun umnida" (A faithless child cries), an early hit by the composer Yi Jaeho, with lyrics by Kim Yeong-il. The male singer Jin Bangnam debuted the song in 1938, when Mun Pilgi was around thirteen and working in her parents' shop. This was five years before she was taken to Manchuria.

In the song a mother's child mourns her passing and looks back with guilt and regret, ashamed of her faithless treatment of her mother.[13] Ever since she left for the war, Mun Pilgi had very personal reasons to remember this song, and she sang it in her own personalized version. During the war and its immediate aftermath, the season of her deepest attachment to the song, she was wracked with guilt when she thought about her parents, especially her mother. "Every time soldiers bothered me I wondered why I hadn't listened to my parents, and ended up like this . . . and I was filled with regret. I would think to myself how I had only myself to blame for this fate. When the sun went down, thoughts about my parents would tear at my breast. I'd think to myself 'I should have listened to them when they told me to get married; what was so great about studying that I allowed myself to be tricked by someone who told me they'd find me a school, and brought to this place, to lead *this* sort of life' . . . and when I thought that,

I despaired" (Hanguk jeongsindae munje daechaek hyobuihoe and Jeongsindae yeonguhoe 1993: 116).

After the war her feelings of guilt and regret only intensified. Her mother told her that she was the reason for her father's untimely death. Spurning her mother's efforts to marry her off, she left home and wandered. In 2003 she spoke to me of her abiding anger at her father, and told me that she had long ago stopped visiting his grave to pay traditional respects (*jesa*) at the Harvest Festival and the New Year. But she still keenly felt the tragedy of her broken relationship with her parents, especially her mother, who had tried hard to give her a good life.

When Mun Pilgi sang "A Faithless Child Cries" for me for the first time, in 2004, she told me that it had been her "'number eighteen' signature song a long time ago." She described it to me as a "letter to someone's mother":

> *Though I cry, though I call, your sweat and blood flowed*
> *I shout my resentment and strike the ground weeping.*
> *My mother who can't come again, you've finally left this world*
> *Mmm—did you go?*[14] 🌀 14

When I heard the original I was struck by the extent to which Mun Pilgi had selected and reworked the lyrics of the song. Her text was a synthesis of the song's first two verses, a composite of the texts in boldface below:

> **Though I moan, though I cry,** mother can't come . . .
> **I shout my resentment and strike the ground weeping.**
> **Mother who can't come again,** this unworthy child
> Throws itself at your feet in sin.
>
> **Your sweat and blood flowed** till your hands and feet cracked.
> You longed for this untrustworthy child's honorable return,
> And suffering, my mother . . . **did you go**
> in tears, mother for whom I long?

Line by line Mun Pilgi had omitted any reference to the "faithless child" (*bulhyoja*), leaving those lines that express a longing for her mother and observe the mother's passing. It is as if the song has been swept clean of the guilt that she professed on so many occasions, but which she had long wished to overcome.

One might assume that because of the mass-mediated and seemingly fixed nature of popular songs, such a transformation would be impossible.

But the principles of flexibility that originated in Korean folk song adhere to the practice of popular song as well among Koreans of Mun Pilgi's generation. Over the many decades since she learned the song, she had remade it through a process of forgetting and remembering. She often complained, "I've forgotten everything!," but what she remembered and what she forgot told a story of her long struggle for selfhood. In "A Faithless Child Cries" she recalled those things that would allow her to improve the relation between the child and her mother and make the song a suitable expression of fondness and sadness, which did not cleave too close to the bone of her guilt and regret.

Mun Pilgi transformed the song as an act of reaching for the purity of familial love and the idealized relationships it sustained. As we shall see, her singerly style was characterized by a passionate search for such ideals and by the acts of cleansing that allowed her to reach them.

Mun Pilgi's modification of the melodic aspect of song was consistent across her repertoire. She was faithful to the basic contours of the original song melody, but she simplified it, removing vibrato, cry breaks, and other ornamental stylings of professional singers in order that the melodies would suit her amateur voice.[15] Sometimes she made these modifications herself; in other songs she adopted the simplifications of her friends and others.

Her modification of text was a more complex and long-range process. In "A Faithless Child Cries" and elsewhere she worked through reduction and imaginative recombination, but in other songs she also composed lines. She gradually changed lyrics by filling in sections that she had forgotten and by omitting or changing lyrics that didn't suit her. In this long, gradual process she negotiated the similarities and differences between mass-mediated cultural forms and her own feelings and experiences, which were already in part the products of mass culture. In so doing she burned her history, her self, and her sense of the world into these mass-cultural objects. And she reinvented herself in an ideal fashion, remaking a sense of purity that she felt the experience of Japanese military sexual slavery had stolen from her.

Mun Pilgi's "number eighteen" showpiece song changed over the years, as she fell under the spell of new songs that addressed her past and her present-day needs. She updated her repertoire to keep alive a connection to the present and popular trends, and she did so as she discovered new songs that she felt particularly resonated with her experiences. Her patterns of remembering developed in parallel and under the influence of the trends of the evolving genre with respect to the past.

Through the decades of the postwar her showpiece song had been "Ureora Gitajura" (Cry, guitar string), originally sung by the famous male *teuroteu* singer Son Inho in the 1950s. It was a centerpiece of her song world and a medallion of her creative and singerly style. It was one of many hits by the *teuroteu* composer Yi Jaeho, whose career spanned from the later decades of the Japanese colonial period until his death in 1960.[16] The song describes a wanderer, drifting in a foreign land, reminiscing about lost love while strumming a guitar. She sang the song for me many times, with subtle differences between each version. One day in the summer of 2004 she sang it for a friend and me in the living room of the House of Sharing.

> In a strange, foreign land, that night, that young woman,
> Somehow it won't let me, let me forget.
> A love strung along a guitar's string, a wanderer's love—
> Cry, oh guitar, oh my guitar.
>
> Every night, every road I follow in dreams, my home is in the shadows—
> Somehow it won't let me, let me forget.
> A love strung along a guitar's string, a wanderer's love—
> Cry, oh guitar, oh my guitar.[17] 🔊 11

Mun Pilgi had learned this song as she wandered around the South Korean countryside working off and on in drinking houses. In such places she became a part of the vast pleasure industry of postcolonial South Korea. The industry, which had its roots in the colonial era, proffered drink, song, dance, and women to South Korean men as antidotes to the stresses of postwar devastation and intensive industrial development. It offered a model of play and power to contrast with most Korean men's everyday lives of toil and subordination. The drinking houses were also places where businessmen could make deals and where they could transform professional relationships into personal ones through play and through collective transgression of social mores. All of this was made possible by women's entertainment and sexual labor.

As a hostess Mun Pilgi had to pour drinks, make conversation, sing, and sometimes dance with her male clients. As bottles went around, patrons belted out their own favorite *teuroteu* hits and cajoled her to sing for them. The drinking houses became one source of her repertoire, one arena in which she would cultivate her personal style of singing and her versions of popular songs. The radio, and later cassettes that she bought and swapped with friends, were other sources. She clung to these technologies as sonic windows into the normal life of a woman of the common classes. She was excluded from this life, working inside the entertainment industry that was its mirror image, a disavowed zone of play and transgression on which "normal life" nonetheless depended.

In the postcolonial era, living and working on the margins of society and struggling with the wartime experiences that cast the shadow of shame upon her, Mun Pilgi long lived the life of an outsider. Like other survivors, she kept the secret of her wartime experiences. But the secret that they kept was a public one. It was passed on discreetly in stories and rumors whispered from door to door. It circulated in the subtexts of popular music's imaginary, dotted with instances of women's suffering at the hands of men and of outcast wanderers like the protagonist of "Cry, Guitar String." Like so many secrets of its kind, the public secret of the "comfort women" system burrowed into the heart of cultural intimacy and national identity, rooted as they were in colonial victimization by Japan. In this way the cultural work of public secrecy paradoxically canonized victims as it demanded their silence and ostracized them from respectable society. Mun Pilgi, like other survivors, moved in public as a person balanced on the threshold of validation and erasure in public consciousness.[18]

In this atmosphere song and mass culture became a way for her to sustain a sense of social existence. *Teuroteu* was deeply implicated in the mechanism of public secrecy and flavored with the character of repression, and so she could use it to establish a link between herself and oppressed others in society. At the same time it was so imbued with these qualities that it only granted her a half-existence, and it was up to her to struggle to make herself whole in song.

"Cry, Guitar String" was a preeminent example. In the song she had found a piece that expressed, in the figure of the wanderer, the displacement that she had experienced, the repressive atmosphere in which she lived, and the repressed self that this life had produced. The wanderer in "Cry, Guitar String" drifted through a shadowy foreign landscape, holding onto music, love, and guitar strings as tendrils of social connectedness. The song resonated with both her wartime experiences and her present-day life on the run from that past and the torment of her postwar exploitation.

The wanderer disappears into the distance, passing beyond the reach of society's gaze, leaving only footprints and memories of the sound of his guitar. From the perspective of the "normal life," the wanderer has only a temporary presence and a spectral identity. But in the wanderer's narrative of isolation she remains whole, if wholly displaced; she does not disappear to herself, only to the society whose eyes and ears follow her until she disappears beyond the horizons of sight and hearing. Mun Pilgi had accepted, to a degree, the place that society had given her, and so she embraced these two perspectives on the wanderer: its vanishing and its durable self. The tension between these two selves destabilized both and made the work of selfhood for Mun Pilgi and others like her a threatened and unfinishable process. This was the very special form of double con-sciousness[19] the survivors of the "comfort women" system would live with in South Korean postcolonial society under the conditions of public secrecy.

As with "A Faithless Child Cries," Mun Pilgi had remade "Cry, Guitar String" and the figure of the wanderer to suit her experiences, her outlook, and her self. She had simplified some lines, perhaps as memories of the original grew faint.[20] But she also altered and omitted lyrics to personalize the song. Sometimes she followed the original version, in which the wanderer is male, but often, she changed the object of the wanderer's desire from a young, unmarried woman (*cheonyeo*) to a young, unmarried man (*chonggak*), allowing her to sing it from her own perspective. She omitted an original couplet: "my burdens strung along a guitar string, wandering thousands of miles / Plucking my guitar as I cry." Perhaps she did so because playing the guitar was something that she, and most women of her generation, would be unlikely to do. Whatever her motivation, her omission made the song less about playing the guitar than about listening to it. And as we have seen, listening to music—to radio, to cassettes, to singing friends—was an important part of her life and a keystone of her participation in her social world. Mun Pilgi's singing style, and her manner of personalizing songs, was one that was inseparable from those acts of listening. Perched on the threshold of the listening fan and the admired singer, she used song for her own particular reasons while simultaneously reaching outward to the collectivities of fandom.

At the most extreme, Mun Pilgi's modifications of songs were outright compositional gestures. The second verse of the original "Cry, Guitar String" began, "On every night, on every road I follow in dreams, in shad-ows sorrowfully drifting up, for this mottled figure I long." When Mun Pilgi performed it for my friend Yukiko and me, she sang, "Every night, every road I follow in dreams, my home is in the shadows." We talked about the meaning of this ethereal line, whose ending she had rewritten. Yukiko asked her about her unusual characterization of the hometown (*gohyang*), a trope of *teuroteu* in the wake of a Korean twentieth century of forced relocation, migration, and urbanization. In *teuroteu* the hometown is almost always portrayed as a lost, idyllic place, but the home of Mun Pilgi's "Cry, Guitar String" was a "home in the shadows."

> Mun Pilgi: Shadows . . . I . . . "the shadows are my home." I'm going into the midst of shadows—that's what it means.
> Yukiko: Where to?
> Mun Pilgi: I follow my dream road, like that. . . . I follow the dream road often, you know . . . so this song says "the shadows are my home."

Over time, as Mun Pilgi and I kept singing and talking about songs, something began to dawn on me: there seemed to be a connection between her "dream road" and her history of traumatic nightmares. "Cry, Guitar String" was a romantic saga of a drifter searching for a lost, unfindable love in dreams; for Mun Pilgi it provided, among other things, an alternative dream world to her dreams of soldiers and sexual violence. She mapped this world by wandering, remembering, and searching through the dream roads and shadowy hometowns of *teuroteu* and popular culture. In her song world she replaced memories of sexual terror that lingered in the silence of her life with a coherent narrative of devotion in love that filled acoustic space with song and its society. The alternative world bore the stamp of the real, however; it was not a terrain of sunshine and happiness, but of shadow and romantic tragedy.

Mun Pilgi told me, "My body is dirty, but my heart is clean." She said that her body had been defiled during her term as a sexual slave, and that it was possible for her to be pure only in spirit. Over the course of her postwar life she had been drawn to religious doctrines and practices of spiritual purification of the body, from Christianity to Buddhism. At a Buddhist ceremony commemorating Kim Sundeok's death in the summer of 2004 we sat together in the House's shrine and I listened to her chant the name of the Historical Buddha (Namuamitabul). She said she liked chanting mantras because it "made one's heart clean." The next day she took my recorder and spent a minute chanting mantras into it, switching back and forth between the Buddha's name and the name of the Bodhisattva of Compassion (Gwanse-eum bosal).

Mun Pilgi told me that she found a sense of spiritual cleanliness in heartfelt loyalty (*ilpyeon dansim*).[21] One day in 2004 she showed me a watercolor that she had painted at the encouragement of the House of Sharing's art therapy instructor, which expressed this sentiment. It was a series of red, orange, and green horizontal stripes, which, taken individually, each look like the Chinese character for the number 1: 一. The overlapping stripes produced new colors, which also look like the number 1. The stripes were of many variations of width, density, and texture. I asked her if the painting had a title, and she told me, "It's called 'My Heart/Mind, the Number One' [*Ilja ne maeum*]." When I asked her about the meaning of the title she said "it means *ilpyeon dansim*—staying beside you with a singleness of heart/mind." Although the "singleness of heart/mind" can suggest devotion to any number of things—the expression shows up in the national anthem to suggest loyalty to country, for instance—Mun Pilgi associated it with romantic love.

The painting was something she had done at the House of Sharing at the request of others. But she had sustained an ideal romantic love for many

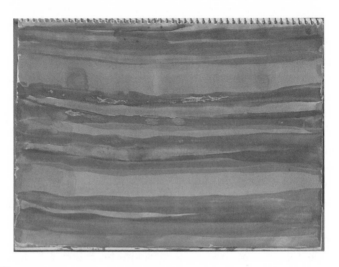

Figure 3.3.
"My Heart, the Number One," by Mun Pilgi (2004).
Photo by Yajima Tsukasa.

decades before that through her daily singing of *teuroteu* songs. The wanderer of "Cry, Guitar String" drifted in a memory-cloud of lost love and clung to that feeling as though it were her lifeblood, and so did she. About a year after she first sang it for me, she told me, "It's about my old love. . . . We parted long ago." The song enshrined love and its tragedy; the love was too perfect to last in the flesh, but it was infinite in the realm of the spirit. So Mun Pilgi's tragic romance had the coherence of an ideal and produced an idealized self. She continually sought love's object and bore its burden in the realm of the spirit, wandering every night along shadowy dream roads. The self that carried the weight was constantly constituted in the act of doing so, and in the ongoing forfeit of the physical world that it required.

This strategy was opposite to that of Pak Duri, who had made recourse to narratives of unhindered sexuality to reckon with the experience of sexual violence and gender domination. Mun Pilgi, collecting herself and her world in the transcendental practice of an interminable quest for lost love, forfeited her body and sought to escape the traumatic memories that inhered in it. Hers was a particularly bitter example of the creation of subjectivity through exclusion of the "abject" (Butler 1990: 181),[22] that part of experience that revolts us by threatening our understanding of the world, and thereby threatens our membership in the social group that shares that understanding. By the normative rules of her social world, her body had been defiled. She embraced these rules and forfeited her body in pursuit of cleanliness of spirit and in her quest for traumatic recovery. Such strategies of selfhood and belonging are found often among survivors of sexual violence, especially women, the world over.

But Mun Pilgi's traumatic experiences and the body that bore their traces both had a materiality that would prove unerasable, and they would continually intrude in dreams. This further spurred her efforts to make herself whole through the tragic sacrifice of *teuroteu* and to connect with others in the ideal, heartbroken spaces of song. She kept wandering, and searching, in songs and in life.

As part of this search, she sifted continually through popular culture for songs capable of harmonizing her thoughts, feelings, and experiences with normative ones, and capable of renewing her sense of social connectedness in the present. As such her song world would change dramatically over the decades. Her early favorite songs had been ruminations on family, on wandering, and other subjects close to her heart; by the last decades of the twentieth century the love theme was wholly ascendant. She, like popular culture in general, was growing more remote from the immediacy of the traumatic experiences of the colonial period and the Korean War and moving, by degrees, into a shrine to ideal love. This pop cultural evolution in the direction of romantic love is a commonplace story; similar and often related trends have characterized much of the world's popular music in the twentieth century. Mun Pilgi embraced this trend as she wove a universe of romantic tragedy and rumination around herself.

Mun Pilgi sang her more recent favorites with little modification, most likely because they were fresher in her memory, receiving daily reinforcement from her television and cassettes. But there is likely another reason: the gradual ascendancy of the theme of romantic love in popular culture, as a trend toward an ideal and as a marketing strategy, meant that songs grew less and less specific, and identification with the various singers and the various characters in songs became easier and easier. As more and more people identified with the characters in songs, the songs articulated larger and larger social formations. Outsiders such as Mun Pilgi were able to edge closer to normal positions in society, based not on the "vanishing presence" she had been allotted during the long public secrecy about Japanese military sexual slavery, but on commonplace kinds of consumption and appreciation of mass-cultural forms.

Mun Pilgi told me that her next "number eighteen" showpiece song after "Cry, Guitar String" was "Anyway, the One who Left" ("Eochapi ddeo-nan saram"), a song that became famous in the 1980s as sung by stars such as the male singer Seol Undo and Jeong Jae-eun, the daughter of the queen of *teuroteu*, Yi Mija. Mun Pilgi sang the piece for me on many occasions, often pairing it with "Cry, Guitar String."

Did I show you my tears?
Did I cry out loud?
No, no, I just got wet
In the silent rain, that's all.
You left saying "I hate you," you left saying "I loathe you,"
So why should I cry?
I must forget, I must forget, anyway, the one who left.[23] 15

In her sung musings on love from the last decades of Mun Pilgi's life, the years of her participation in the "comfort women" movement, she seems less interested in creating alternatives to traumatic memory, such as we saw in "Cry, Guitar String," and more prone to different kinds of confrontation with traumatic experience. Songs such as "Anyway, the One Who Left," for instance, record injury suffered at the hands of men assimilated to narratives of romantic tragedy. This song and "One Night's Puppy Love" ("Harutbam putsarang," another hit by Son Inho, the singer of "Cry Guitar String") explore the unforgettability of tragic love. Unforgettable love seems like a coherent, tragic version of the recurrence that also characterizes inchoate, traumatic memory.

The inability to forget the lost love is an archetypal theme in late twentieth-century South Korean popular music and *teuroteu* in particular.[24] Most of these songs were written by male composers for female vocalists. In their original forms such songs will into reality a male fantasy of a woman's undying love, which acted as a balm to postcolonial realities of shattered social relationships and disparities of power among men, and provided an opportunity for men to grieve and console themselves at their own failings and reaffirm their social power. But in the hands of women who made these songs their own, the songs became cinematic renderings of the experience of being used and abandoned. They gave voice and sense to suffering. Mun Pilgi used such songs to express her own experiences of love and loss. This work was ongoing, as the work of self-purification and self-making were founded on the practice of seeking and remembering. But this unfinishability did not put the lie to the coherence that she had carved out of a lifetime of exploitation and struggle. Rather Mun Pilgi's wandering toward ideal love guaranteed the perfection of that spiritual innocence.

In 2002 a book of photos published by the Korean Council had this to say about Mun Pilgi:

Grandmother Mun Pilgi, of Seoul's Deungchon neighborhood, who made her debut as a professional singer as a "comfort woman" victim, is even now frightened awake every night by a dream in which she is fighting with Japanese soldiers. Ten years ago her face was smooth, but line-by-line her wrinkles grow deeper, as her fight with the Japanese government grows longer. (Hanguk jeongsindae munje daechaek hyobuihoe 2002).

Mun Pilgi was one of the earliest survivors to join the "comfort women grandmothers movement," registering as a survivor and giving testimony in June 1992. She participated in testimonials and protests in both Koreas and Japan, putting herself and her traumatic experiences forward with characteristic articulateness and grace, and with the aura of innocence that surrounded her and lay at the core of her song world of romantic selfhood. She flourished in this spotlight, making friends and cherishing public attention and acknowledgment.

In the course of her participation in the movement Mun Pilgi sang often in public. "Before, people said I was a good singer. Wherever I went, when I was at the Korean Council, if we'd go somewhere they'd look at me and say 'Start with a song,'" she told me with pride. The Korean Council encouraged all of the women to sing, to promote self-expression, the sharing of experience and emotion, the development of self-confidence, and collective enjoyment. But Mun Pilgi was particularly keen. Throughout the 1990s she became more and more well-known as an enthusiastic singer in the social life of the movement, and her notoriety would soon spread to the media representations of the movement and the "comfort women" issue.

In 2001 the electronic musician and singer Yi Sanghun saw a program about the "comfort women" on television and was struck by a painting that figured in the program. It was *Ppae-atgin sunjeong* (Stolen innocence) by Kang Deokgyeong, a House of Sharing resident who had painted an immense symbolist oeuvre in the last few years before her death in 1997. A copy of the painting hangs in the art gallery of the House of Sharing's museum, and the original is archived there.

The centerpiece of Kang's painting is an old cherry blossom tree in late bloom. The tree is sprinkled with flowers and leaves, which are falling, and it is phantasmagorically dotted with red and green hot peppers. At the base the tree's root mass spreads like tentacles over a mound of earth. Beneath the earth in cutaway is a pile of skulls, some faded and some black. The black ones are larger and appear to be only the closest of a large mass of skulls buried beneath the tree. The trunk of the tree contains a uniformed Japanese soldier, eyes shielded by his visor, who reaches out with his right hand toward a naked girl, lying on the ground covering her face with her hands, surrounded by fallen leaves and flower blossoms. The *sakura* (cherry blossom), symbolic of Japan, feeds on the dead to produce its blossoms and

Figure 3.4.
Stolen Innocence, by Kang Deokgyeong.
Courtesy of the House of Sharing/Museum of Sexual Slavery by the Japanese Military.

its ultra-phallic fruit; *gochu* (hot pepper) is common Korean slang for the male sex organ. This hellish tree will soon consume the girl, who will soon join the other skulls below ground.

Yi Sanghun had been an apolitical "admirer of Japanese music" uninterested in Korean music and history, but he described how the painting had awakened him with a "shock that words could not describe" (Silhom 2001). The painting appeared to him in his dreams for several days, and he wrote a song with the same title. He organized a concert and made a record so that young people did not forget "our mothers' mothers' flood of painful blood and tears" (Silhom 2001).

The result was 2001's *Tribute to wianbu halmeoni* (Tribute to comfort women grandmothers). The disc, which is a concept album, combines songs and programmatic instrumentals. It tells the story of an unspecified woman or women's experience of Japanese military sexual slavery, and its denial and rediscovery in the postwar era. The ballad "The Land of Morning Quiet" gives way to the instrumental "Dragged Away," modeled after another painting of the same title by Pak Duri's friend Kim Sundeok, which is followed by "Opening Mother's Diary." Electronic meditations and dance beats give way to piano musings, children's voices, samples of *teuroteu,* and electric guitar. In the finale a scorching solo guitar blasts out the Korean national anthem, "Aegukga" (Song of patriotism) in rote form, in an orgy of power and affirmation, a radical misreading of Jimi Hendrix's agonistic "Star Spangled Banner." In this way the album's tribute to the "comfort women grandmothers" appropriates their stories to a defiant and triumphant national narrative.

There have been other tribute projects in South Korea and elsewhere, such as an independently produced Korean album *Sharing the Pain of the Jeongshindae* and the CD *I Will Not Forget* (*Watashiwa wasurenai*), the product of an Okinawan choral group.[25] But what distinguished Yi's project was its first song, called "Stolen Innocence" after Kang Deokgyeong's painting, which featured a survivor singing. He had sought out a survivor to sing on the track and had found Mun Pilgi.

"Stolen Innocence" begins with a wash of keyboard sound over which we hear the melody of the piece on the keyboard. The rhythm is 6/8, a time signature that references the prevalence of meters based on threes in Korean traditional music. The texture slowly builds: a synthetic *gayageum* (a twelve-string plucked zither) enters to double the melody, playing arpeggios in between phrases, and a synthesized drum track enters.

Finally the synthesized melodic parts disappear, and Mun Pilgi begins to sing in her mild and warbling voice.

I hurt. I cried.[26]

Then she is joined by a children's choir in unison:

Flowers bloom . . . Flowers bloom.[27]

This line provides a sequel to the famous painting *Unblossomed Flower* by Pak Duri's "big sister" Kim Sundeok, which inspired the statue of the young girl in the center of the House of Sharing grounds.

This first verse repeats verbatim, followed by an instrumental break. Yi Sanghun sings the next two verses:

I hurt. I cried.
Flowers bloom . . . Flowers bloom . . .

You threw me away. You trapped me.[28]
Flowers bloom . . . Flowers bloom.

Another instrumental interlude follows, and then the drums stop. Menacing synth sounds introduce the sound of children laughing against a somber synth background. Suddenly the children's laughter fades and is replaced by the voice of a young girl, Yi Eunhye, who sings:

I hurt. I cried.

Three gun-like snare strikes signal the reentry of the whole instrumental ensemble and the choir. The children repeat together the whole text of the song:

I hurt. I cried.
Flowers bloom . . . flowers bloom . . .

You threw me away. You trapped me.
Flowers bloom . . . flowers bloom.

Finally the instrumental accompaniment breaks down and the child soloist reiterates the last, triumphant line:

Flowers bloom.

In this song, as elsewhere in public culture, the mildness of Mun Pilgi's voice was read as an aura of innocence (*sunjeong*) that contrasted dramatically with her experience of Japanese military sexual slavery. She was taken to be a living embodiment of the dyad of the innocent girl and the wrinkled grandmother that pervaded the discourse and imagery of the "comfort women" in the South Korean public sphere, which I had found represented so starkly in the courtyard of the House of Sharing. In the combination of her warbling voice and the simple, almost childlike quality of the textual expression, her singing encompassed both childlike innocence and woundedness. Her voice contrasted with the voices of the children, as the verse structure contrasted the woundedness of the first couplet with the renewed blooming of a resurgent innocence in the second.

The song is not content to let be the static interdependence of innocence and woundedness that characterizes Mun Pilgi as a representative "comfort woman grandmother." The tension of this opposition sets in motion a process of rebirth, audible in the song's changing soundscape of voice.

This transformation has three parts. First, we hear Mun Pilgi's voice, representing woundedness, invoking the feeling of stolen innocence, and suggesting the potential for its retrieval. Because she sings "I hurt, I cried" alone, we learn that she is capable of representing woundedness alone. But when she is joined by the children's choir to sing of flowers, we find out that she is incapable of a total representation of innocence because of the supposedly unhealable nature of her wound. Of course in other aspects of her life Mun Pilgi accomplished just that, over and over again, and she had won that innocence through a lifetime of searching and trial.

After the first verse Mun Pilgi's voice disappears, not to return. Now, in verses 2 and 3, the second part of the song's transformation, Yi Sanghun and the young children take full possession of the experience of woundedness. All of the other solo voices from here forward sing the lines about suffering without Mun Pilgi's assistance. This is the "sharing" of the experience of the wound that I discussed in the chapter "Beginnings." It is the process by which "the virtual experience involved in empathy gives way to vicarious victimhood, and empathy with the victim seems to become an identity" (LaCapra 1999: 699). The participants have retained the spirit of the "comfort woman grandmother," but her body has passed on in its brokenness. The wound bursts the bounds of its singularity in a Big Bang that expands into the shape of South Korean national consciousness.

In the final stage of the transformation the wound is excised by the triumphant blooming of flowers, symbols of human flourishing and young womanhood. The "comfort woman's" destroyed potential for flourishing is resurrected and activated by the children and the national whole. The whole, however, excludes the survivor's voice. When the children's choir returns for the last two verses, the space of Mun Pilgi's solo voice is now taken by a young girl, who collapses the plurality of voices into one transcendental blooming flower. The universe of the Korean imaginary collapses back in on itself, remaking the singularity in its image.

As Mun Pilgi's voice disappears, the song renders her experience a sacrifice. It is a sacrifice that, although a tragedy, is cast as a fundamental part of the historical process of Korean national identity. The sacrifice provides the energy, the outrage, and the moral authority for national resurrection. She becomes a national martyr, as she did elsewhere in the discourse of the "comfort women" issue.

But as she did so in this song, she became part of a generic representation, an archetypal "comfort woman grandmother." The song was a patchwork of different women's expressions and experiences: the title was taken from Kang Deokgyeong's painting *Stolen Innocence*, the blooming flower motif was a reference to Kim Sundeok's *Unblossomed Flower*, and the voice was Mun Pilgi's. It is not surprising that on the album's release the *Donga-Ilbo* newspaper claimed that she was "expressing the *han* of all the 'comfort women grandmothers'" (October 3, 2001).

There were two reasons why Yi Sanghun found Mun Pilgi so ready-made to represent woundedness and the "comfort women grandmothers." First, in the course of her participation in the movement, she had taken part, as had Pak Duri, in the ongoing creation of the archetypal "comfort woman grandmother." Second, in her quest for self-reconstruction and social belonging, she had been trying for years to harmonize her life with available popular cultural representations of colonial suffering and the experience of military sexual slavery. Her search for lost love and ideal social relationships, in its sacrifice of the body, was a personalization of a broader narrative, latent in the *teuroteu* genre, in which Koreans sacrificed the material aspects of life in pursuit of national flourishing and the prosperity of younger generations. For both of these reasons she had developed a public persona that was similar to the generic representation.

The dyad of woundedness and innocence and the logic of sacrifice found in the song "Stolen Innocence" bore some similarity to aspects of Mun Pilgi's ways of understanding her past, herself, and her place in the social world, which she cultivated in her beloved *teuroteu* songs. But her cleanliness of spirit and the resurgent "stolen innocence" of Yi Sanghun's song were different in numerous ways. Mun Pilgi had sought and found her innocence through a lifetime of song and struggle, and her innocence bore the traces of that struggle and of her age. It was something she had made, an ideal product of having suffered, loved, and lost.

But in "Stolen Innocence," as Mun Pilgi's voice was replaced by the children's choir and finally a single girl's voice, her spiritual cleanliness was reframed as a primordial purity. In its rebirth it was stripped of Mun Pilgi's arduous history of searching and finding. It was born again, as if for the first time. The song's "stolen innocence" was an elemental "springtime of youth" (*cheongchun*) that bloomed anew in the light of South Korean early twenty-first century modernity. It was inexorably connected to youth, and Mun Pilgi could not fully share in it. Mun Pilgi the person, the elderly woman with wants and needs and an identity of her own, had no place here; she had a place in the public sphere only as a symbol of past victimization. The nation returned to her, or rather to the archetypal figure that she had become, only occasionally, to restock its cohesion and its moral authority.

Mun Pilgi was frustrated by the periodic amnesia that plagued South Korean society with regard to the "comfort women" issue, as were many others in the movement.[29] She was frustrated at the sudden annual resurgence of interest in the "comfort women" issue in the nationalist fervor surrounding *Gwangbokjeol* (Independence Day), the August 15 holiday celebrating independence from Japanese colonialism in 1945. Every August, she said, her heart hurt and she shook. She would forget about the past and go on with life, and then, only in August, people would show interest, and she was made to remember. But then the interest would fade until the following year. Unsurprisingly the album and Mun Pilgi's song were released to coincide with Independence Day.

This idea of sacrifice for the nation manifest in Yi Sanghun's "Stolen Innocence" and which explained the fickleness of national interest in the "comfort women" issue nonetheless gave meaning and purpose to Mun Pilgi's wartime experiences. She found satisfaction and strength in the acknowledgment and the role that public culture allotted to her, and she moved deftly in that role. She spoke often about her activism and was both proud of and committed to it. She felt very strongly about Korea's colonial exploitation by Japan, she told me, and she felt that she was an example of that exploitation. She longed for the day when she and the other survivors might receive an official apology and reparations from the Japanese government. She was an ardent though not uncritical nationalist and derived symbolic power from her status as a representative.

After years of being shunted to the margins of society and treated like a ghost, Mun Pilgi seemed to take great satisfaction in the public recognition she enjoyed for the very particular sacrifices she had made. In the attention, applause, and accolades, she experienced broad social confirmation of the voice she developed in *teuroteu*, and a confirmation of herself as its creator. And although the public sphere erased the particulars of Mun Pilgi's identity in this way, she came into being and sustained herself and her social world precisely through her musical and political acts of sacrifice. She borrowed the core structure of her sentimental sacrifice in the search for lost love for her passionate search for justice. Hers was, in more ways than one, an impassioned activism.

The movement was important to her for another reason: within it she sought and found social connections which she had also sought in song. She was a regular participant in the Wednesday demonstration, but also in the many outings arranged for the survivors by different activist and social welfare organizations.

In April 2003 I again found myself on a bus with Mun Pilgi, on a Korean Council trip to the Korean Folk Village (Hanguk minsok chon) near Suwon, about an hour south of Seoul. As on the bus to Jeju Island, the onboard microphone circulated, and the women sang in turn. Mun Pilgi was sitting with her "little sister," Kim Yushim, who rarely left her side during vacations and who was with her when she had berated me for not being able to dance. They were sitting up front, close to the PA and the young woman staff

Figure 3.5.
Mun Pilgi giving testimony to a group of Korean students, 2005.
Photo by Yajima Tsukasa.

member of the Korean Council who was serving as emcee, calling on the women to sing one by one.

The young woman passed the mic around in a wide circle. It came to Mun Pilgi and Kim Yushim last. Mun Pilgi took it first and sang a long medley in her light voice, which, although less powerful than it had once been, had lost little of its radiance. Kim Yushim sang appreciatively by her side, alternating between singing the lyrics and shouting rhythmic interjections: *kkung-jjak kkung-jjak, chan-chan-chan,* and others. She sang loudly, clearly audible underneath the sound of Mun Pilgi's gentler, amplified voice.

Medleys such as this one are common practice in *teuroteu;* many cassettes contain two sides of ceaseless medley. This pattern originated in social singing, but now, under the influence of such cassettes, *teuroteu* fans reproduce recorded medleys in their own singing. Medleys are sometimes associated with travel, as many of these cassettes are for sale at rest stops along the expressway and provide the recorded soundtrack for express bus travel and the musical material of singing parties on private tour buses (Son 2006).

Mun Pilgi sang "Anyway, the One Who Left," "Tears of Mokpo," and many of her other favorite songs. She chose well-known classics and recent hits, leaving aside her more obscure favorites so that Kim Yushim and the other survivors could join in singing the *teuroteu* canon. It was of course her personal version of the canon, centering on songs of loneliness and love. Many of the other women clapped and sang, calling out the rhythmic syllables; others nodded off or sat lost in thought, watching the passing scenery of the expressway. Some of the young people too sang along on well-known verses and choruses. If there was a lull Kim Yushim would call out the first line of a new song, which for most women their age served as the song's title and a clue as to how to begin. After a while Kim Yushim took the microphone from Mun Pilgi, and beneath the distortion and the reverb of her booming voice Mun Pilgi sang softly in support.

As the two took turns and supported each other they were knitted together as friends, fans, and survivors. And singing brought them together with those other survivors, activists, and volunteers around them who sang along or listened appreciatively. This was a community in formation in the moment of performance, united in the collective appreciation of *teuroteu* songs and the evolving story of love, despair, and intimacy found there. It was also a community of survivors, of women, and a transgenerational community bound by fragile and tentative collective understandings. The Korean Council and other organizations had long struggled to bring that community of survivors into being, and to sustain it. There was an infrastructure of institutions and funds that supported it, and the sense of security and the opportunities for sharing that it made possible. But it also depended for its survival on moments like this.

The song party on the bus also made official the links that survivors had long cultivated with public culture and society. Although the bus was closed unto itself within the racing space of the surrounding expressway, it was enveloped in a network of vehicles: car stereos blasting *teuroteu* radio and cassettes, buses with passengers singing and dancing in a flurry of colored lights, tendrils in the web of *teuroteu* fandom. And on the bus there were the video cameras, digital cameras, cell phone cameras, and microphones, the whole recording apparatus of the movement and the media, which recorded this moment for circulation in private and public. Candid photographs would begin circulating electronically almost immediately. Within days written narratives of the trip would appear online. Several months later pictures taken that day by a professional photographer would be published in a photo book.[30] Both the national fandom of *teuroteu* and the multimedia apparatus of movement, media, artists, and scholars linked Mun Pilgi to the imagined community of the nation and her social world.[31] These networks transposed her creations—her voice, songs, stories, and self— for that world, continuing the cycle that began when she adopted popular culture for herself.

After Mun Pilgi moved into the House of Sharing in the fall of 2003 she was in constant contact with other survivors, activists, social workers, volunteers, and researchers. There were daily opportunities for sharing song and memories. On a warm night a year after she moved in she and I sat up late in the courtyard of the House of Sharing. We were sitting at picnic tables and singing with Bae Chunhui, another survivor with whom Mun Pilgi had recently become close, and a group of young activists and volunteers—House staff members, Korean college students, and Japanese volunteers. Mun Pilgi and Bae Chunhui had become friends camping out in front of the TV set in the living room and staying up late on occasions like this, "playing" with staff and visitors, at which times they could be somewhat competitive for the attentions of others.

Bae Chunhui sat at a picnic table with a small group of young volunteers; Mun Pilgi, myself, and a few others sat at the adjacent table, talking about singing. I had started the conversation, and she seized the topic eagerly. She sang a Japanese song, "Aizen yakyoku" (Nocturne of Aizen).[32] "I don't know if you'll know this one," she said.

> The Promise Tree's blooming Spring—
> Why does the storm . . . mmm-hmm . . . resent it so?[33] 🔊 16

Bae Chunhui, listening on in the background, translated for the Korean volunteers and gave Mun Pilgi a prompt when she paused before the last word. Bae Chunhui remembered everything because she rehearsed songs in her thoughts and made mental and handwritten notes to help her remember. Mun Pilgi, on the other hand, was excavating things from her past and grudgingly welcomed the helping hand.

I asked her when she had learned the song. "In the Japanese colonial period," she replied. "Well, I didn't learn it . . . I basically just sang it together with soldiers."

Koji, a long-time Japanese volunteer at the House, asked her what part of Japan the song was from. She told us that it was from the film *Aizen Katsura* (The tree of Aizen), Hiromasa Nomura's 1938 epic. She described going to see the film with the doctor she had known at the "comfort station."

> We went once, secretly, secretly. If someone found out I'd have been beaten. . . . We saw it secretly, and let me tell you what was amazing about this song: so there's a Japanese soldier, and he goes to war. And his rank is lieutenant colonel. But he's got a daughter. He's got a daughter, and his family name is Warakin. So that's how it is and it's goooooooing like that,[34] and as the movie's going on, this song, "Aizen Katsura," they sing it, is what I'm saying. I can't even tell you what a great song it is.

Bae Chunhui started singing the song again from the beginning, at the table next to ours.

Mun Pilgi went on:

> So as the movie's going on the guy goes waaaaaaaaaay off to the front lines. So the woman and her baby have to live apart from him. So she criiiiiiiiiies, and that's how it is. And she couldn't see him off, and she couldn't go to welcome him back. Because she couldn't go over there, to see him.

The evening closed in around us as Mun Pilgi spoke of another instance of love's tragic perfection. In the song "Nocturne of Aizen" she reached into the well of her time in Manchuria and brought out something beautiful to show us. She had climbed the mountain again, cut down a pine tree, and scraped out its nourishment, and given some to us. She had brushed once more against traumatic experience and wrested from it an ideal self that was the keeper of an ideal love.

Mun Pilgi's life at the House of Sharing and in the "comfort women grandmothers movement," despite its frustrations, was replete with opportunities to perform this self and its creations, and to do so in the company of others. A few weeks later we were sitting together at one of the outdoor tables with two college seniors from Seoul and a Japanese exchange student. The three students had been visiting the House on weekends. Bae Chunhui was there as well, keeping up her monologue at the adjacent table. Mun Pilgi, at the encouragement of the two students, sang a short medley of her favorite *teuroteu* songs and talked with us about each of them. She started with "Cry, Guitar String" and followed it with "One Night's Puppy Love."

> *Staying up all night in puppy love—*
> *A nail is stuck in love, and these flowing tears*
> *Soak a handkerchief, leaving only regret*
> *Breaking up without a word . . . oh, unforgettable one.*[35] 🔊 17

I would find out later that Mun Pilgi had added that last part about the "unforgettable one," making this another song explicitly addressed to unforgettable love in its pristine preservation. I would also find a video of Ju Hyeon-mi, a female *teuroteu* singer who debuted in the 1980s, singing these two songs consecutively, along with other Mun Pilgi favorites. And I discovered a greatest hits record by Son Inho, the original singer of both songs, which included both pieces.[36] Son Inho and Ju Hyeon-mi had obviously made a tremendous impression on her, and perhaps the latter had influenced the way she organized songs in sequence. But Mun Pilgi rarely mentioned singers; she talked principally about songs and how she came to make them her own. She had done so through the various modifications she had made as she sang them over the years.

As we sat in the courtyard frogs began to sing in the nearby rice paddy. Kari, the Korean male student, told Mun Pilgi that the frogs sang in response to her singing, and Saeyong, the young Korean woman, agreed, complementing her on her voice.

The pair clamored for another song, and Mun Pilgi obliged with "Anyway, the One who Left." 🔊 18

After her final line—"I must forget, I must forget . . . anyway, the one who left"—Kari said earnestly, "Oh, Grandma, I really cried, oh, oh."

Mun Pilgi: What?

Josh: He cried, just now.

Mun Pilgi (to Kari): You cried? "Crying, why cry?"

In her reply Mun Pilgi referenced a recurrent phrase in *teuroteu* song, which she had just sung a variation of in "Anyway, the One Who Left": "Crying, why do I cry?" But now she removed the "I," suiting the line to Kari. In so doing she turned the line into a reference to another *teuroteu* hit of that name, "Crying, Why Cry?," by the male singer Na Hun-a.[37] Her speech was shot through with popular song texts and references; this was one way the solace and understanding she found in song was woven into the texture of her everyday life.

The young Japanese exchange student, who had been quiet until now, chimed in from the sidelines. She sang a germane fragment of a song from somewhere across the landscape of contemporary Korean pop, too commonplace and short for me to identify: "Why did (you) cry?"[38] Everyone laughed. As she sang (1:34 on audio track 18) she tapped out the pulse on the table. She stopped singing, but kept on tapping.

Mun Pilgi listened for a moment in silence to the student drumming on the table, and then began to sing with the rhythmic sound. She sang her version of Kim Minseong's "Far, Later Days" ("Meon hunnal"):

Even if you find me by chance, and go without seeing me
Don't get caught up in an old love . . . (without) speaking . . .[39] *just please leave.*
Although I think of the thing called love,
The distant future will still be a future which that person has left.[40]

"Gosh."

The young student's short quotation and her tapping became a shared pulse, and Mun Pilgi seized on it as a scaffold for her own song. The pulse became a kind of synchronicity with another. It was an agreement about time, and a rhythmically organized moment of intergenerational, and international, conversation about love.

"Hey, Grandma, all of these songs are love songs!" said Kari. Mun Pilgi looked slightly embarrassed. There was a short pause. "Grandma, what is love?" Saeyong asked in her spaced-out but earnest way (at 2:51 on the audio track). Mun Pilgi laughed. "Oh, I don't know," she said, smiling. "Let us—you've got to let us know," I said. "I don't know, you do it! Show me somebody who doesn't know love!" she said with good-natured heat.

"Grandma, what do you think love is?" said the persistent Saeyong, trying another tack. "Love is what I think it is," she said, turning her question into an answer. She went on to say more, but as if by design my minidisc recording is suddenly corrupt at this moment. I can't remember what she said. I expect it will come back to me when the time is right. But when the recording becomes intelligible again, about ten seconds later, you can hear Saeyeong asking "What is love?" again, apparently unsatisfied. Or perhaps she was following Mun Pilgi's advice and looking for love in the asking.

After sitting quietly for a few minutes Saeyong asked Mun Pilgi to teach her a song. The pair spent an hour under the stars, the old woman teaching the young woman the words and the melody to "Anyway, the One Who Left." As Saeyong sang the song back to her, Mun Pilgi's eyes shone. Then they sang it together a few times, to be sure Saeyong had it right, and they picked up with the song the next day. That weekend Mun Pilgi was a teacher, a singer of songs who shared her wisdom with her juniors. Saeyong was her newest friend, fan, and student, the most recent person to benefit from her lessons in life and love, and the latest point on the web of relationships that connected her to her social world.

In the last years of her life it seems Mun Pilgi was in the process of adopting "Can Everyone love?," which we had listened to together a year before in her apartment, as her new "number eighteen." The song explains that love is something that people make together, rather than something one finds in whole cloth: "The joy of meeting and the pain of parting are things that two people make."[41] Mun Pilgi kept making these things in the act of searching, along her road in shadows, for ideal love. In this search she sustained the purity of a remade self and found a place for that self in her world. When she died one late winter morning in 2008 she finally completed her journey to the ideal realm that she had made.

One year after Mun Pilgi died I was watching YouTube reruns of *Old Miss Diary*, the popular Korean sitcom that ran from 2004 to 2005.

Figure 3.6.
Mun Pilgi singing with Pak Ongnyeon, summer 2004.
Photo by Yajima Tsukasa.

The show follows the long courtship of two workers at a radio station. In episode 74 Chi PD (Production Director Chi) finally screws up his courage and tells his coworker Mija that he loves her, after seventy-three episodes of hesitating. It is a classic story of romantic *ilpyeon dansim*, keeping one's heart for another. That sort of pure, untrammeled love, finally requited, reminds me of Mun Pilgi, whose life and society saw her excluded from the possibility of such realization. But I remember the ideal love that she found in song, a purity that she possessed more completely than almost anyone. She was one among many marginalized women in South Korea and elsewhere who made popular culture their own, and made themselves a part of that culture, despite its daily attempts to shut them out. And not just a part, but the secret heart of that culture, thoroughly broken, yet as whole as the number one.

Bae Chunhui

A phoenix among birds,
Before the gate of longevity,
a bird of the bountiful harvest
　　　　　　　　—Bae Chunhui, "Ballad of the Birds" 🌀 19

It is an unusually warm day in January 2003, and we are at the Wednesday demonstration. Eight survivors have come, seven of them making the trip by van from the House of Sharing. The members of the Korean Council address the women and the small crowd of supporters. It's a good day for protesting because it's not too cold, but few people have come.

Bae Chunhui sits on the end, warming the air she breathes with an air-filtering flu mask. I am standing behind her. Although the mask provides partial anonymity, her body is wrapped in the Council's smock, and her rainbow of clothing announces her presence. She is looking at the camera.

Bae Chunhui had this perplexing place and presence in the "comfort women grandmothers movement." She regularly participated in the protest at the Japanese Embassy, but she often wore a mask and always sat on the left end of the row of survivors, so that she was never surrounded. In the ten years in which she had been living in the House of Sharing she hadn't given a detailed testimony to the staff or the members of the Korean Council about her experience of the Japanese "comfort women" system; despite her encyclopedic memory, she spoke of this part of her past just enough to confirm that she had been a sexual slave of the Japanese military. She spoke fondly of Japanese people, food, and commercial products. She waited every day for Japanese guests to visit the House of Sharing. "Any guests today?" "Yes, Grandmother." "Japanese?" "Not today."

Figure 4.1.
The Wednesday demonstration, January 2003.
Photo from the Korean Council website. Used by permission.

"*Aiiiiiiiigo* [Good grieeeef]." What was the "comfort women grandmothers movement" to make of Bae Chunhui? She seemed to both want and reject a place in the movement and at the House; she had one foot in but was always ready to withdraw. She occupied a place in these conspicuous realms that was surrounded by a mist of question marks and exit strategies.

Movement activists and social workers told me that she could certainly contribute to my project on song in the women's lives. Each staff member recommended Bae Chunhui to me in a different way.

"Oh, you want to study the grandmothers' songs? You want Bae Chunhui."

"She is the *best* singer here, a professional."

"She sings songs in Japanese . . . Chinese . . . Russian . . . and of course Korean."

The staff of the House of Sharing described Bae Chunhui's character and gave me hints about her history, but I was clueless as to what all this meant. They could do little more, they said, because her life was cloaked in mystery, because she was reluctant to talk about her wartime experience. They advised me not to ask direct questions about the war. They also told me that she could be somewhat difficult: she insisted on doing everything her way; she took great pleasure or great offence in small things; and she liked and disliked people quite intensely. Because I liked music, one of the staff told me I would get along. It would be better, the museum director said, if I spoke Japanese. Years later, as Bae Chunhui and I switched in and out of Korean and Japanese depending on who was around and what the subject was, I found out just how right he had been.

On my first few visits to the House I scoured the museum archives for information about Bae Chunhui but found little. There was a one-page biography in the handbook of the Historical Museum of Japanese Military Sexual Slavery (Nanum ui jip yeoksagwan huweonhoe 2002). The book provided short biographic and character sketches of the women who were living at the House upon my arrival in the summer of 2002. It also provided entries for former residents who had passed away.

Bae Chunhui's entry was shorter than those of the other women. In contrast to all of the other mini-biographies, there was very little there about her childhood and her wartime life. But, making up for the lack, the description of her life at the House of Sharing was the longest among all the biographies. The entry is short enough to quote in its entirety:

Grandmother Bae Chunhui

Born on March 12, 1923, in Seongju-gun, North Gyeongsang Province. She had one elder brother by a different mother. In 1941, when she was eighteen, as her mother had already passed away, she was living by helping out with housework. She went to a friend's house to visit, and there she met two men, a Japanese and a Korean businessman. She fell for their words "we'll find you employment" and was forcibly taken to Jiamusi in China.[1] She lived there as a "comfort woman" until the liberation.[2] There were approximately twenty-seven Korean women at the comfort station, and every day they each received about ten to fifteen soldiers. There wasn't enough to eat, so they suffered terribly from hunger.

After the liberation she wasn't able to return home directly, and she remained for a time in China. She knew that liberation had happened, but after the (comfort station's) manager and the others scattered and disappeared, she was left alone and did not know a means of returning. After passing through a resettlement camp and roaming from place to place, she crossed to Japan in 1951, where she lived for thirty years.

She returned to Korea in 1981, and soon after met her family and they lived together. But she was swindled by her half-brother, who was her only flesh and blood at the time, and she lost all of the money she had brought back with her from Japan, and was left penniless. Possibly due to this experience, she became unable to trust others. After this, in order to carry on living, she worked in restaurants and in drinking houses; she worked as a housemaid and as a kitchen maid; she says there is no type of work she hasn't done and no type of suffering she hasn't endured. She didn't marry. She moved into the House of Sharing in October of 1996.

Grandmother is very interested in political affairs, so she watches the news with enthusiasm and is a fan of President Kim Daejung.[3] She has the character of an excellent entertainer, and is a particularly excellent singer. If someone requests a song, she always sings after all the other women have taken their turn; and if somehow she gets hold of a drumstick, she sings continuously, connecting song after song together, oblivious that the sun is rising. For a woman of her age, her manner of dress is bright and youthful, and she always pays meticulous attention to her makeup.

She speaks fluent Japanese and Chinese and sometimes she demonstrates a good command of Russian. But whether or not it's because she hasn't gotten used to our language again,[4] if an argument breaks out among the grandmothers of the House of Sharing, she stares with a bewildered expression, as if she doesn't know what's going on or why she is there—this picture is memorable. And sometimes she makes the whole group laugh with her clever wit.

She is also a good painter, and so she passes time by painting pictures on the rocks around the House of Sharing. She pays great attention to the warm reception of Japanese and other visitors, and she takes great pleasure in speaking Japanese, and so she stays in touch with some people by exchanging letters. Since volunteer Yonekura Mayumi returned to Japan in 2001, she takes informational queries by phone from Japan, and she also guides Japanese visitors around the House as well. (Nanum ui jip yeoksagwan huweonhoe 2002: 143–44)

This passage left me with many questions. What was Bae Chunhui's life like before she turned eighteen? Presumably she learned Chinese in Manchuria, but how did she come to speak Russian? Why did she leave China for Japan? What did she do in Japan for thirty years? And I wondered how and where she learned to sing songs "continuously, connecting song after song together, oblivious that the sun is rising."

I wondered why these questions were not addressed in the biography. The glossing over of her childhood and her thirty years in Japan seemed rather conspicuous. And why would the author speculate that Bae Chunhui had not "gotten used to our language again" after twenty-one years back in Korea, when she had sufficient talent for language to master Chinese and Japanese and make occasional displays of competence in Russian?

This biography of Bae Chunhui had been edited twice over, first by Bae Chunhui herself, and then by the staff of the House. Later I spoke with her at length over many years about her life in China after liberation and her decades in Japan. Whether by design or from sheer habit, things were omitted from her biography that didn't assimilate easily to the archetypal image of the colonial "comfort woman" victim. Her history, her attitudes, her carefully cultivated, stylish and youthful appearance, her polyglot virtuosity in song and language, and her skilled painting perplexed the public's cults of woundedness and decrepitude; her fondness for Japanese people and cultural forms frustrated the nationalist sentiments that the "comfort women" issue was used to fuel.

Just as Bae Chunhui sat on the end of the row of survivors at the Wednesday demonstration, she deliberately set herself apart in her biography and in her everyday life at the House. She avoided House arguments, she sat far back in the van, and she avoided talking about her past as a victim of the "comfort women" system. She maintained a strategic distance between herself and other people and institutions, partly out of habitual mistrust, and always out of a belief that she was utterly exceptional.

Bae Chunhui set herself apart in many other ways in the course of her daily life around the House. For much of the 2000s, she ate breakfast, lunch, and dinner alone on the sofa in front of the television outside of Pak Duri's room, unless one of the staff decided to eat with her or there was overflow from the main dining room. In conversation she contrasted herself to the other women at the House: "These grandmas, they don't know their letters, they don't know anything. Their parents wouldn't let them study when they were young, so they got stubborn and stupid, and their heads turned to stone."[5] She was critical of what she considered to be the other women's monoculturalism: "These other grandmas don't know anything but Korea. I've been abroad, you see, I lived in China and Japan, so I know that there are all kinds of ways of living, and there are different cultures, languages, and so on.... These grandmas don't know any of that. So they're always Korea this, Korea that, Korea's the best, *aigo* [good grief], it's no good."[6]

Bae Chunhui told me that she had learned from her international experience that there was good and bad everywhere (something that Mun Pilgi had told me as well). It was her ongoing project, as we shall see, to gather the good things together. The biography in the museum handbook had described accurately how she waited expectantly for Japanese visitors, but in fact she waited for internationals of any stripe. She also waited for artists, for musicians, for anyone she considered colorful and interesting. She was an admirer of children and animals, both of whom seemed to be untouched by human vulgarity. And she amassed to herself anything that seemed to transform the mundane or the unpleasant into art: dance, story, and music, which made art from movement, language, and sound; melodrama, which made poetry out of the frustrations of love; and westerns and gangster movies, which choreographed and aestheticized violence. Like the authors described as "magical realists," she filled her everyday world with fantastical elements. She was the collector, architect, and alchemist of an enchanted reality, a magical real. Her room was crammed, wall-to-wall, with the fruits of these long labors.

It was in this capacity that Bae Chunhui met me in the summer of 2002. To her I was a music lover and a singer; I could contribute as she turned ordinary evenings into landscapes of song. As we sat together she would rue our certain fate: "Singers, you know, end up alone and with nothing." I was interesting to her as an American who sang Korean courtesan songs, which

Figure 4.2.
Bae Chunhui in front of the rice paddies next to the House of Sharing, January 2004.
Photo by Yajima Tsukasa.

I had studied during my master's fieldwork years before. This meant, she said, that I had international musical experience, because these songs were incommensurable with music from elsewhere. She said we shared the experience of trying to cross the musical boundaries of culture. She helped me generously, teaching me about Korean and Japanese folk and popular culture and language. We stayed up late into the evening swapping stories and songs, often with the volunteers and staff with whom she liked to "play." She would read the fortunes of her young companions from the year of their birth and help out with matchmaking and career decisions. She would drink one, or perhaps two short glasses of beer, and she would take vicarious pleasure in the drinking and smoking of her young cohort. "A man who smokes is a stylish man," she would say. She chided me for cutting my hair: "When you first got here all those years ago you looked like a folk singer, or Jesus or something," she said. "But now you look like a middle-aged Korean guy."

Over the course of many long evenings over eight years Bae Chunhui sang more than a hundred songs for me and talked with me about them, and so I was able to record a significant but unknown percentage of her vast musical encyclopedia. She sang for me with great attention to detail and respect for original or canonical versions, hardly ever altering original texts or melodies. We listened back to my sound recordings of this massive collection of songs and conversations, and recorded songs again if she was dissatisfied. In this long process she began to clarify for me some of the mysteries of the museum's short biography, such as how she knew all those languages and all those songs. And she began to show me a very different sort of person.

Bae Chunhui, it turned out, was not reticent about discussing her past, as some staff at the House had told me she would be. She was just reticent about discussing the war and her experience of the "comfort station," parts of the past they wanted to know about. She was quite talkative about some aspects of the past in which they weren't particularly interested.

Bae Chunhui had spent many of her thirty years in Japan as a professional cabaret singer, singing in evening shows with a house band. In the cabaret she built an identity as a cosmopolitan professional. The story she told me was not the tale of her life as a "comfort woman" and a survivor, but of her arduous path to her career as a professional singer, and of the long years of that singer's retirement. It was a saga that encompassed much of the music history of twentieth-century Japan and Korea, and pieces of the modern music history of China and elsewhere. It was also the tale of her spiritual journey back, after forty years, to a Korea she was both inexorably drawn to and deeply mistrustful of. And finally it was an epic of her tragic fate, by which she ended up "alone and with nothing" at the House of Sharing.

Bae Chunhui's way of telling her life story was born in the world of the Japanese cabaret, and it bore the patina of that world. Entranceways—doors and names, for instance—were hazy. But art forms, and the dancers, musicians, and singers who performed them, came clearly into focus under the bright lights. The haze protected that world and its mystique, but once you stepped inside, its spectacle shone with a blinding brightness. At the same time those same stage lights washed away the audience. Bae Chunhui told a story that blotted out spectatorship, like the bright lights that made the performer oblivious to the objectifying gaze of the male clientele of the postwar Japanese cabaret.

Although Bae Chunhui was obviously an important character in her own story, she was also present in the story as a performer who expertly rendered others' stories and channeled other's sentiments. When I asked her what her "number eighteen" signature song was, she replied, "What number eighteen? I've got too many songs for anything like that." She kept a professional distance from songs in this way. She rarely spoke of identifying with the protagonists and other characters in songs, although she gave occasional clues that some songs bore on certain aspects of her experience. As a performer she was thus able to control tightly what others knew about her and always keep a hand in the process of her public representation. As she danced on the line between telling her story and the stories of others, sometimes she sang of her past, and at other times she sang to demonstrate her competence and mastery as a performer in the present.

Bae Chunhui said very little about her childhood. She told me that her father had allowed her to go to school as a child, although she hadn't learned music there. She was forthright about having been a "comfort woman," but she never spoke to me or to others whom I met about the intimate details of her experience. The staff of the House of Sharing had reason to believe that her four years as a sexual slave had been severe.

Bae Chunhui told me that she sang now and then while she was a "comfort woman," but that this was unrelated to her "work" at the time. She learned a few Japanese folk songs, *gunka* (military songs), film songs, and other popular songs. But she had no great desire to sing until afterward, and didn't learn songs on purpose. "They just went into my ears," she told me.

Her story of life after the war was comparably clearer. The Japanese army abandoned her and many other women in Manchuria, and she remained there for the Soviet army's one-year occupation of Inner (Chinese) Manchuria. She left rural Jiamusi and went to Harbin, the bustling and diverse "Moscow of the Orient," to work in a restaurant. The Soviet occupation lasted until the following year, when the Chinese Nationalists forced the Soviet army out. Resident Russians and Soviet troops would come to eat at the restaurant where she worked, and she spent a good deal of time with them, drinking, singing, and talking, picking up Russian phrases and songs here and there.

One of the jewels of her cosmopolitan repertoire was "Katyusha," a Russian popular song composed in 1938 by Matvei Blanter with lyrics by Mikhail Isakovsky, famously performed by the popular Russian folk singer Lidiya Ruslanova during the Second World War. For years during the war Ruslanova had toured the front performing for soldiers. "Katyusha," a tender diminutive for Ekaterina, was her most popular song. It told the story of a girl who longs for her beloved, who has gone away to fight in the war. She walks on a riverbank, thinking of him, praying that he "may protect his native land, as Katyusha protects their love."[7]

The song was massively popular, and its name was given to a Soviet multiple rocket launcher that was brought into service in 1941. In 1945 the song reached a new height of popularity as the tragic resolve of the young woman and her soldiering lover was rewarded with victory.

Drinking in Bae Chunhui's restaurant, soldiers sang this song over and over again, and she found Soviet Koreans to translate the song for her. Being able to sing in different languages was an asset for a "restaurant girl" in cosmopolitan Harbin, and so she mastered a number of "Katyusha's" verses. She had become part of an entertainment industry where women were expected to provide not only food service but also company and entertainment. Unknowingly, she had begun the long process of transformation by which she would eventually become a professional singer. 🔊 20

Until now Bae Chunhui's experience of foreign cultures had been indistinct from her experience of foreign power and violence. Here, in the immediate postwar period, she encountered new cultural forms in the season of her liberation. She learned songs as a way of learning about the world, which shone the best light on people and places by turning terrible experiences into shimmering melodramas, and by sifting the world for beautiful things. And she took to learning songs as a way to be with, relate to, and entertain the people around her. She told me, "At the next house there were Chinese grandmas, and then if you went over to that house over there, there were Soviets. So it was then that I thought it'd be nice to learn some songs."

In 1946 the exiting Soviet forces handed over the weapons of 700,000 Japanese POWs to the Chinese Communist Party. Thereafter Manchuria became a principal staging ground for the Communists' organizing efforts in their bid to defeat the Guomindang (National People's Party) nationalists. The area became a hotbed for Communist organizing and activity, and Bae Chunhui was privy to this world as well. In the restaurant setting and beyond she learned Mandarin and a fair number of Chinese songs— lullabies, popular songs, and propaganda pieces, including a Chinese version of "The Internationale." By the end of her tenure in northeast China her repertoire had grown to include Korean, Japanese, Chinese, and Russian pieces. But she was just beginning to amass her world of songs.

During my time with Bae Chunhui she sang many Communist songs that she learned during this time and afterward. She leaned to the left in matters of South Korean politics, but living in China in the wake of the revolution, she soured on Communism as she saw it implemented. There were perhaps many reasons for this; among them was the fact that the new government was fundamentally opposed to many aspects of elite and popular culture that Bae Chunhui loved. She rued the end of colonial Shanghai, a place that she remembered as a fashion show of lanterns, kimonos, and Chinese fiddles. This image of the place derived partly from experience and partly, as we shall see, from the cinema and songs of the Japanese imperial imagination of occupied Shanghai.

In 1951, she told me, two years after Mao declared the People's Republic, she caught a ferry from Shanghai to the western Japanese port city of Shimonoseki. She was twenty-eight. She never said why she went to Japan and not back to Korea; she told me and others only, "Of course I couldn't go back to Korea then." That might have meant she couldn't return because the Korean War was under way, or she might have been reluctant to return for reasons that she chose to keep to herself.

One day soon after Bae Chunhui took the boat to Japan, she was eating dinner in a restaurant. A middle-aged woman approached her and asked if she wanted a job in a cabaret. She hesitated, but the woman told her it wasn't hard work, so she agreed to give it a try. The proprietors soon discovered her talent for song; her career as a professional singer had begun. For the next several decades she would live in many different places in Japan, singing for a living.

Bae Chunhui spoke to me often about her life at the cabaret. "Cabaret" (*kyabare*) was a name that designated in Japan both music-theatrical revues and the restaurants or bars that featured such shows. This part of Japan's entertainment industry began in earnest in the heat of Japanese imperialism, inspired by cabaret scenes in the colonies, especially that of colonial Shanghai, but it mushroomed in the postwar period, during and after the Allied occupation of Japan.

The Allied occupation, which lasted from 1945 to 1952, brought hundreds of thousands of Americans and other Allied troops to Japan. Much as it had instigated the wartime "comfort women" system, the Japanese government created the Recreation and Amusement Association in order to prevent the rape of local women by the occupying forces.[8] The RAA recruited tens of thousands of geisha, café waitresses, barmaids, and prostitutes into sexual servitude for the Allied forces (Chung 2004: 166), often, seemingly by deception, functioning very much like the "comfort women" system (Tanaka 2002: 147). The organization fostered an enormous sex-and-entertainment industry, with dance halls, cabarets, officer's club "comfort stations," "an officers' cabaret," and numerous "cabaret and comfort stations." According to Tanaka, the number of performers at individual cabarets ranged from ten in an establishment in the Santama area to four hundred in Tokyo's Ginza district (143–45).

In March 1946, in the midst of a near-epidemic spread of venereal disease among American troops and women in the sex industry, the General

Headquarters of the U.S. occupying forces issued a nonfraternization policy. The RAA was promptly shut down, but according to Chung (2004: 168), many establishments that had formerly barred entry to Japanese quickly opened their doors to Japanese men. This signaled the beginning of the cabaret boom, which lasted until the 1970s and coincided with the rise of the Japanese nightclub (*naito kurabu*), also introduced to cater to Americans and now absorbed into a thriving sex-and-entertainment industry for Japanese men. It coincided as well with another mainstay of the industry to this day: the hostess bar.

Cabarets, nightclubs, and hostess bars were frequented by Japanese businessmen and politicians who came to forge friendly relations with each other through collective socializing with women. They would bring foreigners as well, or anyone who they wanted to impress. The business clientele came from both legitimate enterprise and organized crime. One of Bae Chunhui's favorite stories was about watching one of her *yakuza* (Mafioso) friends from the cabaret eat ten bowls of ramen in one sitting.

Nagoya, the scene of Bae Chunhui's longest residence, had a lively cabaret, nightclub, and hostess bar scene, described in this passage from *Fodor's Guide to Japan and East Asia* of 1964 (340–41):

> As for cabarets, the biggest and by far the noisiest is *All Stars Nightly Mikado*, which puts on three shows nightly and has two bands, though of course they don't usually play at the same time. . . . Nearby the Mikado is *Monterrey*, a lounge where you may pay a high price for your highball but it includes the attentions of a hostess, who will give you reassuring pats if you buy her a drink or two. The *Club New York* is one of those madly modern places, or so it likes to think. There are the usual two bands but only two shows nightly. . . . In the basement of the Imaike Building is the *Three Aces*. Here the floor show is not emphasized, but of course the bands provide background music all the time. The lights are dim and the hostesses are bright. A rather different atmosphere prevails at the *Club Zombi*, where the food is good and the drinks are not too expensive. . . . It is the sort of place to which you can take your wife.

Bae Chunhui never named the place where she worked, but as she talked the inside of the club came into sharper focus. It was a large entertainment hall with around eighty women on staff. Guests ate as they watched the show. There were only two shows per night, one in the early evening, around seven o'clock, and one later, around eleven. The shows involved songs, dance, and skits, and when they were finished the women were expected to socialize with the clientele. Bae Chunhui spoke of sitting and chatting with customers and of singing songs for privileged clients and friends when the show was over.

She spoke at length about her part in the show and about her fellow musicians. The club had a full band, consisting of a horn section, made up of trumpet, clarinet, and saxophone, plus drums, piano, guitar, and perhaps other instruments. The trumpet player, Mr. Okuda, was the bandleader. They were quite close. As she reminisced about him she hummed the melody to Gershwin's "Summertime," praising his playing. But he was a hard drinker, and he had a bad stomach, she said, "as all trumpet players do"; she watched him drink too much for years, after each show was finished, into the early morning hours. She told me he had passed away in 1986, just a few years after she returned to Korea.

Bae Chunhui came on stage to the accompaniment of the band, dressed in a fine *hanbok* (traditional Korean dress) or a *kimono*, to sing a changeable set or medley of Japanese and Korean folk and popular songs. She sang Korean folk songs wearing the *hanbok* and playing the *janggo* (Korean hourglass drum). She had taught herself to play the hourglass drum and Korean folk songs in her first years at the cabaret, with the help of other Korean residents in Japan, including other performers in the cabaret scene.[9] Many of these singers and musicians were visiting performers who came for a week or so to add Korean music and dance to the revue. She sang popular folk songs and professionalized pieces, often called *sori* (literally "sound"), the musical legacy of early twentieth-century Korean courtesans. She learned these from recordings and other performers.[10]

To a male Japanese audience Bae Chunhui, dressed in traditional Korean clothing and singing Korean folk songs, was a feminine and eroticized representation of Korea. This was the 1960s and 1970s, the era of Japanese postwar economic resurgence, when a perspective on the world was evolving that cast foreign countries, cultures, and peoples as objects for epicurean consumption. It was also the era of the *gisaeng gwan-gwang* ("courtesan tourism") industry in South Korea,[11] an enormous sex tourism industry that evolved to cater to men in economically revitalized Japan. Despite all of her virtuosity and her vast repertoire, Bae Chunhui inevitably served, for some, as an advertisement for Japanese investment in South Korea and for the new culture of cosmopolitan consumption and its related sex tourism. All of these industrial developments would help to spur the South Korean economy out of its post–Korean War devastation.

But on the stage and in less formal settings as well, Bae Chunhui seems to have cultivated and performed a complex cosmopolitan identity that, if rooted in its exoticism, nonetheless resisted assimilation to reductionist Japanese fantasies of an exotic Korean Other. It was an identity that was simply too complex, too changeable, and too overwhelmingly competent to submit to reduction, and she foiled attempts to do so. She cultivated her multilingual and multicultural medleys, which thirty years later would lead the anonymous author of her biography at the House of Sharing to wonder if she would sing until they would see the sunrise. She strung the folk songs of Korea and Japan together, often based on themes, as in her medley of fishermen's work songs, which fused the Korean folk song "Baetnorae" (Boat song) with the northern Japanese fisherman's song "Sôranbushi." 🌀 21

She performed Japanese and Korean popular songs in addition to folk songs, and she sang in Chinese and Russian as well. She strung songs together like beads on a necklace: six songs about rivers, five songs from gangster movies, folk songs of the world. She collected songs voraciously, learning them from tapes, radio, friends, and patrons, as she had learned "Katyusha" years before. She sang many pieces, including "Katyusha," in bilingual versions that included the original text and a Japanese translation. And she paid attention to other, international genres that it was beyond her language ability to perform, such as American jazz, folk, and pop, Hollywood musicals, and Hawaiian popular music. In this way, just as she would avoid sitting in the middle of a row of survivors at the Wednesday demonstration thirty years later, she resisted being typecast or rendered a stereotype at the cabaret. She presented herself as a cosmopolitan professional, aware of the shared aspects and the particularities of culture, a collector and transmitter of cultural forms rather than a consumable form herself.

Bae Chunhui's complex new identity was made possible and influenced by the cosmopolitanism of the cabaret atmosphere and the postwar Japanese popular music scene. The Japanese popular music industry of the day was fascinated with jazz and other American genres but also had multifaceted interests in the popular music of the Pacific, continental East Asia, Southeast Asia, and the Middle East.

This was a cosmopolitanism fraught with a history of imperialism, which would shape Bae Chunhui's musical storehouse and her cosmopolitanism as well. Since at least the Meiji Restoration (1868) there had been a manifold tradition of tune- and idiom-borrowing in Japanese popular music, which complemented the government creation of a music education system based on Western models. The Robert Burns songbook and many others were mined for tunes: "Comin' through the Rye" became "Kokyô no sora" (Hometown sky) and "Auld Lang Syne" became "Hotaru no hikari" (The glow of the fireflies; Tsurumi 1987: 99–100). Such songs were ubiquitous in Japanese music education and in society as well. Songs were also composed in Western musical idioms. Such practices date from the beginning of the Restoration, but they had a particularly significant presence at the moment of the proliferation of popular music via the Japanese mass media in the early decades of the twentieth century, and they would leave a tremendous imprint on Japanese popular music history.

A number of foreign music fads swept the country in the late teens and early twenties. Jazz came to Japan as part of a rising social dance craze.[12] The French revue was imported as well, and would influence all-female revues (J. Robertson 1998: 4). This was the beginning of Japan's cosmopolitan modernity, dominated by ideas of the "culture life" (*bunka seikatsu*), predominantly focused on the West and the appropriation of Western modernity and its accoutrements.[13]

One of these was imperialism, and Japanese cosmopolitanism in the 1920s also developed a paternalistic and Orientalist attitude toward its colonies in East Asia and elsewhere throughout Asia and the Pacific. This "Oriental Orientalism" (Kikuchi 2004: 123) would attain its height in the war era, in the aspiration to the Greater East Asian Co-prosperity Sphere.[14] Imperial ideology held that Japan needed to unite East and Southeast Asia against Western imperialism in order to usher in an "Asian modernity" to China and Korea, which were thought to be overburdened by history, and other places in Southeast Asia and the Pacific, some of which were thought to lack history altogether. In tandem with this, songs from around Asia and songs composed in exoticist imitation of foreign idioms increased in popularity.

The most popular Korean song in Japan at the time was a Japanese version of the most popular song in modern Korean history, "Arirang."[15] In the late nineteenth century "Arirang" was a tune family of Korean folk song, a collection of regional variants of a similar musical and textual material scattered throughout the Korean peninsula. In 1926 "Jeongseon Arirang," a traditional version originating in central eastern Korea, was simplified and harmonized for Western instruments and used as the theme song of the 1926 film *Arirang* by the Korean actor-director Na Un-gyu, widely considered to be Korea's first film masterpiece. At viewings a singer would typically sing the piece on stage in the final scene, in which the protagonist sings it, and audience members, who received printed programs, were invited to sing along (Atkins 2007: 652). This version became universally popular in Korea throughout the colonial period, and attained concurrent popularity in imperial Japan via radio performance and SP recordings of Japanese versions. Through this process the version of "Arirang" became canonical, and remains so to this day. Several survivors of Japanese military sexual slavery mentioned having sung the song for soldiers. Bae Chunhui knew many regional variations of the "Arirang" tune family, but she also knew many versions of the canonical modern version in both Japanese and Korean, and she performed them in the cabaret.🔊 22

At its peak the cultural fascism of wartime Japan banned "Western" music, a broad category of pieces and styles associated with the West, including jazz, Hawaiian music, music that made use of the English language, and anything stylistically Euro-American, with the notable exception of German and Italian music. But the cultural nationalist policies of the height of the Asia-Pacific War saw the immense popularity of "Oriental Orientalist" pieces aimed at representations of the colonies. In the center of this work of representation was the film star Li Xianglan (born Yamaguchi Yoshiko), a Japanese national born in Manchuria and raised there and in Beijing who played Chinese roles.[16] Her movies and their songs would become particularly important in Bae Chunhui's memories of China, her wartime past, and its aftermath, and they would come to be important to her understanding of herself as a cosmopolitan and a professional.

Li, or Ri Kôran in Japanese pronunciation, was a Japanese national who appeared as an ethnic Chinese in a number of famous movies in Japanese-occupied Shanghai, released by the Toho and Shôchiku film companies. The films paint an imperial Japanese characterization of China as a ruin of ancient civilization overrun by bandits and peppered with alternately savage and flower-like women in need of discipline, cultivation, or rescue (see also J. Robertson 1998: 107). In the films Ri's character typically falls in love with a Japanese man who tames, nurtures, or rescues her. His effort and her submission and gratitude render the Japanese imperial project in a metaphor of intercultural love.

In the course of this common story Ri sings Chinese songs or Japanese *enka* that use Chinese instruments and musical features to make appropriately dissipated and exotic representations of China, songs that Bae Chunhui sang for me as we spoke of her time in China and her postwar life at the cabaret. Songs such as "China Nights" ("Shina no yoru") and "Suzhou Nocturne" ("Soshyû yakyoku"),[17] both from the 1940 film *China Nights*, feature slippery glissandos and pentatonicism in imitation of Chinese popular folk song. The text of "China Nights" is smattered with hazy images of lanterns, fiddles, flowers, and willows:

China nights, China nights
In the purple night of the port lights
Junks sail up, dream boats.
I can't forget the sound of fiddles—
China nights, the dreamy nights

China nights, China nights
Lanterns sway in a window by a willow,

A Chinese girl with a red birdcage,[18]

Inconsolable love songs—

China nights, the dreamy nights.[19]

"China Nights" and its partner "Suzhou Nocturne" number among the most popular songs in the history of Japanese popular music, loved throughout the empire, postwar Japan, and postcolonial East Asia. They set the standard stage for the postwar Japanese imagining of China and East Asia. Bae Chunhui would inherit this imaginary and call these scenes to mind when remembering her time in China and reckoning with her own sense of foreignness in Japan and later in Korea. 23

Such imperialist Orientalisms mellowed in the postwar era but did not disappear. They became part of the memorialization of the imperialist project and the war, laced at times with nostalgia, regret, and sincere interest in understanding the exotic people and places to which they referred. The postwar period saw Japan's tremendous economic revitalization and expansion, and with this the reintensification of unequal cultural exchange in East Asia. Exoticism flourished as a way of imagining others and fantasizing about alternatives, and the exotic, cosmopolitan milieu of the cabaret thrived as well. It was at this time that the Soviet "Katyusha" became popular, along with many other international pieces, and Bae Chunhui added the Japanese version of "Katyusha" to her repertoire.[20] She also added the Ri Kôran pieces to her jukebox around this time.[21]

Her repertoire took its particular wildly cosmopolitan shape at this time, as she fashioned herself as a cosmopolitan professional capable of both satisfying and evading her audience. These two goals were ultimately inseparable.

Bae Chunhui would come to derive a sense of self-confidence from her remarkable abilities to remember, understand, and virtuosically perform her many songs. Hers was the twofold competence of the cosmopolitan described by the anthropologist Ulf Hannerz (1990): it involved a general talent for living in different places and entering into different cultures, which for her included a talent for learning and performing language and song, and it involved facility in particular cultural scenarios—the Chinese, Russian, Korean, and Japanese. Competence in culture was inseparable from fluid movement in and control of certain terrains of memory and rendering these provinces of memory into an aestheticized vision of the world. Hence ultimately Bae Chunhui's sense of self as a social actor centered on her competent musical rendering not only of cultures, but of her experiences, herself, and her world as works of art. This rendering was mobile and could be moved without losing net value (Hannerz 1990: 246); in this way it consisted of a relatively stable identity in the midst of a life under great strain and constant transformation.

The many international genres that Bae Chunhui learned and performed in Japan contributed to her project of competent self- and world-making in numerous ways. The songs interrogated the world and replaced suffering or reorganized it into art. The Russian and Chinese pieces were like items from a highly selective scrapbook of her experience of Manchuria. The non-Japanese songs were a way that she marked, translated, and generally dealt with her own foreignness in Japan. One such piece was the Chinese "Zai na yaoyuan de difang" (In that far-off land), rendered in Japanese as "Sôgen jyôka" (Love song of the steppe). This song was written in 1939 by the prominent pop songwriter Wang Luobin, who had become famous in China for writing Mandarin-language songs inspired by the melodies of Chinese ethnic minorities. In his travels he had become enamored with a Tibetan woman, and he wrote or adopted the song from a folk song for her (see Rees 2003: 154–5). Bae Chunhui sang it for me one night early in the winter of 2003:

(Japanese) *In that far away place way out there,*
There's a pretty girl whom everyone admires
There's a pretty girl whom everyone admires

(Mandarin) *In that far-off land,*
There is a nice girl
When they pass the curtain of her room,
They all turn their heads and stare. [22] 🔊 24

In Japan the "Love Song of the Steppe" had a layered exoticism: the Japanese version was an Orientalist feminization of China, which lay on top of the Chinese version's Orientalist feminization of Tibet. Bae Chunhui, as a Korean cabaret singer in Japan, seems to have looked to China and available Orientalist representations of the Chinese exotic, as Mahler had looked to China in his *Das Lied von der Erde*, as a way of understanding, expressing, and rendering intelligible her own alienness: "By the euphemism of foreignness the outsider seeks to appease the shadow of terror" (Adorno 1992: 150).[23] She made similar use of the Ri Kôran songs, identifying with Ri as a singer poised between familiar and exotic selfhoods.

"In That Far-off Land" / "Love Song of the Steppe" speaks of how the young woman is stared at; perhaps we find here a trace of Bae Chunhui's awareness of and critical thoughts and feelings about being watched as a foreigner and a performer. Or perhaps not. This, however, is a question she might rather we pass over. In any case her command of these songs, quite independently of any subjective identification with them, and her rendering of them in Japanese established several kinds of competence that undermined, in her Japanese present, the capacity of that "Oriental Orientalist" gaze to fully detect and control her, although at the same time they rendered her intelligible, for a moment, to her audience. Walking the diva's tightrope she alternated between a persona that defied explanation and an exotic intelligibility.

As a performer of the exotic, Bae Chunhui focused mostly on songs from the places and cultures with which she had had direct contact and "Oriental" melodies given Japanese lyrics. But as a listener, appreciator, collector, and at times as a performer, she far exceeded these boundaries. In Japan she became acquainted with American jazz standards and popular songs and figures such as Louis Armstrong, Paul Anka, and Simon and Garfunkel. She had an extensive knowledge of Hollywood films and film music, especially those of the 1960s and 1970s, when, she told me, she would "go to the movies every day." She had a particular fondness for the music in westerns, especially *Johnny Guitar* (1954) and *High Plains Drifter* (1973). She spoke about French *chansons*, and she hummed the melodies to several Hawaiian pop songs that had been popular in postwar Japan. She expressed regret that she hadn't been able to learn songs in French and English because she never had a chance to develop proficiency in these languages.

Bae Chunhui went about her life in Japan beautifying the world and cultivating her autonomy through collecting the foreign and exotic, but she also learned and performed a massive repertoire of Japanese songs. In so doing she made artistic sense of her immediate surroundings and balanced her performance of otherness with a deep familiarity. She learned and sang *enka*, folk songs, children's songs, and even popular military songs (*gunka*) from the war. She studied new Japanese material to perform at the cabaret, both in shows and at after-show parties with customers and friends. Her competent performance of Japanese songs allowed her to demonstrate mastery of an aspect of the society that framed her as an outsider and to forge connections and make comparisons between her life in Japan and her life abroad.

This deeply cosmopolitan repertoire formed the backdrop for Bae Chunhui's performance of Korean folk and popular songs in the cabaret. She typically sang songs in both Korean and Japanese, thus balancing aspects of an unintelligible Other and a translated Other prepared for consumption. Many of the Korean pieces, such as the ubiquitous "Arirang" and the "Baetnorae" (Boat song) of Korea's central western Gyeonggi Province, had long been popular in Japanese versions, and as she sang these she fit herself into well-established Japanese patterns of encountering and consuming an exotic Korea.

But her performance of Korean pieces had manifold significance for her beyond this work of presenting identity. The folk pieces sustained her Korean past, and the popular pieces renewed her connection with the country that she had been taken from so long ago and to which she wondered if she would ever return.

Bae Chunhui learned folk and popular songs as a member of the Korean resident community in Japan, an oppressed and fractious group made up of first-, second-, and third-generation Koreans who had come to Japan willingly or by force during the colonial era, along with more recent migrants. This community was, and remains, divided into groups loyal to South and North Korea. Both groups imported Korean popular culture, and so Bae Chunhui learned popular songs of both the North and the South. As she learned Korean popular songs, she fostered her membership in the expatriate community and kept up to date with new musical and cultural developments and sentiments in South Korea. And for Bae Chunhui, staying contemporary was also a way of staying young; together with her colorful dress and meticulous makeup it give her a patina of perpetual youth.

Keeping up with trends in Korean popular music would only become easier in Japan as the late twentieth century progressed. In 1965 Japan and South Korea established formal relations, and a new era began of increased importation to Japan of South Korean popular films, music, and television.[24] A number of South Korean pop stars, such as Patti Kim and Jo Yongpil, had bilingual or Japanese-language hits in Japan, often remakes of previously released songs. These South Korean *teuroteu* hits, in their newfound Japanese popularity, recirculated colonial, *enka*-derived *teuroteu* to Japan. The songs provided postwar Japanese with a new encounter with Korea that was already doubly patterned by systems of colonial cultural and human circulation, and they helped to forge the new post-colonial relationship between South Korea and Japan, characterized by further migration, investment, trade, and sex industrialization.

Bae Chunhui told me that despite the differences of timbre, ornamentation, and signification between Korean *teuroteu* and Japanese *enka*, the genres could "communicate with each other, because they had similar origins": they had arisen in similar historical circumstances and in a circuit of transnational influence.[25] While she was in Japan she took Korean-Japanese songs and Japanese-influenced Korean popular songs in general as opportunities to locate herself within the structure and affect of their twofold circulation—their transnationally mediated movement through public cultural space, and the colonial and postcolonial circulation of human beings to which they so often referred, in keeping with the *teuroteu* tradition of reflecting on the experience and sorrow of displacement.

One such song was Jo Yongpil's "Dorawayo Busanhang-e" (Come back to Busan Harbor), a landmark *teuroteu*-rock fusion that debuted in 1975 and became a hit in Japan several years later as "Pusanhan-e kaere" (Return to Busan Harbor):

> Spring has come to Camellia Island, where the flowers bloom
>
> But at Busan Harbor, where my sibling left, there are only seagulls crying
>
> With every ferry going back to Oryuk Island
>
> I call out with choked throat, but you, my sibling, don't answer
>
> Come back to Busan Harbor, oh sibling for whom I long.²⁶

The song wove together colonial and postcolonial sentiments of separation from one's family and combined *teuroteu*-style melody with synthesizers and rock instrumentation. Certainly, thirty years after the end of the war, most Koreans waiting for their siblings to return from overseas had given up hope; but as we have seen in Mun Pilgi's case, there are real reasons to keep hoping beyond hope. At the end of the second verse, in a very un-*teuroteu*-like turn, the lost sibling actually comes back to Busan Harbor: "You've returned to Busan Harbor, oh sibling for whom I long." Such gestures of closure were becoming more and more imaginable as the twentieth century marched along.

Because Bae Chunhui was always so intentionally opaque about her identification with the characters in her songs, I don't know what she felt as she sang the original Korean "Come Back to Busan Harbor" in Japan. When she sang it, she had to do so from the perspective of the sibling waiting for a brother or sister such as herself to return. Perhaps she contemplated returning to Korea as she sang "Come Back to Busan Harbor" in Japan; if there is anyone who would let a song change her life, it would be Bae Chunhui.

After around thirty years in Japan Bae Chunhui fell very ill. In the throes of sickness she was visited in a dream by Shakyamuni, the Historical Buddha. He told her that she would die unless she returned to Korea and started attending a Buddhist temple. So in 1981, forty years after she had left Korea, and six years after the Korean debut of "Come Back to Busan Harbor," she gathered up the money she had saved and went home.

She moved back to the Southeast, where she was reunited with her sister and half-brother. But as the House of Sharing booklet mentioned, the half-brother made off with all of her savings. Adding to her troubles, she became alienated from her sister. She lived alone and cobbled together a living from countless odd jobs. She worked in drinking houses and as a maid. She took work as a hired entertainer, frequenting public parks and other venues in Daegu as a singer and drum accompanist for picnics and parties.

Out on her own in Korea Bae Chunhui continued to learn new material. She memorized a massive number of Korean popular songs from tapes and from the radio, and she learned songs while she worked as a hired drummer and singer and at drinking houses. She added to her old *teuroteu* repertoire, and she learned contemporary *teuroteu* hits, such as Sim Subong's 1988 "Miwoyo" (I hate), Ju Byeongseon's 1989 "Chilgapsan" (Chilgap Mountain), and scores of others that she sang for me over our years together. She got hold of new Japanese materials that were circulating on the black market, which traded in Japanese audio, video, and print culture during the South Korean ban on the importation of Japanese popular culture, which lasted until 1998. And she kept rehearsing and remembering the Japanese pieces and international pieces, both privately and with nostalgic and sympathetic middle-aged and elderly patrons and friends. She survived the last dark decade of South Korea's authoritarianism with her songs and her drum, sustaining and developing her performing self and modifying her enchanted world to suit her new surroundings.

In October 1996, fifteen years after her return from Japan, Bae Chunhui came forward as a survivor of the "comfort women" system and moved into the House of Sharing. She was seventy-four, and the years of scraping by had taken a toll.

When I met Bae Chunhui she had been living at the House for five years. She was the fourth most senior resident there, a contemporary of Pak Duri, but younger than the senior matriarchs of the House, Kim Sundeok and Pak Ongnyeon. She spent most of her time alone, chatting with young people, or watching television, often with fellow survivor Han Dosun. Some years later she would become friends with Mun Pilgi in this way as well.

Bae Chunhui, like other residents, had complex feelings about the House of Sharing. Some were drawn to their hometowns, from which many had long been estranged, and all of them had left homes elsewhere to take up residence at the House. Bae Chunhui was alienated from her family and missed Japan, so her feelings toward the House were mixed. She considered it a lonely place, a place where she was fated to end up. But she enjoyed the constant schedule of activities and the constant stream of domestic and international visitors, and she told me she considered her life to be quite comfortable. Indeed the House was uniquely suited to someone of her cosmopolitan disposition.

After years of hard-scrabble living on her own around South Korea, Bae Chunhui's life at the House of Sharing was financially more stable. Life at the House brought her from the margins of society into a new spotlight, with quite different expectations from those she had been accustomed to during her time in Japan and after her return to Korea. She shunned the role of the "activist grandmother" that Pak Duri and Mun Pilgi embraced. But she nonetheless had more of a visible presence than many women at the House, although it was an atypical one. She anchored herself by the television in the living room for hours each day. I found out later that there had been a cassette player there as well, which Bae Chunhui supervised, but it had been removed after several fights broke out over musical taste. There was enough to fight about on the television alone, and plenty of music programs besides.

There were several reasons why Bae Chunhui made a place for herself next to the television. She watched the news, an avid follower of South Korean and world politics. She was a great fan of Kim Daejung, the democratization activist who served as president from 1998 to 2003, and she supported his Millennium Democratic Party. She was a sworn enemy of the conservative Grand National Party, whom she often referred to with the mild and colorful curses of women of her age. She had her own considered and idiosyncratic beliefs about the "comfort women" issue; unlike many of the other women, she felt that through various means most South Korean victims of Japanese sexual slavery had already received sufficient financial compensation, but she wanted an apology from the Japanese government. Bae Chunhui considered herself an educated citizen: she was proud of her faithful voting record, her ability to follow political issues, have her own opinions, and locate herself in her own web of political understanding. The television was her tool in this respect.

Bae Chunhui also avidly watched shows focused on music, dance, performance, and art. She faithfully watched the song competition on Sunday, in which a long cue of contestants would sing *teuroteu* and other pop songs for cash prizes. She made sure to watch the Korean Folk Arts Competition for Foreigners, a song competition where non-Koreans sing Korean folk and popular songs broadcast on the public Korean Broadcasting System at the Occidental New Year; we figured out that she had watched the 1998 program, which I had won while I was doing my master's research on folk song.[27] She knew almost all of the songs and sang along when so inclined. She also watched concerts, such as the Secret Garden performance we watched together in June 2010.

Bae Chunhui watched many shows that were preoccupied with Korean life and Koreanness, including dramas and the song contests, but she also sought foreign programs and programs with international themes. When no one else was around, she would switch over to the state-supported Japan Broadcasting Corporation and watch children's shows, documentaries, performances, and whatever caught her eye or her ear. She scanned for Chinese programs, which catered to fans of Chinese media and the large

Chinese minority in Incheon. She watched Japanese, Chinese, and American films, and she faithfully watched a number of travel shows. She pursued this cosmopolitan array of television programs as part of her general interest in things from elsewhere and as an act of culling things to include in her enchanted world. These foreign elements in the physical heart of the House of Sharing's social life helped her to cope with her own sense of foreignness and rootlessness in the House, and in a South Korea that she nonetheless considered home.

Bae Chunhui's cosmopolitan television viewing, however, was but one species of her pursuit of the fantastic through TV. Another was her preference for shows having to do with animals and children. Her interest in such things was inflected by Japanese "cuteness" (*kawaisa*) culture, itself motivated by sentimental discourses of lost youth, and by Korean discourses of lost youth such as those we have encountered thus far.

One day in the summer of 2004 we sat together before the living room television, watching a program about a parrot whose owner had taught her to sing famous *teuroteu* songs. As the bird sang Na Hun-a's "Gajimao" (Don't go), Bae Chunhui clapped along; I rarely saw her look so happy. In front of the television she was a detective collecting evidence of the wondrousness and the redeemability of the world.

Figure 4.3.
Bae Chunhui at her spot in front of the television, watching a parrot sing "Gajimao" (Don't go), 2004.
Photo by the author.

Bae Chunhui often joined in or even initiated song parties with House staff and volunteers. She sang and played rhythmic accompaniment for the other women on the hourglass drum, much as she had done in the parks in Daegu. She also was an enthusiastic participant in the many excursions and social events set up by the House of Sharing and the Korean Council. Such occasions were opportunities to play and perform with other survivors and were some of the most powerful moments when she distinguished herself from the other women as a performer and showed us the contours of that role and identity. She dazzled others with her trained performer's voice, as she meticulously reproduced original or canonical versions of song melodies and texts. She balanced difficult pieces with ones that others could sing along to, and obscure songs with popular ones, but she avoided singing songs that were very popular among the other women, such as the new folk song "Arirang," the colonial Japanese hit "China Nights," and canonical *teuroteu* pieces like "The Tear-Soaked Duman River," which was Yi Okseon's "number eighteen" showpiece song. She astounded others with the vastness of her memory for melodies, texts, titles, and music history. And in the manner of a star she wavered between performing and refusing to participate in song circles with the other women, holding herself apart from the proceedings.

When we toured Jeju Island with the Korean Council in September 2002, Bae Chunhui was on the same bus as Mun Pilgi and me. It was the very same day on which Mun Pilgi had chastised me for not knowing how to dance "like an American." As we hurtled around the island on our way to Mount Halla, the Jeju Folk Village, and other attractions, the tour guide narrated the journey. But some of the women grew tired of the narration and clamored for the singing to begin. Presently a staff member of the Korean Council took up the emcee's role and called on each woman in turn to sing. Bae Chunhui was sitting close to the front, so her turn came up soon, but she refused. The microphone continued to circle around for a few more songs.

Around ten minutes later Bae Chunhui suddenly got up and approached the mic. She stood behind Kang Ilchul, waiting for her to finish singing her "number eighteen," the colonial-era *teuroteu* ballad "A Drinking House with No Address."[28]

Bae Chunhui then sang an unfamiliar song about Jeju Island. The other women and the young activists and volunteers looked at each other, searching for someone who recognized the song. It was "Arirang Jejudo" (Arirang of Jeju Island), a *teuroteu*-style ballad popular among older generations of Korean residents in Japan loyal to North Korea (Kim Yeon-gap 1988: 4357–58). Its Japanese origin was the reason why she alone knew it.

The piece celebrated the natural and civilizational wonders of Jeju Island, a landscape suffused with love and melodrama. Just as boats leave from south Jeju's Seongsan Harbor, sang Bae Chunhui, "following time and tide, my love goes, and my love comes."[29] The song references the seafaring traditions of Jeju Island, which have been separating lovers for centuries. In this way it shared the preoccupation with separation found in folk song and in other *teuroteu* songs and songs of the resident Korean community in Japan, where it originated. As with so many such songs about Jeju Island, this one was tainted by the memory of the brutal suppression of the leftist Jeju Island Uprising in the late 1940s and early 1950s, which claimed the lives of thirty thousand to eighty thousand islanders (see Cumings 1998). During this time as many as thirty thousand islanders escaped to Japan (Ishikida 2005: 53), and many joined the pro–North Korean resident community, which explains the origins of the song in the North-leaning Korean community in Japan. The lover who leaves and comes back could be one of these émigrés to Japan, but like the Japanese version of "Come Back to Busan Harbor" and many other songs, the song is sung in the voice of one left behind. 🔊 25

Bae Chunhui's postcolonial life was a similar story of human circulation, so as she sang of the diasporic experience to which the song alludes, she may have been marking her own homecoming. Whatever the case may be, Bae Chunhui sang this song because it suited the situation, and it revealed her astonishing knowledge of song. As she sang that song that no one knew she took a step forward that was also a step away from everyone else, an act of distinction. But as she did so she also revealed a hidden soundtrack to the world, moving through the physical landscape of the island to a terrain of cultural and personal memory. This song, like her many others, was like a special looking glass that she used to reveal the hidden world of wonder, romance, beauty, and sorrow. That magical real, that enchanted world shone out of it, not repressing history and memory but extracting art from them.

In moments like this Bae Chunhui stepped forward into the spotlight as the architect and guardian of that magical real. But at the final dinner and song party on the Jeju trip she flatly refused to sing, despite pleas from the Council staff. In this seemingly retiring gesture, she became once again the obstinate center of attention, the compact nucleus of a swirling galaxy of singers and songs.

Back at the House of Sharing Bae Chunhui had more social power and typically less competition from other women, so her performances at song parties were more extensive. Survivors, staff, and volunteers gathered in large and small groups in the media room, where the drum that Bae Chunhui used sat tucked in a corner.

On January 23, 2003, the Korean Council brought a group of around thirty-five women to the House to celebrate the coming Lunar New Year.[30] After lunch the survivors and the Council staff played *yunnori*, a traditional stick-throwing game traditionally played around the New Year, a derivative of traditional divination practices that farmers used to forecast their fortunes in the field. Some of the women began to tire of the game, and the staff of the Council suggested a song party.

Bae Chunhui was dressed for the occasion, made up with great care and wearing one of her many dresses of *gaeryang hanbok* ("modernized" Korean clothing). She rose and walked to her self-appointed place in front of a short microphone stand, then sat with the drum in front of her.

The second mic began to circulate, and Yi Yongnyeo, a former resident of the House who now lived at the foot of the valley, began the singing. She was a bit flush from a private stash of *makgeolli* (unfiltered rice wine) and the beer that the Council was serving, and it showed as she took the microphone and began to sing her florid version of the "Ballad of the Traveling Entertainer," Pak Duri's favorite song. Bae Chunhui called out the name of the song, identifying it for everyone. At this Yi Yongnyeo stopped: "You're asking me to sing the 'Ballad of the Traveling Entertainer?'" Bae Chunhui grumbled at the persistent ignorance of amateur singers of the proper names of songs. She replied temperamentally, "I'll play the drum for you. I said I'll play the drum for you." Yi Yongnyeo looked confused. Frustrated, Bae Chunhui looked to her and snapped "Dance, dance!" and proceeded to begin her day's medley.

The first song was "The Ballad of the Birds" ("Sae taryeong"), a famous southwestern folk song that, much like the "Ballad of the Traveling Entertainer," had been canonized in a version made popular by *gisaeng* (professional female entertainers) and professional male singers throughout the peninsula in the late nineteenth and early twentieth centuries. She sang this vocally-acrobatic piece in its most famous version, articulating the well-known text precisely while accompanying herself on the drum.

Bae Chunhui sang of a spring bustle of songbirds, waterfowl, and magical birds, heralding the New Year and the renewal of the world and bringing tidings of the year's harvest:[31]

Birds are flocking this way
All kinds of different birds are flocking this way.
A phoenix among birds,
Before the gate of longevity, a bird of the bountiful harvest
Over people-less high mountains and through deep valleys
Flying in the deep forests, water birds

Flying in pairs, singing back and forth a cheerful spring song
Saenggeut saenggeut *flying this way.*[32] 19

Bae Chunhui sang the piece because it was relevant to the New Year, and hence it was another opportunity for enchanting the everyday, for weaving her magical reality. She also performed it before the other women because of the different kinds of virtuosity it allowed her to display, emphasizing her place in that magical real. She deftly wound her way through the rich and archaic Sino-Korean texts, and she handled the song's florid melody with the grace of a professional singer. In the second half of each verse she sang long melismas on the word "cry." Her voice balanced here between narrating and imitating the ecstatic vocalizations of the birds. Finally she let loose with the song's famous imitations of particular birdcalls, in which she assumed, unambiguously, the voice of a bird. Bae Chunhui imitated the sound of a Korean mountainous turtledove,[33] followed by a long melismatic passage:

> *Going to this mountain,* ssuk-kkuk, ssuk-kkuk
> *Going to that mountain,* ssuk-ssuk-kkuk, ssuk-kkuk
> *Eo heo—Eoi hi—Eo—*
> *Drifting left and right and singing.*[34]

Her imitation of the dove required a leap of more than an octave, and a leap into falsetto. The long melismatic passage involved intensive microtonal shading, the practice of pitch-bending common among trained singers and less utilized by amateurs. It ended with a long downward tumbling to the last line, describing the ambling motion of the bird. In this line she assumed again a third-person relationship to the drifting and crying birds. She repeated the whole process of transformation in the second verse, where she assumed the voice of a Chinese oriole (*kkoegori*): *kkoekkol, kkoekkol.*

As Bae Chunhui showed off her vocal pyrotechnics in song, she performed a metamorphosis that was a core aspect of her sense of self, from the medium of a magical real to a productive part of it. She also demonstrated her power as a performer to effect such transformations. Here was the transformation of a human voice into bird song and a human being into a bird, and back again. It was a ritual moment in a cultural schema of mythic transformation that made sense of the relations between humans and nature, and music and sound.[35] It was a moment in which this cultural scheme and Bae Chunhui's personal work of myth-making intersected, in which she demonstrated her power to reveal and affect her enchanted world. In the first half of the verse she narrated the world as art; in the second she merged with that world, in the voice of a bird, before gliding back down to the role of the narrator. Bae Chunhui's portrait of the world as art, her secret soundtrack that was the truth of the world, showed the other women her place in it, and, consequently, their places as well. It explained the relations not only between humans and nature, but between her and her peers. She was "a phoenix among birds."

After her first song Bae Chunhui changed her tone. The rest of her set was composed of popular *teuroteu* ballads and one *sinminyo* (new folk song), all known by the majority of the other survivors. She had already established her supremacy; with these pieces she showed us that she was not above singing common songs that express common sentiments. Now she became a different sort of medium, channeling the feelings of others, singing, in part, on their behalf. As before, when her voice became the voice of a bird, her voice was opaquely identified with the aestheticized mass-cultural sentiments she conveyed when she sang. There could be identities of self with the characters and sentiments of song, or her voice could be that of an unidentified and divested storyteller.

In the practiced manner of professional singers of *enka* and *teuroteu* Bae Chunhui smiled as she sang songs of sorrow, for she had that special power of the performer to identify with sorrow, to become the art of sorrow, or to relay it from elsewhere. She sang Sim Subong's 1988 "Miwoyo" (I hate): "[I] hold tight to my drink, I hold tight to a song of love . . . men, men, how I hate the tears of men."[36] Who was it who did the loving and hating? Where, in the room, in public culture, in the country or the world, was she? We can only venture to guess, and that is precisely the point. Bae Chunhui enjoyed the power of flexible identification and differentiation. She took part in a tradition of opacity in popular music that enabled such flexible identifications, and in so doing allowed many people to participate. In this way it made possible the moral education of women, men, young and old, and gave birth to the abstract categories of culture: subjects, genders, peoples, ethnicities, sexualities. Steering this process, she left her imprint, however small, on those categories. And she created a fantastical identity for herself as a performer, with a wardrobe of costumes and masks that revealed as much as they hid.

Bae Chunhui had rather cool relationships with most of the other women at the House of Sharing, but her performer's role did not go unappreciated. On a midsummer's day in 2004 I sat on the second floor of the residence hall passing time with survivors Yi Okseon, Kim Gunja, and Pak Ongnyeon. We were in the hall to catch the cross-breeze that came down from the mountains, in through the rear windows, and out southward down the valley to the river. Pak Ongnyeon and some others insisted on the benefits of this natural breeze and rarely resorted to electric fans, much less air conditioners.

I had just given them each a copy of the booklet for the exhibition of the fifteen survivors' portrait photographs and songs that the Japanese photographer Yajima Tsukasa and I had put on in August of that year. Yi Okseon was reading through the different song texts, and she came to a rest on Bae Chunhui's photo and the text of her song. The song was "Dance Song of Youth" ("Qing chun wu qu"), a Chinese folk song arranged in 1938 by Wang Luobin, the composer of "In That Far-off Land," which she had sung for me at the House of Sharing in the spring of 2004. It had become popular again in China when it was sung by the female lead of the melodramatic film *Susanna* (1967); the film became popular in Korea, and Jeong Hunhui debuted a Korean version, "Cheongchun mu-gok," in 1970.

This song was also about birds, here harnessed to the trope of lost youth. Yi Okseon read the lyrics, in Korean translation, under her breath:

(Chinese) *The sun descends over the mountain and rises the next morning*
Flowers wither and bloom again the same way next year
The beautiful baby bird flies away without a trace
Just like the baby bird, the spring of my youth doesn't return.
This mustn't be so . . . this mustn't be so—
The spring of my youth flies away like the bird and doesn't return.

(Korean) *The sun rises again*
Flowers bloom again with the coming of spring.
But like the baby bird, who flies up and goes far,
The spring of my youth does not return,
The spring of my youth does not return.

(Chinese) *This mustn't be so . . . this mustn't be so—*
(Korean) *The spring of my youth does not return.*[37] 26

Yi Okseon looked up at Kim Gunja and said, "You wanna hear what Bae Chunhui sang? 'Like the baby bird, who flies up and goes far, the spring of my youth does not return.' How about that? 'The spring of my youth does not return.'" Kim Gunja looked up and said, reluctantly, heavily, "She's good." The room grew very quiet, as though everyone had stopped breathing.

"Goooooooooood," Kim Gunja repeated.

Despite Bae Chunhui's status as a perpetual outsider at the House of Sharing, indeed perhaps because of it, she was able to evocatively express this sentiment, so palpable in the lives of the women. She sang of the lost springtime of youth that was a trope of the "comfort women grandmothers movement" and many of the women's songs, like Pak Duri's versions of the "Ballad of the Traveling Entertainer." But while Bae Chunhui sang of the springtime of youth as a baby bird that flies off, never to return, she had held fast to the bird, becoming the bird of spring and youth in "Ballad of the Birds" and in her beautiful costumes. Her very name meant "Spring Princess," and she had grown into this role. She resisted age and time itself, with remarkable success.

In the song Bae Chunhui both identified with and kept a distance from spring, the lost springtime of youth, and the birds, as well as the many characters and sentiments of her other songs. This was her place at the House, simultaneously possessed of great expressive power, admired for her expressive ability, and yet outcast from full membership in the community and its cult of lost youth. This had been the place of the performer and her social world in South Korean society for centuries, and in many other parts of the world as well. It went a long way toward explaining the solitary fate of which she so often spoke.

In this way Bae Chunhui lived simultaneously at the margins and at the center of survivor society at the House. Her visibility and curiosity led to relationships with House visitors and the young staff and activists that made her a centerpiece of much of the House's daily goings-on. She reveled in the queries and attentions of the many guests to the House, whom she waited for in the living room and in the yard, where she listened to music on the PA system and smoked cigarettes, until she gave them up in the late 2000s. She spent countless evenings drinking, talking, and singing with guests, and she was a fixture at song parties.

As a result Bae Chunhui was quite popular with young people at the House. They appreciated the way she reached out to them, asking questions, fascinated by the new and seeking opportunities to renew her own sense of youthfulness, and they shared her love of play. Many Japanese guests arrived at the House with immensely complex feelings—of shock, guilt, or awkwardness. Most, besides, were unable to speak Korean and hence unable to communicate with most of the women without the aid of a translator. They were obviously quite pleased to meet Bae Chunhui, a survivor of Japanese military sexual slavery who was fluent in Japanese, a fan of Japanese culture, and waiting for Japanese guests with whom to sing and chat.

One day a young Japanese woman walked out of the museum sobbing and sat down at Bae Chunhui's side in the courtyard. Bae Chunhui put an arm around the woman until she stopped crying. For someone who monitored her personal space with great care, this was an immense gesture, even if the woman had practically collapsed on her shoulder. I never saw her do anything like that again.

Many of her meetings with Japanese visitors turned into correspondences, and these new friends and acquaintances would send or bring her cassette tapes and other things she asked for from Japan. In this way her semiprivate meetings with guests and volunteers at the House helped her gather the materials she employed in her musical revelation of the magical real. The work of making these relationships was, for Bae Chunhui, a work of making intercultural communication possible and generating a sociality from her vast cosmopolitan identity. It was also a means by which she recharged her own identity as a cosmopolitan professional and as a relevant participant in the world.

Song parties were one such place where she forged and revitalized senses of self and society. In October 2002 she went to a party in the education room for Tsukasa, the Japanese photographer. He had been visiting the House for two weeks and was returning to Japan, with plans to return to the House of Sharing as a staff member in January of the coming year. In that short time Bae Chunhui had warmed to him considerably; at the party she gave him a stylish neotraditional Korean shirt and pants set as a going-away present.

The round of singing began rather late, in the quiet and private hours after ten, when most of the other women had retired for the night. Bae Chunhui asked each of us to sing first. Tsukasa sang a classic Japanese pop love song, "Ue wo muite arukô" (Let's look up and walk), and Bae Chunhui sang along. Jeongsuk, the administrator who most of the women called the "Office Girl," sang the well-known *teuroteu* "Namhaeng yeolcha" (Southbound train). I sang a northwest Korean folk song I had been learning called "Neurigae taryeong" (Slow ballad). Bae Chunhui played the drum to accompany each of us in turn.

Bae Chunhui responded to my song with a medley of Korean folk songs from across the peninsula, starting with "Monggeumpo taryeong," a ballad of the scenic spot Monggeumpo northwest of Seoul, a song from the same region as mine. She sang each of the folk songs and then translated her favorite parts for Tsukasa, explaining aspects of Korean traditional culture to him and explaining the often archaic lyrics for all of us. She went on to Japanese folk songs and translated the lyrics for the museum director, myself, and the administrative assistant. From there she proceeded to Korean folk songs that had been translated into Japanese.

In a long stretch she sang two verses of a Japanese version of the canonical "Arirang." The piece had been melodically Japanized by rendering the formerly neutral third above the central tone as a minor third,[38] thus giving the melody a pentatonic (five-note) minor feel reminiscent of many

Japanese folk songs and *enka* pieces. She reproduced this modal transformation carefully and accurately, although she discarded the Japanized Korean of the refrain and sang the canonical Korean text in its place, bookended by Japanese verses.

(Korean) *Arirang, arirang, arariyo*
Crossing over Arirang pass.
(Japanese) *When we're far apart and wish to meet*
Would that the moon would become a mirror.[39] 22

The museum director marveled at the beauty of the Japanese lyric. The song spoke of two lovers separated by a tremendous distance by combining a (Japanized) Korean melody and a Japanese lyric to express this longing. The song thus acted like a mirror, longing to realize the union it accomplished in its privileged domain. So did Bae Chunhui's long performance, of which this was but a culminating moment; taken as a whole, her long medley was symmetrical, bouncing back and forth between Korean and Japanese songs and languages, and now with the Japanese "Arirang" she blended the two cultures together. She concluded by telling us, "The basic ideas of Korean and Japanese 'Arirangs' are all the same." She was herself akin to the mirror of the song, as she joined and blended the two cultures in rippling reflection.

That night, as the four of us listened to Bae Chunhui's necklaces of song, we came a little closer to her and to each other. The song's aspiration—that we might finally be able to meet across the vast gulfs that separate us—edged closer to being realized. She went on to sing a number of Japanese versions of Korean pop songs: "Come Back to Busan Harbor," "Don't Go" ("Gajimao"), "With Pain in My Breast" ("Gaseum apeuge"), and others.

We were all amazed at the songs themselves, but also because of the harmonization of selves and others that Bae Chunhui used the songs to create in this moment of play. Much of the amazement focused on Bae Chunhui, who made all this possible and who put the lie to the idea of cultural discreteness that reified Korean and Japanese culture as perfectly separate. On many evenings such as this one Bae Chunhui sat magisterially at the center of a palpable social reality, in this temporary union of her international cohort, this tangible form of her ongoing acts of world creation. At other song parties she would perform other international repertoires, whatever she thought best for creating this enchanted sociality. If her mode of play was a means of generating a social world according to her tastes and with herself at the center, it was also an ethical activity that encouraged mutual interest, understanding, and harmony,

Figure 4.4.
Bae Chunhui singing at the House of Sharing, Spring 2010.
Photo by Yajima Tsukasa.

three things that she often told me were important and sorely lacking in South Korean society.

In the everyday context of the House of Sharing the Japanese, Chinese, and Russian songs were in part means by which Bae Chunhui expressed her sense of foreignness at the House and in South Korea. They were elements by which she distinguished her own sense of self from South Korean national identity and from her contemporaries at the House. But in the context of these international song parties she made the songs and herself at home in the cosmopolitan atmosphere that she wove around herself. And although this was a temporary social world, in need of constant renewal, the seeds of its renewal and flourishing were omnipresent, like the inevitability of spring that she described in "Ballad of the Birds." All she had to do was find them, again and again—on television, in the

ambivalently cosmopolitan atmosphere of the House of Sharing, in the
mail, and in thin air.

We will end this chapter and most likely our lives without dispelling the
mysteries surrounding the relationship between Bae Chunhui's world
of song and her traumatic experiences. "Good purposes are often served
by not tampering with vagueness," wrote Quine (1960: 127), the
philosopher of language. Bae Chunhui, in pursuing a policy of opacity
with respect to the relationship between her personal life, her heart, and
her songs, reaped an immeasurable harvest. So might we, if we focus on
what she wanted us to see and hear.

Bae Chunhui turned my attention, again and again, to the world as
art, and to her gestures revealing that world, by which she explained life to
herself and others. The magical real was not just a collection of cultural
artifacts, but a special kind of social space. It was a space that balanced
particularity and universality. When it attained its ideals, people rooted in
their particular cultures and histories acknowledged each other in their
particularity, but were nonetheless capable of moving beyond national and
generational culture into spaces of togetherness. Doing so was the stuff
of reconciliation that has evaded Northeast Asia ever since the Asia-
Pacific War. Understanding Bae Chunhui meant grasping a sociality that
encompassed elements of the secret cultural histories of transnational
circulation of people and culture in East Asia, but this sociality was
beyond nations and cultures, facilitating their reformation and reconciliation in the terrain of a magical real.

We have all seen attempts to make similar magical realities concrete.
Everland is South Korea's largest theme park, located an hour south of Seoul
near the town of Suwon. A supporter of the House of Sharing was in upper
management at the park and often arranged for the women to visit for free,
and I have been twice with them.

I visited Everland with Bae Chunhui and several other survivors in the
spring of 2003. We were going specifically to tour the annual Flower
Carnival, a tulip festival. We rode the "flower train" together through the
tulips of the park's Netherlands Village. In a mockup of a small Tudor chalet
we watched a short song and dance revue performed by anonymous white
people, who looked half-present, like characters out of a fantasy. We toured
the petting zoo, rode carousels, watched an elephant show, and took in the
Carnival Fantasy Parade, in which more phantom Caucasians appeared as
fairy-tale creatures covered in electric lights. Bae Chunhui reveled in the
exoticism, the cultivated natural splendor of the gardens, the cuteness of
the animals, the omnipresence of icons of youth, and the large numbers of
children at play.

But there was something wrong with this place, some reason why Bae Chunhui didn't talk about it and why she never seemed so enthusiastic about going. The song and dance show was a hasty amalgamation of popular Western melodies, which were sung, without love, to the accompaniment of canned music. The chalets and castles were made of cheap prefab materials. Everland, whose title is a reference to Peter Pan's timeless Neverland, was out of the world, even though its website spoke of the park as a "union of human and nature."[40] In sharp contrast, Bae Chunhui's magical real was based in her ability to reveal the world as art, not to escape it into fantasy.[41]

Everland was divided into sections called "European Adventure," "American Adventure," "Global Fair," "Zoo Topia," "Caribbean Bay," and "Magic Land." The scheme was borrowed from American theme parks, although there was very little of the exoticist representation of third world and aboriginal peoples that is so common at Disney's parks, from Paris to Anaheim to Tokyo (see Marling 1992). The park was a South Korean corporate fantasy of Europe, America, a people-less Caribbean, the natural world, and the wonderlands of primarily European fairy tales and children's stories. There were few representations of Asia, except in the section called "Global Village," where various Asian traditional costumes were displayed.

Inside the fantasy of Everland, of course, Asia was lurking; the park was a fantasy of difference that offered all the amenities of home, and hence neutralized the differences it projected. South Korea had a hidden omnipresence.[42] The Café Amsterdam was a fried rice (bokkeumbap) specialty house. So unlike Bae Chunhui's world, Everland was not the fantastical spine of the world, which worked resolutions of selves and others; it was a fantasy of otherness that hid within it a fantasy of essential Koreanness, an essential ethnic and national subjectivity. Everland inserted Korea covertly into a fantasy of European otherness; Bae Chunhui gave the manifold selves and others she encountered a place in her fantastical world. Everland produced the self through convincing fantasies of otherness; Bae Chunhui extracted structures of enchantment from the stuff of experience. So she felt both at home and estranged at Everland, as she felt in South Korea in general.

On our visit to the annual tulip festival the signs of early spring were everywhere. The forsythias and azaleas were in bloom, and we admired them as we walked slowly up the low hill to the rear entrance of the "European Adventure" part of the park. I was escorting survivor Pak Ongnyeon, who was now eighty-five, as she walked slowly, stooped from endless years of hard labor. She was teaching me the order in which flowers bloom in the Korean spring. Magnolia, forsythia, azalea, Rose of Sharon....

Bae Chunhui was coming up the hill a bit faster with Tsukasa, the Japanese photographer. As they approached the rear door a few white acrobats came out for a break. As they passed, we heard them speaking a Slavic language. Bae Chunhui stopped, and spoke in Russian to a tall blond young man.

He was from Ukraine, as were most of his coworkers. She asked him if he knew "Katyusha," the Russian song she had learned back in Harbin. He said yes, and they sang the first verse together.[43]

For most Korean visitors to Everland, the Ukrainian was a generic white; it didn't matter where he was from. He performed and facilitated fantasies of the West; he lived his professional life under the persistent gaze of Everland's quality control apparatus and its expectant visitors.[44] Bae Chunhui, drawing on her own trove of experiences, found something as close to his experience as she could. She engaged the generic Other to discover his history, his culture, and his particularity. And she found that she shared something in common with him, the common knowledge of a song, which they had arrived at through very different histories of encounters with Russia.

In this effortless gesture she threw into question the South Korean logic of self and Other that had such vicious concreteness at Everland and that shaped the South Korean everyday and formed the backdrop of the "comfort women grandmothers movement." In the everyday process of tirelessly discovering and renewing the fantastical world, Bae Chunhui became its medium, one capable of engendering a fantastic sociality worthy of it. She and the acrobat sang of unfaltering love:

Apple and pear trees were blooming
The fog swam over the river
Katyusha walked on the bank,
On the high, steep bank.[45] 20

Epilogue

"Don't grow old," Pak Ongnyeon said, beginning one of her favorite jokes. "Because as you grow old you get stupid. And then you say stupid things," she paused. "Like don't grow old, because as you grow old you get stupid . . ." and as she looped back around we all laughed.

Pak Ongnyeon, now nearing ninety years of age, had been taken during the war to Rabaul, a township in eastern Papua New Guinea, as a sexual slave of the Japanese military. When defeat drew near the Japanese attempted to evacuate. She lived through two shipwrecks; out of an initial group of fifty, she was one of four women who lived.

Returning to South Korea she married and had two children. She farmed and did other kinds of hard work during South Korea's long road to recovery from the colonial era and the Korean War.

Now, at the House of Sharing, she walked with a bent back but farmed and exercised regularly. On her daily walks she would suddenly take off running, to make you jump or to get a laugh. She berated me for smoking, snatching Balloon Flower herb-tinctured cigarettes from me and smoking them with a kindly leer. In all the world, she said, she feared nothing, except for boats. "Can't do boats," she said.

Pak Ongnyeon and I were in the garden on a hot, clear day in the fall of 2003. The hills around the House of Sharing were just starting to exchange their blanket of deep greens for the burnt and brilliant colors of fall, dotted with dark green pine trees. We spent an hour or so bringing in a bumper crop of squash (*hobak*). As I set down the last sack load on the floor outside her room she beamed. "My goodness, that's a big one!"

"It's the king," I said.

She bowed reverentially, smiling. "The king."

It was hot, and so she handed me an energy drink and a banana to thank me for my help. The drink was electric red and very sweet, one of many visitors' gifts shared among the women, which they shared in turn with volunteers and friends.

We sat down among the squashes, admiring them and singing. She sang a few songs from the era before *enka*-derived popular song held sway in Korea, when North American popular and religious music exerted the preeminent foreign influence on popular music in the Korean peninsula. There was "Song of Hope," one of the very first popular songs of Korean composition, which wandered along in a lilting waltz time, emulating the threes of Korean folk song. And she sang a Korean version of "Clementine," which she had learned at night school as a child; she pronounced the girl's name "Clementink." The story of Pak Ongnyeon's finely wrought song world, like that of so many other women, has yet to be written.

She began to talk about one of her favorite tunes. It was one of her many verses to the popular central Korean folksong "Norae garak" (Song-tune), of which Pak Duri was also fond. She explained that it was about a dead tree that comes to life. Perhaps at some darker moments in her life it had served to remind her that scenes of devastation would renew themselves, and she had renewed her life, countless times. Today she talked me through it and sang it in her cigarette-stained voice, a voice inseparable from the world and the life it described.

She paused for a disclaimer. "These days I can't sing. My voice is all messed up." Then she sang:

> By the universe's greatest sea
> Sprouts a rootless tree.
> Its branches are twelve,
> And its leaves are three hundred and sixty.
> When that tree bears fruit,
> The first month of the year has come.[1] 27

There is more to a person than suffering, more than victimization, more than survival and flourishing. These are only a few way stations in an endless cycle of blooming and falling—a wheel of time.

This book is about three women's courage and creativity, which are made perpetually necessary by social forces that perpetuate suffering. Perhaps the wheel is that circle of suffering and endurance, a hell of infinite repetition, with no end to the cycles of sexual violence or exploitation, an infinite recursion without soul or justice.

But the wheel in Pak Ongnyeon's song is not just that. It is an endless process of remaking ourselves and refashioning the world in our image, and being remade as a likeness of that world. It is a fine song, prized again and again from the heart of a pine tree. It is a "song I sing every day," as Pak Duri called her "Ballad of the Traveling Entertainer," that enjoins us to live well while we can and comforts us toward the end. It is Mun Pilgi's song of perpetual searching for love, a love too perfect for the world that she made and kept in her heart. It is the infinite exposition of an encyclopedic songbird like Bae Chunhui. Finally it is a horizon that stretches on beyond these pages, a project of listening to others that we must not allow to end.

Pak Duri's Testimony

BEATEN BY THE OWNER AND THE MANAGER, I LOST MUCH OF MY HEARING

"Without a hearing aid, I can't communicate in everyday situations."[1]

I was born in 1924 in Cheongdo, Miryang administrative district, South Gyeongsang Province. My father was a farmer, and the situation in our house was somewhat comfortable. But my father and his older brother ran around with women and squandered all our assets. After that we had to move back and forth many times between the Cheongdo area of North Gyeongsang Province and Miryang,[2] because of my father, who had started work as a carpenter. Of seven siblings, I was the oldest, born when my father was eighteen. The next eldest, a brother, was five years younger than me; in the middle there were two other brothers and after that there were three sisters.

I never got to go to school, even once. In those days there weren't many girls in my neighborhood going to school. So I'm completely unable to read.

My mother raised us kids in a house with three rooms. I helped by looking after my younger siblings. At that time my youngest sibling was two years old. My twelve-year-old younger brother didn't go to school so that he could help my father with his carpentry work. Times were hard and we got by eating wild greens that we picked, but we didn't go hungry.

I WANTED TO EARN MONEY IN A JAPANESE FACTORY IN ORDER TO HELP MY FAMILY, BUT . . .

When I was dragged off my family was living in the Samnangjin area in Miryang. In those days my father was working for a construction company called Nakamura Gumi as a carpenter. The company was in the middle of building a railroad that went all the way to Bukcheong.

My parents wanted to marry me off, but there wasn't anybody who I thought was right, so I didn't marry. I was thinking of getting married a little later.

I know that I was taken away in 1940, the year I turned sixteen. But I don't remember when it was during the year. All I know is that it wasn't hot or cold. My second oldest brother was in his first year of elementary school.

One day three men came to our village. The three divided up and went around town collecting females.[3] The man who came to our house was a tall Japanese who looked like he was around fifty. This Japanese man appeared to be the person in charge out of the three men. He spoke in Korean but his Korean wasn't clear. So my parents and I thought he was a Korean living in Japan, and it was only when I got to Taiwan that I found out that he was Japanese. The other two men seemed to be Koreans. He said that he would place me in a Japanese factory. I told him that I wanted to make money in Japan and send it to my parents. My parents didn't doubt his intentions and didn't oppose my wish, because they really thought I was going to a Japanese factory to make money. . . .

Those men took around ten girls from our village with them. I have no memory of how we got to Busan. . . .

In Busan we got on a large ship with two stories. There were many soldiers and civilians. There were about ten women here and there about the ship. The boat didn't stop in Japan; it went straight to Taiwan. It was the first time for us to travel by boat, so the girls all grew nauseous and vomited violently. The wind blew strong. On the boat I got two or three blankets.

We got off at some port. I couldn't remember the name of the port and I was very upset about it, but hearing the editor [of this testimony] list the Japanese names of Taiwanese cities, I remembered: Shôka [Changhua] . . . Shôka. Some of the females got off with me at Shôka and others went on to somewhere else.

BEATEN BY THE OWNER AND THE MANAGER

After arriving in Shôka I might have been there for a week, maybe for a few days, I don't know—that's how nauseous I was from the ship. I don't know what I rode in transport from the port to the house where our bodies were sold,[4] but I saw commoners' houses. The place I was taken to was a Taiwanese person's house, a big one-story house. There were bars on the windows.

There was a sign on the house. When you wanted a sign for your business, you had to have permission [from the Japanese military], they told me. No matter how much I think, I can't remember the name that was written on the sign. There were hills in front of the house, and there were bananas and mandarin oranges growing there.

At the large front entrance there was an office where the owner and the manager sat, and in front of that there was a corridor. Rooms for the girls ran the length of the corridor on both sides. And across from the office there were rooms for girls as well. In the middle there was a small courtyard that the girls' rooms were ringed around. There was a dining room to the left of the office. There were flowers and trees planted next to the main entrance. We all lived in our own rooms but blankets and clothes were kept in another small room. The house wasn't clean inside, and there was only one bathroom. Girls would put on makeup and change into clothes and then come out and sit in a room to the right of the office.

The Japanese man who had taken me away at Samnangjin was the owner of the house. He was a capable man and he maintained good dealings with soldiers well. There were already five or six girls there. They were all Korean. Those of us who were new were waiting to be sent to a factory.

But soldiers started coming. The owner suddenly came to us and ordered us to receive "guests."[5] That's when I knew that I had come to a place where I had to serve soldiers. I was so surprised. This was my first time with a man. I thought of trying to escape but without being able to read, and without knowing my way around, I couldn't. If I'd gone out I would have died. Without knowing a soul . . . I thought dying would be better but I had to suffer through it.

As soon as the soldiers would come in they'd grab a female they fancied and take her into a room. Lots of soldiers and civilians waited outside the main door. Some guests would come alone, others in groups of two or three. I received around ten guests a day. Sometimes there were soldiers who would stay for the night. Army and navy, everybody came. It seems like there was a base close by. The colors of their uniforms were different, so I knew that all kinds of soldiers were coming.

There were both Japanese and Taiwanese civilian guests. Civilian customers as well would come in and sleep for about an hour and then leave, but each month a few civilians would spend the night. The civilians who came to me were mainly Taiwanese. They spoke some language other than Japanese, their skin was darker, and they smelled, so I knew they were Taiwanese. They wore average civilian clothes. They were crude and filthy. Those Taiwanese didn't go to the other females.

But there were more soldiers than civilians. If there were lots of soldiers, civilians would stop by and then go home. Because soldiers couldn't come frequently except when on leave, we had to take soldiers whether they had much or little money. They came both by day and by night. In Shôka there were lots of houses like that, and so soldiers went elsewhere as well.

In particular, many came on Saturday and Sunday. Because soldiers didn't have a lot of money, they'd come when they got their monthly pay. Among the soldiers I obtained *najimi* [steady customers], but when the company moved they stopped coming. I didn't have any affection for any one particular Japanese soldier.

There were regulations for how much it cost a soldier to take me to a room for a night, or for an hour. The manager woman received the money, wrote down the amount in the accounting book, and gave the money to the owner. Since she'd follow us and take the money from the soldiers I didn't know how much it was. The manager was a Japanese woman in her thirties, and she was in charge of telling us when to clean and everything. She was also the one who brought us food, and although at the most there were two managers, usually she did everything alone. The owner would get the money from the manager and add it up, and figure out which of us was bringing in the most business.

I didn't get a break even during menstruation. My back hurt so much that I couldn't even get up. Soldiers brought condoms with them. There were a small number of soldiers who didn't use condoms as well. The older woman who was with us went here and there with the movement of troops.

Some soldiers who stayed for the night would ask how I had gotten there, and they'd pity me and leave money [about 1,000 or 2,000 won by today's standards[6]]. In those days I didn't smoke or drink, so I didn't waste money. The soldiers didn't hit me.

When I started business there the owner gave me a *nemaki* [a robe for sleeping in] and an *obi* [cloth belt].[7] I had to prepare each of around three or four sets of the differently patterned kimonos that I would wear when I did business. So I had no choice but to use the pocket money the soldiers gave me. I'd give the manager money and she'd buy me makeup and clothes.

My hair was long to my lower back, but when I started that business I went to a beauty shop and had it cut. That was the owner's wish, so I had to do it. Girls who had some spare money because they had lots of guests would get perms as well.

The female owner was also Japanese. She'd tell us to buy cosmetics and make ourselves up beautifully. We *definitely* had to use makeup. She told me I was ugly and so that if I didn't use makeup it was likely that no one would come. My Japanese name was Fujiko. The owner made up the name for me.

When guests would sleep for the night and leave, we'd wake up, wash and clean up. Whether I had a guest or not, I couldn't sleep at night. I had to sleep until one or two in the day so that I could wake up to do business at night again.

The owner of the house I was in brought lots of other females from Korea other than us. All of them were country girls, and they were all around fifteen years old. There were typically around twenty females there. But some of the females went off to other places and so sometimes there were around ten.

In the house if one person made a mistake, we all were beaten, like they did in the military. We'd be told to sit on our folded knees and the owner and the Japanese female who managed us would beat us on our inner thighs with a rod. They'd beat us that way so that guests couldn't see the marks. It hurt so much. It'd make a black line. It wasn't because of something I did— if one among us drank a lot and said that she couldn't do business, we'd all be beaten, whether there were ten of us or twenty of us. Or if anyone said something bad about the owner. For my part, if the owner was good I didn't compliment, and if the owner was bad I didn't say so. If we didn't do good business we'd get yelled at, but we never got beaten for having only a few guests. I got in trouble a few times for not sending guests off in the morning by the required time. I got whipped again for not being able to wake up my guest. The owner and the manager beat me fiercely. I think the reason I've lost so much of my hearing now is because of how they beat me back then.

Every morning the manager examined us by putting a medical instrument in our genitals. Then, after the examination, she disinfected us. She gave us pills, saying they were for contraception, and told us to swallow them. I put those pills in my room and took them occasionally. The manager would tell us to be careful because if we caught a sexually transmitted disease it could pass to the guests and we'd have to stop doing business. If one of the females got a disease the owner would take her to the hospital. The owner said that if the females got sick and passed it to the guests that the camp would be shut down. If a female caught a disease she got shots at the hospital. That hospital was huge and there were many soldiers and civilians. The doctor was Japanese. There were females who got treated at the hospital and got better right away, there were those who had to be admitted for a few days, and there were those who were operated on. I also had an operation.[8] Because I had to receive so many guests my right thigh swelled up and I went to the hospital and they said I should have an operation. I still have the scar from it. Someone told me that my evidence that I'd lived in a house where I had to serve Japanese soldiers wasn't clear, but the mark of that wound [the interviewer confirmed a five-centimeter scar] is my very immediate evidence.

I WAS SO HUNGRY . . .

The hardest thing about my life in Taiwan was that I was unable to eat properly. In that house they didn't provide us with a proper diet. Rice was rare and sometimes we skipped meals. That's the age when you want to eat the most food. . . . They'd give us a bowl of rice, miso soup, and some anchovies just twice a day. Because I'd have to stay up all night doing business I couldn't eat breakfast. I couldn't go out, and even if there was something I really wanted to eat I didn't have any money to buy it with. The owner promised to give me the money I'd earned later, but never paid me even once. In just under five years of living in Taiwan I never got as much as a penny from the owner. All I got was food.

The owner demanded that we speak Japanese. I remember *irasshaimase* [welcome in], *arigatô gozaimasu* [thank you], *osake* [alcohol], *tabako* [cigarettes], *hari* [needle], *ito* [thread], *kome* [uncooked rice], *mugi* [barley], and other things. In about two months I was able to have simple conversations with soldiers in Japanese.

We had a vacation once a month. But even during the vacation I wasn't able to go out often. In addition I was never once able to go to the coast. They prevented us from going out on our own freely, so I only went on outings with lots of other people.

The manager got a certain amount of money each month from the owner. I think it was Japanese money. I'd sleep and come out in the daytime, and I was bored until the guests came. Once I went out, following somebody who was going on a shopping trip. We slipped through the barbed wire but as we picked bananas we were caught and the owner beat me to a pulp.

I made some friends in that house in Taiwan. I was sadder to part with one of them than I had been to part with my mother and father. I don't know how much I cried. I missed her more than if I'd lost an arm. I didn't eat—I just cried for three or four days. I'm not sure where those friends with whom I parted went. I suspected they had been sold off. Just like they sell off girls nowadays.

I sent photos that I took with friends in the courtyard to my parents. With the help of a friend who could read and write I was able to send letters at the post office. Of course they told us to write that we were doing well, and to say nothing of our suffering. Not knowing whether my family had moved, I sent the letters to the school that my younger sibling had been attending when I was taken away. After a while I got a letter from him asking me to send pencils and notebooks. When my brother attended elementary school we were really poor. So I sent a package to the school that my brother had transferred to, Hwayang Elementary School in Cheongdo.⁹ I only had a little money and so I couldn't send much.

After I had the operation, I was moved from the house to a new one. The new owner was Taiwanese. Twenty of us all moved together. A Taiwanese told us we'd all been sold. About one year after I had another operation liberation came.

TELLING NO ONE ABOUT MY SUFFERING IN TAIWAN

Right after the liberation the owner and my friends scattered off in all directions. I was happy about the liberation but I was sorely disappointed not to receive any money at all from the owner. I caught a boat for Busan with a Korean man who had been an errand boy at the first house where I had been. I caught a train in Busan and it took me to Cheongdo. The Korean guy, who was from Seoul, took me to my house in Cheongdo. When I got back from Taiwan I was twenty-one. He was ten years older than me. He liked me and I liked him too. I had done his laundry for him in Taiwan. He stayed at our house for a night and went up to Seoul. My parents came before him and asked him if he was thinking of marrying me. But he said that he already had a wife in Seoul and so he couldn't. That was the first time I had heard he was married. After that I got a letter from him suggesting we live together in Seoul but I didn't go. If he's got a wife already how am I supposed to go to Seoul?

I lied to my parents and told them I had worked in a factory. What else could I have done? They thought I should have brought back a lot of money, and they were disappointed that I hadn't, but they trusted what I said about having worked in a factory.¹⁰

Two years after I came home I was married to a man whom I met through an acquaintance's introduction. This was when I was twenty-three. I later found out that my husband already had a wife. At first I too had been fond of my husband, but after he began to hassle me for not giving him a son, I grew to dislike him. Of course, he knew nothing of my suffering in Taiwan. How could I bear to say anything about it? After the first wife died I went up formally on the family register.¹¹ I was thirty-seven. My husband, I, and my (younger) stepbrothers and sisters lived as farmers in a mountainous district of Cheongdo called Maejeonmyeon. Even though my husband wasn't rich he took another young woman as a concubine.

I had a son when I was twenty-eight. Even though I had lived in the same house with my husband for five years I barely was able to. After that I gave birth to three daughters. Two of them died of disease while they were young, and my husband died when I was fifty-one. I took the kids and went to Busan. My son died when I was fifty-eight of charcoal fuel fume poisoning. That was when I started smoking and drinking. What else could I have done? My headaches got much worse. When I was sixty-five there was more worrisome trouble. The young concubine had given birth to a son, who had gone up on my family register; when he got married he split me off of the family register into an independent one, saying that his bride would complain if she had two mothers-in-law. So according to the family register, I was alone in the world.

Without a hearing aid I can't hold a conversation. Using the [Korean] government's support fund I was able to exchange the broken hearing aid I used for a new one. One of my siblings, seeing how I was unable to use my head [ears], thought I was an idiot. My condition got this bad because I was beaten so much by the manager and the owner while I sold my body in Taiwan, but my family didn't know about that.

I told my one surviving daughter that the reason I made a declaration to the government is because I worked in a Japanese factory but I never received as much as a penny. She also believed what I said. If I get compensation from Japan I want to give some of the money to my second eldest younger sibling, through whose efforts I came out, and I want to give some money to my daughter as well.

Although I sold herbs and vegetables in Busan, I wasn't able to make the 200,000 won I needed to live each month.[12] So I came to the House of Sharing. Die, live, either way I'll do it here. Here my heart is comfortable and it's good.

Editor's note [in the original]

Grandmother was born on September 2, 1924, in the Miryang area of South Gyeongsang Province. In 1940, a Japanese man came to her village and promised to place her in a Japanese factory. She went with him, thinking she would be able to earn money to help out her parents. When she arrived she realized she was not in Japan but in Taiwan. She served soldiers for around five years in Shôka (Changhua), Taiwan. For her age, she has lost much more of her hearing than normal. So nowadays she speaks in a very loud voice. There is a very good chance that her hearing loss was due to the beatings she received at the hands of the owner in Taiwan. Her knees hurt in winter, so much so that she is unable to sleep. If she thinks of her life in

Taiwan she can only sleep after drinking alcohol and smoking many cigarettes.

Grandmother came to the House of Sharing in the winter of 1992. Because two of her daughters died as children and her son died in 1982, she only has one surviving daughter.

There are some uncomfortable aspects of community life for her at the House of Sharing, but compared to her difficult life alone in Busan, it is more comfortable in many ways. If she were to leave the House of Sharing she'd have no place to go. All she has are blankets, clothes, and a very old mini-refrigerator. On top of her desk she has pictures of her grandchildren.

Grandmother believes that the Japanese government needs to make reparations quickly because she has so little time left in this world.

APPENDIX

Researched and organized by Okuyama Yoko: born in Japan's Shizuoka Prefecture, graduated from Osaka Foreign Language University (Osaka University of Foreign Studies). She has lived in Seoul since 1984. She majored in East Asian Studies at Yonsei University's Graduate School of International Studies, and she has served as a full-time lecturer in charge of Japanese language, conversation and other subjects at Dongdeok Women's University's Department of Japanese Language and Literature. There are many aspects of the relations between Korea and Japan during the Japanese colonial period that still have not been brought to light. Through this second volume of testimonies, she wishes to educate the young people of both countries about these historical facts, especially the younger generations in Japan.

NOTES

PREFACE
1. Descriptions of this process can be found in Soh 2008 and Kim-Gibson 1999.
2. LaCapra (1999, 2001) discusses these issues involved in witnessing traumatic experience at length.
3. http://www.oup.com/us/companion.websites/9780199759576/?view=usa.
4. For example, in Korean, see Hanguk jeongsindae munje daechaek hyobuihoe and Jeongsindae yeonguhoe 1993; Hanguk jeongsindae yeonguhoe and Hanguk jeongsindae munje daechaek hyobuihoe 1995, 1997; Hanguk jeongsindae yeonguso and Hanguk jeongsindae munje daechaek hyobuihoe 1999, 2001; Hanguk jeongsindae munje daechaek hyobuihoe and yeoseong gukje beopjeong Hanguk wiwonhoe jeungeon tim 2000; Ito 1997; Yoshimi 1993. In Japanese, see Yoshimi 1992, and in English, see Howard 1995; Tanaka 2002; Yoshimi 1995.
5. Examples of English-language sources are Yoshimi Yoshiaki's classic *The Comfort Women* (1995); Tanaka 2002; Kim-Gibson 1999; Howard 1995.
6. See the Council's website for information about the weekly demonstration: www. womenandwar.net/english/menu_02.php, accessed June 11, 2010.

INTRODUCTION
1. Mun Pilgi is pronounced "Moon Peel-gee," without stress on any one syllable (also see the online pronunciation guide).
2.
   Joahajido anhe.
   Geureon kkenne terebi deureonoko radio deureonoko
   Kung, kung, kung...
   Ne neomu waerowaseo,
   Terebi deureonoko radio deureonoko
   Kung~jjak kung~jjak
   Geurae saneun geoya.
   Waeroun kkenne. Simsim hageodeun.
3. Tia DeNora (2000: chapter 3) describes song and music as "technologies of self."
4. Pronounced "Pahk Doo-ri." There is no nasalized "a," as in "pack," in the Korean language; the "a" in Pak is pronounced similarly to the "o" in "rock" (also see the online pronunciation guide).
5.
   Odong namu yeolmae-neun eolmeong-deolmeong hagoyo
   Keun-aegi jeottongeun mongsilmongsil hada.

This couplet is also a popular verse of a southwestern folk song called "Jindo Arirang" (Arirang of Jin Island), and it is likely that Pak Duri has adapted the text from there or elsewhere in Korean folklore to another melody, as she did in other songs.

6. There is a line preceding this last one, but it is obscured by the animated conversation. The song starts at 32 seconds on online audio recording 2. The transliteration follows:

Dangsin eojji naengjeonghan saram
Sagwi-eo dun geosi nae geureuda
Iman hamyeon nal beoril jullo
Na do bandasi aratneunde
[obscured line]
Algodo sokgo moreugodo soga.

7. Pronounced "Beh Choon-hee." See the online pronunciation guide.

8. See the song discography at the end of this book for this and all other discographic information.

9.
Chueok sogui Seukabeuroya
Na eonje dasi mannari
Nae sarang-i salgo inneun
Areumdaun naui gohyang.

10. The large disparity in the estimates is due to the disparity of evidence about how many women were provided per soldier or laborer and assumptions about turnover rates. Yoshimi (1995: 93) bases his upper-figure estimate on official documents of the Coal Control Association's Eastern Department Chief, who reports aims of the Asia Development Agency, the branch of the Japanese imperial government that oversaw the Chinese territories, which led him to believe that at most there was one sexual slave for every thirty soldiers or laborers. He bases his lower figure on a reported ration of one sexual slave to one hundred soldiers in the 21st Army in 1939 (92–93). The Japanese military's systematic destruction of records has made precise estimates difficult.

11. I have written at length about the application of this concept to music and song elsewhere (Pilzer 2011).

12. See, for instance, Trezise (2001) on popular assumptions of the unspeakability of the Holocaust and the consequences for survivors.

13. For a few other examples from across the world of women's song, see Abu-Lughod 1986; Doubleday 1988; C. E. Robertson 1987; Vander 1988.

14. Scholars have published meticulously researched descriptions of the sex-slave system itself (Yoshimi 1993, 1995; Hanguk jeongshindae munje daechaek hyobuihoe and Jinsang josa yeongu wiwonhoe 1997; Hanguk jeongshindae yeonguso 2000). There are many books of survivors' testimonies (Hanguk jeongshindae munje daechaek hyobuihoe and Jeongsindae yeonguhoe 1993; Hanguk jeongsindae yeonguhoe and Hanguk jeongsindae munje daechaek hyobuihoe 1995; Howard 1995; Hanguk jeongshindae yeonguhoe and Hanguk jeongsindae munje daechaek hyobuihoe 1997; Hanguk jeongshindae yeonguso and Hanguk jeongsindae munje daechaek hyobuihoe 1999, 2001; Ito 1997; Yeoseongbu and Hanguk jeongsindae yeonguso 2001). There are several books of survivors' art work (Nanum ui jip 2000, 2004). And there are almost twenty years of novels, books of poetry, news articles, documentaries, artistic tributes, and other media concerning the system, its victims, and the political movement concerned with the "comfort women" issue.

BEGINNINGS

1. In 2007, there were 225 registered survivors of the "comfort women" system in South Korea, of whom 121 remained alive.

2. The Korean-language name of the Korean Council is Hanguk jeongshindae munje daechaek hyobuihoe.

3. A rare exception is made when the New Year or the annual Harvest Festival, Korea's two most important holidays, fall on Wednesday.

4. In Korean, *wianbu undong* and *wianbu halmeoni undong*, respectively.

5. Pronounced "hahl-meoh-nee."

6. www.mofa.go.jp/policy/women/fund/state9308.html, accessed May 11, 2010.

7. The music and speech of Hwang Geumju's generation have long reminded me of the blues, r&b and rock and roll, although her and her contemporaries' cultivated roughness, stylized simplicity, dynamic range, skilled improvisation, and virtuosic expressions of sorrow and joy came to be in a rather different although no less turbulent social world.

8. The exhibition booklet for Ahn Hae Ryong's *Silence's Cry: Voices of Korean Grandmother Veterans of the Japanese Military "Comfort Women"* (2002) includes a photo of Kim Bunseon with a picture of herself as a young woman and Yi Okseon in front of Kim Sundeok's painting *Unblossomed Flower*. An exhibition of photos of the survivors at the House of Sharing shows each woman with a picture of herself as a young girl or a young woman. Drawings or photographs of blooming flowers, symbolic of young women, are often juxtaposed with images of old women: the pamphlet from the 2003 event entitled Nanum ui chukje (Festival of Sharing) held in Hadong, South Korea, shows survivor Choe Gapsun at a demonstration flanked by drawings of lotus flowers.

9. Choi (2002: 110) defines *han* as the sentiment that develops when one cannot or is not allowed to express feelings of oppression, alienation, or exploitation because one is trapped in an unequal power relationship.

10. See Lie 1998.

11. The occasion was an exhibition of portrait photographs of survivors paired with my recordings of each featured survivor's song, held in Seoul August 11–22, 2004. See Pilzer 2006a: chapter 6.

12. There are numerous examples of nationalist assimilations of individual stories to stereotypical figures. Of Hyon Kiron's 1986 short story "Shadow and Substance," about a famous Jeju Island female diver who denied leading an uprising she supposedly led against the Japanese in 1937, Carter Eckert (1999: 365) writes, "Assigning meaning and value to the old woman's story only insofar as it affirms a ready-made ideological stereotype denies the old woman her humanity by reducing her to a caricature." Choi Kyeong-Hee (1999: 223) notes that similar processes have affected Korean women in general: "They have lost their face as women in order to wear the mask of nationality, only to find that in everyday life they must function only as women."

PAK DURI

1. The following biographical account is summarized from conversations with Pak Duri and from Pak Duri's testimony in Hanguk jeongshindae yeonguhoe and Hanguk jeongshindae munje daechaek hyopuihoe 1997: 31–42, which I have translated and included in the appendix of this book.

2. *Hyeongnim* is an expression that, like other family terms, can refer to both family members and others. Among young Koreans this is generally used only by men to refer to elder male sibling figures.

3. The Korean "number eighteen" is from the Japanese *jūhachiban*, taken from Japanese kabuki theater. The term originally referred to eighteen kabuki pieces canonized and copyrighted by the noted actor Danjuro Ichikawa VII (1791–1859).

4. Tia DeNora (2000) discusses this at length in "Music as a Technology of Self," chapter 3 of *Music in Everyday Life*. On music and self-identity, see especially 62–63.

5. First published in 1910 in the Japanese governmental *Standard Elementary School Song Book* (*Jinjyô Shôgaku tokuhon shôka*). See Ue et al. 1910: 22.

6.

   Mureun mureun sireodaga
   Bulnanjib-e gatda jugo
   Horaebi hancha sireodaga
   Pak Duri bang-e pur-eo bara!

7. "Norae hameun siyoooooon ha da" ("Norae ha-myeon siwon hada" in South Gyeonsang Province dialect).

8. Although male shamans are common, the majority of shamans have long been women. There are two reasons commonly given for this: the mostly male pantheon of Korean spirits are thought to prefer to enter female bodies, and the rigid proscriptions placed on female behavior in the neo-Confucian Joseon Dynasty (1392–1910) and modern Korea created the conditions for the mental "spirit sickness" (*sinbyeong*) that set some women on the path to becoming shamans and also made shamanism an attractive alternative for ambitious or unconventional women. For more on Korean shamanism and women's fundamental roles in the shaman religion, see Kendall 1985, 2009.

9. The song bears a strong resemblance to the "Ballad of the Harvest God," a *taryeong* from another section of Gyeonggi Province shaman ceremonies dedicated to the god of the harvest. A version of this song can be heard on *Changbu taryeong geoljakseon*, Jigu Records JCDS-0782.

10. Although in the twentieth century female *gwangdae* had disappeared, there are female and male versions of the *gwangdaesin*.

11. More and more musicologists of Western art music appreciate that this fixity is a wish rather than a natural condition of musical practice. An emergent trend in scholarship takes up issues of performance and change: see, for instance, Barolsky 2005; Millington and Spencer 1999.

12. This is a process that began in 1961 with the creation of the Munhwajae gwalliguk, a government office that designates and oversees "intangible cultural treasures" (*Muhyeong munhwajae*) and that continued after Korean folk performers were given a place at the National Center for Korean Traditional Performing Arts (Gungnip gugagwon) in 1978. Both of these institutions have opposed many artists' stylistic innovations, while at the same time encouraging artists to resurrect older styles that cleanse their repertories of the taint of colonialism and modernity. For discussions of this guided process of codification, see Howard's (1986, 2006) extensive investigations. For a detailed description of the transformation of a single genre, see Pilzer 1999: chapters 3–5.

13. The concept of liminality comes from the work of the anthropologist Victor Turner (1969: 95–96) and denotes the quality of being on a threshold between structures of culture. Turner used it to describe the quality of ritual space, the flexible social space of transformation that exists between the hardened realms of cultural life and its normative moralities. He used the term to stress that such social spaces, which can appear to be external, marginal, or alternative to culture and its normative moralities, are indeed constitutive elements of a cultural system, in-between spaces that allow transformations that a culture requires. These kinds of women's social spaces, for instance, provide an outlet for female expression and education without which patriarchal cultures would cease to function as smoothly.

14. The films are available in many college and university libraries and can be purchased on DVD from Seoul Selection, www.seoulselection.com.

15. Three colonial-era versions of this text appear on tracks 8, 9, and 13 of the CD *Changbu taryeong gyeoljakseon* (Jigu Records JCDS-0782).

16. The propositive *-se* is not used in most contemporary Korean dialects, although it remains common in the Southwest.

17. Melisma is the practice of giving multiple melodic notes to a single text syllable.

18. She did this by following the same melodic contour in each of her couplets with the exception of the ending note; the first ended low and the second ended a fourth above, on the central tone of the mode. In this way one became the question and the other became the answer. This was quite unusual; most singers' opening refrain followed a differently shaped and lower melodic contour than their verses, which began on higher pitches and gradually settled downward. A typical refrain thus acted as a low melodic prelude to the higher-pitched verse.

19. Personal conversation with the author. Kim Dong Won also discusses the idea of *jolbangmi* (拙樸美) in the documentary film *Intangible Asset Number 82*, directed by Emma Franz (2008).

20. For more on these notions of transience in modern Korean Buddhist thought, see "Secrets on Cultivating the Mind" in Chinul 1983; Muller 1999: chapter 5; Sørensen 2010; Yun 2010.

21. *Nurunbap* is scorched rice from the bottom of the pan.

22.

> *Mureun mureun sireodaga*
> *Bulnan jibeda gatda jugo*
> *Horaebi hancha sireodaga*
> *Nanum ui jib-e pureodogo*

Pak Duri: Hancha maneuma galla hama andoena?
Byeon Yeong-joo: Eo.

> *Sewori sewori gageodeullang*
> *Ni honjaman doragaji.*
> *Akkapgo bulssanghan Pak Duri cheongchun-eul*
> *Wa ireohjido deuryeoganno?*

Pak: Maeumeun ajik yeol-daseotsal inde . . . na chilsip-neoiga mwokko?
Byeon: Maeumi yeol-daseosiraguyo?
Pak: Maeumeun, ajik isok ui maeumeun yeol-daseotsal geudaero inde, naga chilsip neoi museun malgo mwo hago imani neulkgo mwo hago imani naireul chyeo mungno?

> *Gae-ya gae-ya geomdung gae-ya*
> *Heuri neongcheong sapsal gae-ya*
> *Nurunbap geulgeoyeo neojuljige*
> *Nae bae-ga bulleoseo neoreul jwonna.*
> *Yabam jung-e gunseobang ogeodeun*
> *Jitji marakko neoreul jwotda.*

Pak: An matna?
Byeon: Matda.
Nurunbap geu jwoya uri yeonggam-i inneunde, uri sillang inneunde dareun sillang-i ogeodeun. An jursuga eopji anjursuya ttan sillangi olgeo aniga? Uri sillang yeo inneunde neomui sillang-i oneunde gaega jijeo ppulmyeon mot oneun geo aniga? Geurae 'nae baega bulleo neoreurjwonna? Yabamjung-e gunseobang ogeodeun jom jitji malgo' itgeora. Geuraeseo nurunbap-eul ni jwonneunde wa uri sillang alguro niga jinno? Uimiga gipeuda geuge!

> *Eolssiguna joko chammallo jonne*
> *Ani noljineun motarira.*

23. *Uri imi osigeodeun.*

24. Herman (1992) discusses this as a general principle, and Choi Chungmoo (2001: 403) draws attention to the importance of reclaiming sexuality and the body in the case of the survivors of Japanese military sexual slavery.

25. Herman's steps also include the establishment of safety, developing relationships that aid in the healing process, processes of remembering and mourning, and reconnecting with society, among others (see Herman 1992, and the discussion that follows).

26.

Bamman mukgo motsalgetgo
Suldo mukgo motsalgetgo
Ni gwa nae-ga gin-gin bam-e

27. "Then I went to Japan" is shorthand for her wartime experiences, even though she was taken to Taiwan.

28. Here is the romanized Korean of Pak Duri's final answer: "Ahyu, gosaeng an han ge eodin-no? Pyeongsaeng gosaeng haetji. Keul ttaedo gosaenghae. Keul ttae chinjeong mot saraga bapdo eodeo meokgo gosaeng haetji. Ilbon gaseo tto gosaenghaetji. Chon-e gaseo tto gos-aenghaetji. Tto ttaro iri busanseo salmyeonseo don nae— iri cheonggwa mwo, sagwa igeo paragajigo meokgo sallago tto—bangse jugo, mulse jugo, jeongise jugo gosaenghaetji."

29. The *ji* sentence ending implies that the speaker believes what she or he has said is obvious.

30. After expressing their sorrows in this genre, singers often continue on to a spirited folk song that mocks the same troubles they had previously lamented (see Kim Hyejeong 2002).

31.

Paljareul deoreopgi saenggyeonaseo
Ilbon gayeo yungnyeon gosang,
Hanguk wa myeonnyeon gosang
Apapi mal mot hago
Nuguhantena hanmareul halkko,
Pak Duri halmae-neun jugeoseodo
Yeohani mansseumnida.

32. Chungmoo Choi (2001: 407) has also noted that the title of this film seems to contradict its content. It is not a little ironic that Pak Duri's plus-size voice is the centerpiece of a film called *The Murmuring*.

33. Attali (1985: 5) famously describes this forecasting function of music in *Noise: The Political Economy of Music.*

MUN PILGI

1. The 'eu' is pronounced like the *u* in "full," and the 'o' is a long *o*. So *teuroteu* is pronounced "tuh-roh-tuh." See the online pronunciation guide.

2. The following biographic material is culled from conversations with Mun Pilgi and also from Hanguk jeongshindae munje daechaek hyobuihoe and Jeongsindae yeonguhoe 1993, the first volume in the Korean Council's series of testimonies, in which Mun Pilgi's testimony can be found on 107–19, and its translation "I So Much Wanted to Study: Mun P'ilgi," in Howard 1995: 80–94.

3. For example, "Da hamkke chachacha" (Everybody cha-cha-cha together) and "Cha-cha-cha Rock & Roll"—both vocalizations and references to the dance.

4.

Uri-ne sayeoneul damneun
Ulgo unneun insaengsa soseol gateun sesangsa
Sesangsa moduga nebakja, kung-jjak.

5.

Olttaeneun maeum daero watdeurado
Gal ttaeneun geunyang motgayo
Neomuna jjalbeun sungan jjalbeun mannam-eun
Manyang aswiwotseumnida.

6.

Sarangiran sarangiran
Mideul su eopseo mideul su eopseo mideul su eopseoyo
Nareul dugo tteonan saram babo gateun namjayo.

7. These are now commonly called *tongsok minyo* (shared folk songs) by music scholars, in contrast to *tosok minyo*, folk songs only well-known locally in specific geographic areas.

8. The story of *enka*'s origins is a complex one. The genre was originally a song-speech performance form that nineteenth-century political groups used to publicize their views and candidates in the early days of the 1868 Meiji Restoration (see Groemer 1994: 260). Many performers of the original *enka* had come from the *yomiuri* tradition of singing the news in the Edo Period and forward, which died out in the late nineteenth century with the spread of mass literacy and print media (260).

    The Japanese state believed that it should assimilate Western culture (including technology, political systems, notions of empire, classical music, and the arts) in a Japanese fashion, in the interests of creating a modern nation-state capable of competing in the global system of nation-states. With this in mind imperial decree made elementary school universally compulsory in 1872. Educators set to work to create a national music curriculum inspired by European models that incorporated Japanese melodic materials. The distinctive *yonanuki* scales that feature in most of today's *enka* songs came into being when Japanese composers of pedagogical music imagined a similarity between Japanese traditional five-note (pentatonic) scales and similar scales in Western music. In this attempt to blend disparate cultural forms, the composers created pedagogical works in five-note major and minor scales that were significantly different from either source music (Okada and Groemer 1991: 286).

    As students graduated and songs in these melodic systems became popular outside of schools, the genre was assimilated by the *enka-shi* political street callers, who often based their singing on popular tunes of the day, in a manner similar to the Anglo-Irish broadside tradition. The Japanese recording and radio industries both rose to prominence in the 1920s, and via the mass-mediated popular music industry the modal system of *enka* gradually overtook Western melodies and melodic modes as the dominant popular style on the air, on records, and on the street.

9. For more about this process, see Lee 2006; Maliangkay 2007.

10. Several practices of translation and composition brought the new musical form to Korea and to its eventual preeminence in the world of Korean popular music. There were Korean translations of Japanese tunes, such as the tune "Hana ga sakimasu" (A flower is blooming), which was translated into Korean by Pak Yeongho and debuted in 1938 as "Cheo-nyeo ilgi" (A maiden's diary). Through verbatim translation of selected songs, the themes of *enka*, like this song's theme of the tentative love of youth, were selectively adopted. There were also collaborations between Japanese composers and Korean lyricists, and songs composed entirely by Koreans. It is the great hits from this last category of songs that would become canonical in the postwar era.

11. Kim Sundeok sang the former and Yi Okseon the latter at the song party with Pak Duri (see p. 38).

12. Younger generations favor newer styles, such as rock, folk, and K-pop. Folk music, or *tong-gita* (acoustic guitar) music, arose in the 1980s as part of the populist movements of the time. K-pop is short for Korean pop and is largely derived from the American

popular music of the 1980s and forward, in particular the American post-soul white boy band tradition.

13. The child's gender is not specified in the text, and I only use female pronouns because I first heard it from Mun Pilgi.

14.

Ureobwado bulleobwado pittameul heullisimyeo
Wontonghae bulleobogo ttangeul chimyeo tonggokhaeyo
Dasi mot ol eomeonim-eun deudieo tteonasyeonne
Nun . . . gasyeonnayo.

15. This melodic simplification was similar to processes we can find among amateur singers of *enka*, North American country music, Indian film music, and other popular traditions noted both for their virtuosic vocalists and for practices of amateur singing.

16. The song was likely inspired by Peggy Lee and Victor Young's 1954 "Johnny Guitar," the title song of Nicholas Ray's film of the same name.

17.

Natseoreun tahyang ttang-e geunal bam geu cheonyeo-ga
Waenil inji nareul nareul monnitge ha-ne
Gitajure sireun sarang tteunaegi sarang
Ureora gitaya naui gitaya

Bammada kkumgilmada geurimja ne gohyang
Waenil inji nareul nareul monnitge ha-ne
Gitajure sireun sarang tteunaegi sarang
Ureora gitaya naui gitaya.

18. In her study of Japanese narratives of modernization, Marylin Ivy (1995) discusses a number of similar sacrificial figures, traditions, and objects whose loss marks and symbolically enables the onset of modernity.

19. W. E. B. Du Bois ([1903] 1994) uses the term "double consciousness" in *Souls of Black Folk* to describe the two sets of eyes through which African Americans perceive themselves: the eyes of white others and the eyes of the self. The concept was further explored by Paul Gilroy (1993) and others.

20. For instance, she changed the original line "Cry, in my memory, oh my guitar" to "Cry, oh guitar, oh my guitar."

21. A Sino-Korean expression, like the "one night's dream of spring" of which Pak Duri sang. *Ilpyeon dansim* literally means "one-side-pure-heart/mind." Heart/mind is a common translation of the Sino-Korean *sim*, or the indigenous Korean *maeum*, both of which refer to the thinking, feeling organ of the spirit, which is not divided into heart, mind, and brain as it is in the English language.

22. This act of casting out, according to Julia Kristeva, is what brings the social world and its symbolic order of roles and relations into being (1982: 65; quoted in Butler 1990: 228).

23.

Nunmureul boyeonnayo?
Naega ulgo marannayo?
Aniya aniya sorieopsi naerineun
Binmure jeojeosseul ppunida.
Siltago ganneunde mipdago ganneunde, ulgineun naega wae ureo
Ijeoyaji, ijeoyaji . . . eocheopi tteonan saram.

24. Postcolonial *teuroteu* songs about unforgettable love are too numerous to list, but the many illustrative titles include "Itji mothal yeo-in" (The woman I can't forget), "Monnijeul dangsin" (Unforgettable you), and "Monnijeo" (Can't forget).

25. The first album is *Jeongshindae ap'eum nanugi*, by Jeong Suja, Kim Jeongil, and Yi Suyeong (self-published). *Jeongshindae* ("volunteer corps") was the name of a series of Japanese governmental organizations that oversaw the labor of colonial subjects and others during the colonial period and the war. One of these was the Women's Volunteer Labor Corps, which oversaw the work of girls and women during the war (Etsuro 2001: 23). Many of the victims of sexual slavery were recruited into the Volunteer Labor Corps for factory labor before being sent into sexual slavery. The term is often conflated, inaccurately, with the system of sexual slavery. Still, because it was the first term used to describe the "comfort women" system in South Korea, it lingers in common usage and within the movement itself. *Watashiwa wasurenai* is distributed by Zatsu Records (ZATSU-004).

26. *Nan apayo. Nan ureotjyo.* The first sentence, "I hurt," is in present tense; the second phrase shifts to past tense.

27. *Kkot pineunde . . . kkot pineunde.* Due to constructional ambiguities of Korean, it is unclear whether this is one flower, or flowers.

28. *Nal beoryeotjyo. Nal gadwotjyo.*

29. Yun Mee-hyang, director of the Korean Council, expressed this same sentiment to me in discussing the inconsistent interest the Korean media show in the survivors and the "comfort women" issue.

30. The book is Hanguk jeongsindae munje daechaek hyobuihoe 2002.

31. "Imagined community" is Benedict Anderson's (1991) well-known characterization of the nation.

32. Aizen is a Mahayana Buddhist deity who transforms lust into spiritual awakening and is a patron deity of love. The song "Aizen Yakyoku" was written by Saijô Yaso, with lyrics by Manjôme Tadashi, and featured in the film *Aizen Katsura* (1938).

33.
> *Aizen katsurano saku haruwo*
> *Nande arashiga . . . mmm-hmm . . . nare nedamu.*

Mun Pilgi substitutes *nare*, which has no meaning in this context, for a word she has forgotten.

34. Mun Pilgi prefaces these words with an elongated *maaaaak (mak)*, an adverb used to indicate intensity. Since there is no equivalent expression in English, I have translated this by elongating the verbs.

35.
> *Harobam putsarange i bameul saeugo*
> *Sarange mosi bakhyeo heureuneun nunmul*
> *Sonsugeon jeoksimyeo miryeonman namgigo*
> *Mareopsi he-eojideon a—monnijeul sarama.*

Haro is Mun Pilgi's dialect for the standard Korean *haru*.

36. The video was available at www.youtube.com/watch?v=qODUYw67NRo on June 6, 2010. The album is *Son Inho: Hit Album* (Oasis OL-12465).

37. "Ulgin wae ureo?"

38. "Wae ureoss-eo?"

39. Mun Pilgi omitted the word "without."

40.
> *Haengyeona nal chaja watdaga motbogo gadeurado*
> *Yetjeong-e meiji malgo mareu . . . doragasaeyo*
> *Sarang iran geureon geot saenggagiya na . . . jiman*
> *Meon hun . . . geu ttae i saram tteonanhu iltenikkayo.*

41. "Mannam ui gippeum do ibyeol ui apeum do dusaram-i mandeuneun geol."

BAE CHUNHUI

1. Jiamusi is a city currently in the Heilongjiang Province of northeastern China. At the time Bae Chunhui was taken there, it was part of Manchuria.

2. The end of the Pacific War and the liberation of Korea from Japanese rule.

3. President of the Republic of Korea from 1998 to 2003.

4. "Our language" is a common expression for the Korean language.

5. An expression that connotes stubbornness, not stupidity. She had both Korean (*doldaegari*) and Japanese (*ishi atama*) versions.

6. Bae Chunhui elaborated on this theme often, in a way which was remarkable for someone of her generation, if not without its issues. Watching an African American woman sing on television, she told me what she thought of the latent racism among people of her generation: "Black people sing very well. The other women around here take one look at a black face and are like—'Oh, look, a black person, ugh!' Good grief. These are more sophisticated people than you, how can you say that? They are people of culture (*bunkajin*). Even in Africa, almost nude, they are a refined, cultured people!"

7.
   Pust' on zemliu berezhët rodnuiu,
   A liubov' Katiusha sberezhët.
   Translation by J. Martin Daughtry.

8. *Tokushu ian shisetsu kyōkai*, literally "Special Comfort Facility Association."

9. From the colonial era until today there have been disproportionately high numbers of Korean Japanese and expat Koreans throughout the Japanese entertainment industry, from the red-light districts to the popular music industry.

10. These songs were professionalized and popularized (via recording and radio) as they became the province of Korean *gisaeng* (professional female entertainers) in the early twentieth century. For more on this process and the *gisaeng*, see Pilzer 1999: chapter 4; Pilzer 2006b.

11. *Gisaeng gwan-gwang* is an appropriation of the traditional term *gisaeng*, a term for a skilled female entertainer, to apply to the sex trade, a terminological change that took place gradually over the twentieth century (see Pilzer 2006b).

12. See Atkins 2001 for a thorough study of Japanese jazz from its origins through the postwar period.

13. See Jordan Sand's (2003) chapters "Cosmopolitanism and Anxiety" and "Culture Villages" in *House and Home in Modern Japan*.

14. Yuko Kikuchi (2004) describes "Oriental Orientalism" in detail in the life and thought of the folklorist Yanagi Sōetsu. She describes the ways "Oriental Orientalism" assimilated Western Orientalist ideas about Asia into Japanese national identity as it placed Japan in a position of cultural and national superiority.

15. See Atkins 2007 for more about "Arirang" in Japan, including its history and its use to represent Korea as an exotic Other.

16. Li's Japanese heritage was largely concealed. For more on her, see Stephenson 2000.

17. Shina is an archaic Japanese expression for the country, similar to the English "China," which was popular in imperial Japan. It has since been replaced in the Japanese language by the Japanese pronunciation of the current common-parlance Chinese name, *Chūgoku*.

18. Importantly, Li sings of "a Chinese girl," simultaneously describing and embodying the feminization of China. Both are examples of what Yano (1998: 257) refers to as the Japanese equation of modernity with a desire for exotic Others that was at the heart of the imperialist project.

19.
   Shina no yoru, shina no yoru yo
   Minato no akari, murasaki no yoru ni

Noboru jyanku, yume no hune
A-a~wasurarenu kokyû no oto
Shina no yoru, yume no yoru

Shina no yoru, shina no yoru yo
Yanagi no mado ni lantan yurete
Akai torikago shina musume
A-a~yarusenai ai no uta
Shina no yoru, yume no yoru.

20. The Japanese version was sung by Saida Aiko and others. See the discography.
21. Of these, during the period I have known Bae Chunhui, from 2002 until the present, she has preferred to sing "Suzhou Nocturne" over "China Nights" because the immense popularity of the latter made it too commonplace. She avoided singing other songs, such as the canonical Korean text of "Arirang," for similar reasons. Here is the text of her "Suzhou Nocturne," sound recording 23 on the book website:
    Clasped to your breast I hear
    The boatsongs of dreams, the songs of birds.
    Does the willow weep
    Because it longs for watery Suzhou's blooming spring?

    Kimi ga mimune ni dakarete kikuwa
    Yume no hunauta, tori no uta
    Mizu no Soshyû no hana saku haru wo
    Oshimuka yanagi ga susurinaku.

22.
    (Japanese) *Haruka hanareta sono mata mukô*
    Dareni demo sukareru kireina musumega iru.
    Dareni demo sukareru kireina musumega iru.

    (Mandarin) *Zai na yaoyuan de difang*
    You wei hao guniang
    Renmen zouguo ta de zhangfang
    Du yao huitou liulian de zhangwang.

23. This is further suggested by Bae Chunhui's fond recital of stories and songs that celebrate classic Orientalist images, such as the Japanese versions of the popular Turkish melody "Uskudar'a Gider Iken" (Going to Uskudar), following the American Eartha Kitt's 1953 release of "Uska Dara (a Turkish Tale)," released in Japan on Nihon Victor Records. Eri Chiemi's Japanese version debuted in 1954. Thanks to Martin Stokes for identifying the song's origins.
24. Meanwhile in South Korea Japanese pop-cultural forms remained banned, although they circulated on the black market.
25. Bae Chunhui was keenly interested in and knowledgeable about the transnational history of musical circulation. On another occasion she told me about the transnational origins of more contemporary Korean cultural imports, such as the K-pop boy band: "All this music originated with black people, you know. Whites imitated blacks doing it, and now the Koreans imitate the whites."

26.
    Kkotpineun dongbaekseom-e bomi watgeonman
    Hyeongje tteonan busanhang-e galmaegi man seulpi une
    Oryukdo doraganeun yeollakseon mada
    Mongme-eo bulleobwado daedap eomneun nae hyeongje yeo
    Dorawayo busanhang-e geuri-un nae hyeongje yeo.

27. I sang "Sanyeombul" (Mountain Buddhist chant) and "Jajin yeombul" (Fast Buddhist chant), a folk song pair from northwestern Korea. The results of my master's research can be found in Pilzer 1999, 2003.

28. "Beonji eobneun jumak," composed by Yi Jaeho, who also wrote Mun Pilgi's beloved "Cry, Guitar String," with lyrics by Chu Mirim, debuted by the male singer Baek Nyeonseol in the early 1940s.

29. *Arirang, saewol ttara, imi gago imi o-ne.*

30. Koreans traditionally celebrate the Lunar New Year; in 2003 the New Year fell on January 31.

31. The song preserved the premodern Korean folk calendar, which began closer to Spring.

32.
> *Saega naradeunda*
> *Waengat japsae ga naradeunda*
> *Sae jung-e-neun ponghwangsae*
> *Man-su-mun-jeon-e pungnyeonsae*
> *San-go-gok-sim muincheo*
> *Su-rip-bi-jo musae-deuri*
> *Nong-chun-hwa-dab-e jjageul ji-eo*
> *Saenggeut saenggeut naradeunda.*

> *Saenggeut* is a mimetic word that represents the gesture of a sweet smile.

33. *Ssuk-kkuksae* in southwest regional dialect, a name derived from the onomatopoeia for the bird's song. The bird's name is *sanbidulgi* (mountain dove) in standard Korean.

34.
> *I saneuro gamyeon ssuk-kkuk ssuk-kkuk*
> *Jeo sanero gamyeon ssuk-ssuk-kkuk ssuk-kkuk*
> *Eo heo~eo i hi~eo*
> *Jwauro danyeo ureum unda.*

35. Steven Feld's (1982) *Sound and Sentiment,* the foundational scholarly investigation of the ethnopoetics of music, seminally discusses the way that songs about birds—through bird song and sound imitation, and through song texts that relate myths about the relations between birds and human beings—forge continuities of sound, language, humans and nature.

36. Like so many Korean sentences, this lyric omits the subject, and we are forced to make guesses from the context. I have guessed that there is an "I."
> *Suljan-eul putjapgo, sarang ui norae-reul putjapgo,*
> *Namja, namja, namja ui nunmul-i miwoyo.*

37.
> *Taiyang xia shan mingtian yi jiu pa shang lai,*
> *Huaer xiele mingnian haishi yiyang de kai,*
> *Meili xiao niao yi qu wu ying zong*
> *Wo de qingchun xiao niao yiyang bu huilai,*
> *Wo de qingchun xiao niao yihang bu huilai,*
> *Bie de na yayou, bie de na yayou,*
> *Wo de qingchun xiao niao yiyang bu huilai.*

> *Taeyangeun dasi tteo-oreugo*
> *Kkocheun bomi doemyeon dasi pineunde*
> *Aegisae naraseo meolli gamyeon*
> *Nae cheongchuneun dasi doraoji anne*
> *Nae cheongchuneun dasi doraoji anne*

> *Bie de na yayou, bie de na yayou,*

Nae cheongchuneun dasi doraoji anne.
Romanization and English translation by Viren Murthy.

38. A neutral third is a pitch that lies between the Western major and minor thirds. In this case the pitch is about two-thirds of the way between, closer to the Western major third than the minor.

39.

Arirang, arirang, arariyo
Arirang, gogae-reul neomeoganda
Tōku hanarete aitai toki wa
Tsukiga kagami ni narebayoi.

40. The park's website is www.everland.com/htm/MultiLanguage/english/htm/Int/IntInt.htm, accessed June 9, 2010.

41. This recalls the pioneer ethnomusicologist John Blacking's (1974: 28) statement that the music of the Venda people of South Africa is "not an escape from reality; it is an adventure into reality."

42. The generic presence of a single social vision seems to be a foundational characteristic of the theme park environment (see Project on Disney 1995). Nooshin (2004) notes that in Disney's "It's a Small, Small World" ride, in which passengers take a slow "boat" ride around the globe and meet the costumed children of the world, the song represents this totalizing presence.

43. See sound recording 20 on the book's website, although this was recorded on a separate occasion. I do not have a recording of Bae Chunhui singing with the acrobat.

44. Project on Disney (1995: 110–62) discusses the many forms of spectatorship to which theme park employees are subject in the essay "Working at the Rat." Also see Marling (1992) for examples of the particular gaze trained on white visitors and employees at Tokyo Disneyland.

45.

Rastvetali iabloni i grushi
Poplyli tumany nad rekoi
Vykhodila na bereg Katiusha
Na vysokii bereg, na krutoi.

EPILOGUE

1.

Daecheonji han bada-e
Ppuraengi eomneun namuga na
Gajineun yeoldu gajiyo
Ip-eun sambaeg-e yuksibira
Geu namu yeolmaega yeoreo il-wol inga.

APPENDIX

1. Source: Hanguk jeongsindae yeonguhoe and Hanguk jeongsindae munje daechaek hyobuihoe 1997: 31–42. I have translated everything in the original text as is: titles, section headings, and footnotes. I have not included the other women's testimonies because Mun Pilgi's is already available in English (Howard 1995) and Bae Chunhui has no full-length published testimony.

2. This is a direct translation, despite the seeming contradiction with the first sentence, which states that Cheongdo is in South Gyeongsang Province. Currently the Cheongdo administrative district (*gun*) lies directly north of Miryang, which has since been incorporated as a city. The border of the two is the border between South and North Gyeongsang Provinces. The proximity likely explains the confusion in the text.

3. The Sino-Korean world is *yeoja*, literally "female person," and does not indicate age, as do "girl" and "woman."
4. Pak Duri says "the house where bodies were sold" (*mom paneun jip*) rather than the military term of the time, "comfort station" (*wianso*). In the original there is a footnote here: "Grandmother doesn't know the term 'comfort station' (*wianso*) and she calls the place a 'house where bodies are sold'" (34).
5. Footnote in the original: "Grandmother calls the men who came to the comfort station 'guests' (*sonnim*)" (34).
6. Roughly a dollar or two.
7. Footnote in the original: "Grandmother calls the work she did at the comfort station 'business' (*jangsa*)."
8. Footnote in the original: "We guess that the disease was lymphogranuloma inguinale. This is a kind of sexually transmitted disease which is very rare today." It is an infection of the lymph tissue in the genital area caused by a strain of Chlamydia trachomatis, acquired through ingestion of contaminated food or water or through sexual contact.
9. Footnote in the original: "The testimony of Pak Duri's younger brother, born in 1931: 'While I was in my second year at Hwayang Elementary School in Cheongdo my elder sister, who was in Taiwan, sent pencils, erasers, and colored pencils twice. I was very happy to get these packages. Because I was young then, I thought that my big sister was off in Taiwan making lots of money. I forgot her Taiwanese address. When my sister began a lawsuit confronting the Japanese government it would have been good if I had remembered the address—I regret that so much. After I got that second package, I went with my mother and younger sisters to northern Korea, where my father and elder brother had already gone. We were there when the liberation [Japan's defeat] came.'"
10. The text says *mid-eo juda*, which means not just that Pak Duri's parents believed her, but that they "gave her their belief," perhaps despite suspicions that she was lying.
11. The official family register (*hojeok*) is a family tree chart, organized around a patriarch; it is now possible to list only one wife on your chart, which means that only one wife and her offspring are legally entitled to inheritance. So when Pak Duri went up on the family register, she and her children acquired this right.
12. Around $165 in 2010.

BIBLIOGRAPHY

Abu-Lughod, Lila. 1986. *Veiled Sentiments: Honor and Poetry in a Bedouin Society.* Berkeley: University of California Press.

Adorno, Theodor W. 1992. *Mahler: A Musical Physiognomy.* Chicago: University of Chicago Press.

Ahn Hae Ryong. 2002. *Chimmuk ui oechim: Ilbongun "wianbu" chulshin halmeonideul ui moksori* [Silence's cry: Voices of Korean grandmother veterans of the Japanese military "comfort women"]. Exhibition booklet. Seoul: Badasaram.

Althusser, Louis. 1971. *Lenin and Philosophy and Other Essays.* New York: Monthly Review Press.

Anderson, Benedict. 1991. *Imagined Communities.* New York: Verso.

Atkins, Everett Taylor. 2001. *Blue Nippon: Authenticating Jazz in Japan.* Durham, NC: Duke University Press.

———. 2007. "The Dual Career of 'Arirang': The Korean Resistance Anthem That Became a Japanese Hit." *Journal of Asian Studies* 66: 645–87.

Attali, Jacques. 1985. *Noise.* Minneapolis: University of Minnesota Press.

Barolsky, Daniel. 2005. "Romantic Piano Performance as Creation." PhD diss., University of Chicago.

Berlant, Lauren, ed. 2000. *Intimacy.* Chicago: University of Chicago Press Journals Division.

Blacking, John. 1974. *How Musical Is Man?* Seattle: University of Washington Press.

Bourdieu, Pierre. 1977. *Outline of a Theory of Practice.* Cambridge, UK: Cambridge University Press.

Brown, Wendy. 1995. *States of Injury: Power and Freedom in Late Modernity.* Princeton, NJ: Princeton University Press.

Butler, Judith. 1990. *Gender Trouble.* New York: Routledge.

———. 1997. *The Psychic Life of Power: Theories in Subjection.* Stanford: Stanford University Press.

Certeau, Michel de. 1988. *The Practice of Everyday Life.* Berkeley: University of California Press.

Chatterjee, Partha. 1993. *The Nation and Its Fragments: Colonial and Postcolonial Histories.* Princeton, NJ: Princeton University Press.

Chinul. 1983. *The Korean Approach to Zen: The Collected Works of Chinul.* Translated with an introduction by Robert E. Buswell Jr. Honolulu: University of Hawai'i Press.

Choi, Chungmoo. 2001. "The Politics of War Memories toward Healing." In *Perilous Memories: The Asia-Pacific War(s),* edited by T. Fujitani et al., 395–409. Durham, NC: Duke University Press.

———. 2002. "The Politics of Gender, Aestheticism, and Cultural Nationalism in *Sopyonje* and *The Genealogy*." In *Im Kwon-Taek: The Making of a Korean National Cinema,* edited by David E. Jones and Kyung Hyun Kim, 107–33. Detroit: Wayne State University Press.

Choi, Kyeong-Hee. 1999. "Neither Colonial nor National: The Making of the 'New Woman' in Pak Wansŏ's 'Mother's Stake 1.'" In *Colonial Modernity in Korea*, edited by Gi-Wook Shin and Michael Robinson, 221–47. Cambridge, MA: Harvard University Asia Center.

Chung, Haeng-ja. 2004. "Performing Sex, Selling Heart: Korean Nightclub Hostesses in Japan." PhD diss., University of California, Los Angeles.

Cicourel, Aaron V. 1973. *Cognitive Sociology*. London: Macmillan.

Cumings, Bruce. 1997. *Korea's Place in the Sun: A Modern History*. New York: Norton.

———. 1998. "The Question of American Responsibility for the Suppression of the Chejudo Uprising." Paper presented at the 50th anniversary conference of the April 3, 1948 Chejudo Rebellion, Tokyo, March 14, 1998. http://www.iacenter.org/Koreafiles/ktc-cumings.htm.

DeNora, Tia. 2000. *Music in Everyday Life*. New York: Cambridge University Press.

Doubleday, Veronica. 1988. *Three Women of Herat*. London: Cape.

Du Bois, W. E. B. (1903) 1994. *The Souls of Black Folk*. New York: Dover.

Eckert, Carter J. 1999. "Epilogue: Exorcising Hegel's Ghosts: Towards a Postnationalist Historiography of Korea." In *Colonial Modernity in Korea*, edited by Gi-Wook Shin and Michael Robinson, 363–78. Cambridge, MA: Harvard University Asia Center.

Feld, Steven. 1982. *Sound and Sentiment: Birds, Weeping, Poetics and Song in Kaluli Expression*. Philadelphia: University of Pennsylvania Press.

Finchum-Sung, Hilary. 2006. "New Folksongs: *Sinminyo* of the 1930s." In *Korean Pop Music: Riding the Wave*, edited by Keith Howard, 10–20. Kent, England: Global Oriental.

Fink, Bruce. 1995. *The Lacanian Subject: Between Language and Jouissance*. Princeton, NJ: Princeton University Press.

Fiumara, Gemma. 1990. *The Other Side of Language—A Philosophy of Listening*. New York: Routledge.

Flam, Gila. 1992. *Singing for Survival: Songs of the Łodz Ghetto, 1940–45*. Urbana: University of Illinois Press.

Fodor's Guide to Japan and East Asia. 1964. New York: David McKay.

Fox, Aaron A. 2004. *Real Country: Music and Language in Working Class Culture*. Durham, NC: Duke University Press.

Garfinkel, Harold. 1967. *Studies in Ethnomethodology*. Cambridge, MA: Polity Press.

Gilroy, Paul. 1993. *The Black Atlantic: Modernity and Double Consciousness*. London: Verso.

Girok yeonghwa jejakso Boim. 1998. *Najeun moksori: How the Camera Waits—Making of* The Murmuring. Seoul: Girok yeonghwa jejakso Boim.

Groemer, Gerald. 1994. "Singing the News: Yomiuri in Japan during the Edo and Meiji Periods." *Harvard Journal of Asiatic Studies* 54, no. 1: 233–61.

Han, Hongkoo. 1999. "Wounded Nationalism: The Minsaengdan Incident and Kim Il Sung in Eastern Manchuria." PhD diss., University of Washington.

Hanguk jeongsindae munje daechaek hyobuihoe. 2002. *Haruga cheon-geum iji . . . Ilbongun "wianbu" halmeonideul ui potodakyumenteori* [One day is a thousand pieces of gold . . . A photo documentary of the Japanese military comfort women grandmothers]. Seoul: Hanguk jeongsindae munje daechaek hyobuihoe.

Hanguk jeongsindae munje daechaek hyobuihoe and Jeongsindae yeonguhoe. 1993. *Gangjero kkeullyeogan Joseonin gunwianbudeul* [Forcibly abducted Korean military comfort women]. Seoul: Hanul.

Hanguk jeongsindae munje daechaek hyobuihoe and Jinsang josa yeongu wiwonhoe. 1997. *Ilbonjun "wianbu" munje ui jinsang* [The facts of the Japanese military "comfort women" issue]. Seoul: Yeoksa bipyeongsa.

Hanguk jeongsindae munje daechaek hyobuihoe and Yeoseong gukje beopjeong Hanguk wiwonhoe jeungeon tim. 2000. *Gangjero kkeullyeogan Joseonin gunwianbudeul 4: Gieok euro dashi sseuneun yeoksa* [Forcibly abducted Joseon military comfort women, vol. 4: History written again from memory]. Seoul: Pulbit.

Hanguk jeongsindae yeonguhoe and Hanguk jeongsindae munje daechaek hyobuihoe. 1995. *Jungguk euro kkeullyeogan Joseonin gunwianbudeul* [Joseon women forcibly abducted to China as military comfort women]. Seoul: Hanul.

——. 1997. *Gangjero kkeullyeogan Joseonin gunwianbudeul 2* [Forcibly abducted Joseon military comfort women, vol. 2]. Seoul: Hanul.

Hanguk jeongsindae yeonguso. 2000. *Halmeoni gunwianbuga mwoyeyo?* [What are military comfort women grandmothers?]. Seoul: Hangyeore Shinmunsa.

Hanguk jeongsindae yeonguso and Hanguk jeongsindae munje daechaek hyobuihoe. 1999. *Gangjero kkeullyeogan Joseonin gunwianbudeul 3* [Forcibly abducted Joseon military comfort women, vol. 3]. Seoul: Hanul.

——. 2001. *Gangjero kkeullyeogan Joseonin gunwianbudeul 5* [Forcibly abducted Joseon military comfort women, vol. 5]. Seoul: Hanul.

Hannerz, Ulf. 1990. "Cosmopolitans and Locals in World Culture." *Theory, Culture, and Society* 7: 237–51.

Herman, Judith. 1992. *Trauma and Recovery: The Aftermath of Violence—from Domestic Abuse to Political Terror.* New York: Basic Books.

Herzfeld, Michael. 1997. *Cultural Intimacy: Social Poetics in the Nation State.* New York: Routledge.

Howard, Keith. 1986. "Korea's Intangible Cultural Assets: A Review of the Sixteenth Festival of Human Cultural Assets." *Korea Journal* 26, no. 1: 61–68, 27.

——, ed. 1995. *True Stories of the Korean Comfort Women: Testimonies Compiled by the Korean Council for Women Drafted for Military Sexual Slavery by Japan and the Research Association on the Women Drafted for Military Sexual Slavery by Japan.* Translated by Young Joo Lee. London: Cassell.

——. 2006. *Preserving Korean Music: Intangible Cultural Properties as Icons of Identity.* Burlington, VT: Ashgate.

Hughes, David. 1990. "Japanese 'New Folk Songs,' Old and New." *Asian Music* 22, no. 1: 1–49.

Ishikida, Miki Y. 2005. *Living Together: Minority People and Disadvantaged Groups in Japan.* Lincoln, NE: iUniverse.

Ito Takashi. 1997. *Jonggun wianbu: Nambuk jonggun wianbu 27-in ui jeungeon* [Military comfort women: Testimonies of twenty-seven North and South Korean military comfort women]. Seoul: Nunpit.

Ivy, Marilyn. 1995. *Discourses of the Vanishing: Modernity, Phantasm, Japan.* Chicago: University of Chicago Press.

Jeon Utaek. 2001. "Urineun mueoseul halsu itneunga?" [What can we do?]. In *Haengbokhan nohu mandeulgi* [Making a happy old age], 50–53. Seoul: Hanguk jeongsindae munje daechaek hyobuihoe.

Kendall, Laurel. 1985. *Shamans, Housewives, and Other Restless Spirits: Women in Korean Ritual Life.* Honolulu: University of Hawai'i Press.

——. 2009. *Shamans, Nostalgias, and the IMF: South Korean Popular Religion in Motion.* Honolulu: University of Hawai'i Press.

Kikuchi, Yuko. 2004. *Japanese Modernization and Mingei Theory: Cultural Nationalism and Oriental Orientalism.* London: Routledge.

Kim Hyejeong. 2002. "Yeoseong minyo ui eumakjeok jonjae yangsang gwa jeonseung wonri: Jeonnam jiyeog-eul jungshim euro" [Characteristics and transmission principles in women's folksong, focusing on the South Jeolla region]. PhD diss., Academy of Korean Studies.

Kim Ji-pyeong. 1987. *Hanguk gayo jeongsinsa* [A psychological history of Korean popular song]. Seoul: Areum.

Kim Yeon-gap. 1988. *Arirang: Geu mat, meot geurigo . . .* [Arirang: That taste, style, and . . .]. Seoul: Jipmundang.

Kim-Gibson, Dai Sil. 1999. *Silence Broken: Korean Comfort Women.* Parkersburg, IA: Mid-Prairie Books.

Kristeva, Julia. 1982. *Powers of Horror: An Essay on Abjection.* New York: Columbia University Press.

Lacan, Jacques. 1977. *Écrits: A Selection.* London: Tavistock.

LaCapra, Dominick. 1999. "Trauma, Absence, Loss." *Critical Inquiry* 25: 696–727.

———. 2001. *Writing History, Writing Trauma.* Baltimore: Johns Hopkins University Press.

Laks, Szymon. 1979. *Music of Another World.* Translated by Chester A. Kisiel. Evanston, IL: Northwestern University Press.

Lee Young Mee (Yi Yongmi). 2000. *Hanguk daejung gayosa* [A history of Korean popular song]. Seoul: Sigongsa.

———. 2006. "The Beginnings of Korean Pop: Popular Music during the Japanese Occupation Era." In *Korean Pop Music: Riding the Wave,* edited by Keith Howard, 1–9. Kent, England: Global Oriental.

Lie, John. 1998. *Han Unbound: The Political Economy of South Korea.* Stanford: Stanford University Press.

List, George. 1963. "The Boundaries of Speech and Song." *Ethnomusicology* 7: 1–16.

Maliangkay, Roald. 2007. "Their Masters' Voice: Korean Traditional Music SPs (Standard Play Records) under Japanese Colonial Rule." *World of Music* 49, no. 3: 53–74.

Marling, Karal Ann. 1992. "Letter from Japan: Kenbei vs. All-American Kawaii at Tokyo Disneyland." *American Art* 6, no. 2: 102–11.

Mehan, Hugh, and Houston Wood. 1975. *The Reality of Ethnomethodology.* New York: Wiley.

Millington, Barry, and Stewart Spencer. 1999. *Wagner in Performance.* New Haven, CT: Yale University Press.

Muller, A. Charles. 1999. *The Sutra of Perfect Enlightenment: Korean Buddhism's Guide to Meditation* (with Commentary by the Sŏn Monk Kiwha). Albany, NY: State University of New York Press.

Nanum ui chukje (Festival of Sharing). 2003. "Festival of Sharing." Brochure. Hadong, Gyeongsang Province, May 9–11.

Nanum ui jip. 2000. *Ilbongun "wianbu" halmoni geurim moeum "Motdapin kkot"* [Collection of paintings by Japanese military comfort woman grandmothers: "Unblossomed flower"). Seoul: Nanum ui jip.

———. 2004. *Ilbongun "seongnoye" pihe halmoni jakpumjip* [Collected works of the grandmothers victimized by Japanese military sexual slavery]. Seoul: Nanum ui jip.

Nanum ui jip yeoksagwan huwonhoe. 2002. *Nanum ui jip ilbongun "wianbu" yeoksagwaneul chajaseo* [On visiting the House of Sharing's Historical Museum of the Japanese Military "Comfort Women"). Seoul: Yeoksa Bipyeongsa.

Nooshin, Laudan. 2004. "Circumnavigation with a Difference? Music, Representation, and the Disney Experience: *It's a Small, Small World.*" *Ethnomusicology Forum* 13, no. 2: 236–51.

O'Brien, Tim. 1990. *The Things They Carried.* Boston: Houghton Mifflin.

Okada Maki and Gerald Groemer. 1991. "Musical Characteristics of Enka." *Popular Music* 10, no. 3: 283–303.

Pilzer, Joshua D. 1999. "Post-Korean War Change in *Sŏdosori,* a Northwest Korean Vocal Genre in Contemporary South Korea." MA thesis, University of Hawai'i.

———. 2003. "Sŏdosori (Northwest Korean Lyric Song) on the Demilitarized Zone: A Study in Music and Teleological Judgment." *Ethnomusicology* 47, no. 1: 68–92.

———. 2006a. "'My Heart, the Number One': Singing in the Lives of South Korean Survivors of Japanese Military Sexual Slavery." PhD diss., University of Chicago.

———. 2006b. "The 20th-century 'Disappearance' of Korean Professional Female Entertainers during the Rise of Korea's Modern Sex-and-Entertainment Industry." In *The Courtesan's Arts: Cross-Cultural Perspectives*, edited by Martha Feldman and Bonnie Gordon, 295–311. New York: Oxford University Press.

———. 2011. "Referential Opacity and the Social Power of Music in South Korea." Unpublished manuscript.

Project on Disney. 1995. *Inside the Mouse: Work and Play at Disney World.* Durham, NC: Duke University Press.

Quine, Willard Van Orman. 1960. *Word and Object.* Cambridge, MA: MIT Press.

Rees, Helen. 2003. "The Age of Consent: Traditional Music, Intellectual Property and Changing Attitudes in the People's Republic of China." *British Journal of Ethnomusicology* 12, no. 1: 137–171.

Robertson, Carol E. 1987. "Power and Gender in the Musical Experiences of Women." In *Women and Music in Cross-Cultural Perspective*, edited by Ellen Koskoff, 225–44. Urbana: University of Illinois Press.

Robertson, Jennifer. 1998. *Takarazuka: Sexual Politics and Popular Culture in Modern Japan.* Berkeley: University of California Press.

Roseman, Marina. 1996. "Pure Products Go Crazy: Rainforest Healing in a Nation-State." In *The Performance of Healing*, edited by Carol Laderman and Marina Roseman, 233–69. New York: Routledge.

Sand, Jordan. 2003. *House and Home in Modern Japan: Architecture, Domestic Space and Bourgeois Culture, 1880–1930.* Cambridge, MA: Harvard University Asia Center.

Scarry, Elaine. 1987. *The Body in Pain: The Making and Unmaking of the World.* New York: Oxford University Press.

Seo Yeongsuk. 2002. *Uri minyo ui segye* [The world of our songs]. Seoul: Doseochulpan yeongnak.

Soh, C. Sarah. 2008. *The Comfort Women: Sexual Violence and Postcolonial Memory in Korea and Japan.* Chicago: University of Chicago Press.

Silhom tongnip manse. 2001. *Tribute to wianbu halmoni* [Tribute to comfort women grandmothers]. CD liner notes. Seoul: Doremi Records DRMCD-1772.

Son, Min Jung. 2006. "Highway Songs in South Korea." In *Korean Pop Music: Riding the Wave*, edited by Keith Howard, 72–81. Kent, England: Global Oriental.

Sørensen, Henrik H. 2010. "Mirror of Emptiness: The Life and Times of the Sŏn Buddhist Kyŏngho Sŏngu." In *Makers of Modern Korean Buddhism*, edited by Jin Y. Park, 131–56. Albany: State University of New York Press.

Stephenson, Shelley. 2000. "The Occupied Screen: Star, Fan and Nation in Shanghai Cinema, 1937–1945." PhD diss., University of Chicago.

Stokes, Martin. 2010. *The Republic of Love: Transformations of Intimacy in Turkish Popular Music.* Chicago: University of Chicago Press.

Tanaka Yuki. 2002. *Japan's Comfort Women: Sexual Slavery and Prostitution during World War II and the U.S. Occupation.* London: Routledge.

Taussig, Michael. 1999. *Defacement: Public Secrecy and the Labor of the Negative.* Stanford: Stanford University Press.

Totsuka, Etsurô. 2001. *"Wianbu" anira "seongnoye" ida* [It's not "comfort woman," it's "sexual slave"]. Seoul: Sonamu Press.

Trezise, Thomas. 2001. "Unspeakable." *Yale Journal of Criticism* 14, no. 1: 39–66.

Tsurumi, Shunsuke. 1987. *A Cultural History of Postwar Japan.* New York: KPI.

Turner, Victor. 1969. *The Ritual Process: Structure and Anti-Structure*. Chicago: Aldine.

Ue Sanemichi et al. 1910. *Jinjyô shôgaku tokuhon shôka* [Standard elementary school songbook]. Tokyo: Mombusho.

Vander, Judith. 1988. *Songprints: The Musical Experience of Five Shoshone Women*. Urbana: University of Illinois Press.

Warner, Michael. 2005. *Publics and Counterpublics*. New York: Zone Books.

Yano, Christine. 1998. "Defining the Modern Nation in Japanese Popular Song, 1914–32." In *Japan's Competing Modernities: Issues in Culture and Democracy*, edited by Sharon A. Minichiello, 247–64. Honolulu: University of Hawai'i Press.

Yeoseongbu and Hanguk jeongsindae yeonguso. 2001. *Hae-oe geoju ilbongun "wianbu" shiltae josajip* [An investigation of the conditions of Japanese military "comfort women" living abroad]. Seoul: Yeoseongbu and Hanguk jeongsindae yeonguso.

Yoshimi Yoshiaki. 1992. *Jugun ianfu shiryôshû* [Military comfort women data collection]. Tokyo: Otsuki Shoten.

———. 1993. *Jonggun wianbu jaryojip* [Military comfort women data collection]. Translated by Yi Gyutae. Seoul: Seomundang.

———. 1995. *The Comfort Women*. Translated by Suzanne O'Brien. New York: Columbia University Press.

Yun Woncheol. 2010. "Zen Master T'oe'ong Sŏngchŏl's Doctrine of Zen Enlightenment and Practice." In *Makers of Modern Korean Buddhism*, edited by Jin Y. Park, 199–228. Albany: State University of New York Press.

DISCOGRAPHY

"Aizen Yakyoku" (Nocturne of Aizen). Kirishima Noboru and Miss Columbia (Nihon Columbia, 30230), 1939.

"Baram gateun saram" (A person like the wind). Kim Gukhwan, *Kim Gukhwan Vol. 8, Baram gateun saram* (Jigu JCS-2788), 1998.

"Bawi cheoreom" (Like a rock). Yu Inhyeok, *Nodong gayo gongsik eumban 2* (Hwaeum Records HD-5040), 1995.

"Beonji eobneun jumak" (A drinking house with no address). Baek Nyeonseol (Taihei 3007), 1943.

"Bulhyoja-neun umnida" (Tears of a faithless child). Jin Bangnam (Taihei 8678), 1938.

"Cha-cha-cha Rock and Roll." Nangnang 18se, *Nangnang 18se* (E&E Media ENEC-031), 2004.

"Chan chan chan." Pyeon Seung-yeop, *Chan chan chan* (Hui Records HRCD-012), 1992.

"Changbu taryeong" (Ballad of the traveling entertainer). Various artists, *Changbu taryeong geoljakseon* (Jigu Records JCDS-0782), 2002.

"Cheonyeo ilgi" (A maiden's diary). Song Dalhyeop (Okeh 12007), 1943.

"Cheongchun mu-gok" (Dance song of youth). *Seujanna* (Ye-geu-rin YGL-703), 1970.

"Chilgapsan" (Chilgap Mountain). Ju Byeongseon, *Ju Byeongseon Vol. 1* (Bando BDL-10), 1989.

"Da hamkke chachacha" (Everybody cha-cha-cha together). Seol Undo, *Seol Undo Vol. 3* (Oasis ORC-1251), 1991.

"Dorawayo Busanhang-e" (Come back to Busan Harbor). Jo Yongpil, *Neomu jjalbayo* (SRB Records SLK-1009), 1976.

"El Cóndor Pasa (If I could)." Simon and Garfunkel, *Bridge over Troubled Water* (Columbia Records KCS 9914), 1970.

"Eochapi ddeo-nan saram" (Anyway, the one who left). Seoul Undo, *Narutbae/Eochapi ddeo-nan saram* (Oasis OL-A-2455), 1982.

"Gajimao" (Don't go). Na Hun-a, *Yakhonnyeo/He-ojyeodo sarang maneun*, split LP with Jo Mimi (Oasis OL-842), 1970.

"Hana ga saku" (A flower is blooming). (Nippo no hon S1016), date unknown.

"Harutbam putsarang" (One night's puppy love). Son Inho, *Hitteu aelbeom* (Oasis OL-12465), 1966.

"Itji mothal yeo-in" (The woman I can't forget). Yi Sangyeol, *71 Oasiseu hitteu ssong seonjip Vol 6* (Oasis OL-976), 1971.

"Kaseum apeuge" (With pain in my breast). Nam Jin, *Araenmaeul ippeuni* (Jigu JLS-120630), 1972.

"Katyusha." Saida Aiko, Victor Josegashodan, and Nihon Victor Orchestra (Nihon Victor A-5117), date unknown.

"Meon hunnal" (Far, later days). Kim Minseong, *Meon Hunnal/Uri-neun seo-roga* (Oasis OL-1987), 1978.

"Monnijeo" (Can't forget). Jang Eunsuk, *Jang Eunsuk Vol. 1* (Universal SIS-78102), 1978.

"Monnijeul dangsin" (Unforgettable you). Yi Mija, *Hiteu gokseon Vol. 13* (Jigu JLS-120484), 1972.

"Miwoyo" (I hate). Sim Subong, *Best Vol. 2* (Hyeondae Eumhyang HDBS-8809), 1989.

"Mokpo ui nunmul" (Tears of Mokpo). Yi Nan-yeong (Okeh 1795), 1935.

"Namhaeng yeolcha" (Southbound train). Kim Suhui, *Kim Suhui Vol. 1* (Asea Records ACD-071), 1989.

"Nareuneun sae cheoreom" (Like a flying bird). Ddua e Mua, *Hit Album Vol. 2* (Universal Records GH00014), 1971.

"Nebakja" (Four-beat rhythm). Song Dae-gwan, *Norae wa insaeng* (Oasis 1618), 1998.

"Norae karak" (Song-tune). Various artists, *Gyeonggi minyo vol. 1* (Oasis ORC-1415), 1994.

"Nunmul jeojeun Duman-gang" (Tear-soaked Duman River). Kim Jeong-gu (Okeh 12094), 1938.

"Ppae-atkin sunjeong" (Stolen innocence). Silhom Dongnip Manse, *Tribute to wianbu halmoni* (Doremi Media DRMCD-1772), 2001.

"Pusanhan-e kaere" (Come back to Busan Harbor). Atsumi Jiro (CBS/Sony 07SH1389), 1983.

"Sae taryeong" (Ballad of the birds). Various artists, *Namdo minyo vol. 1* (Oasis ORC-1417), 1994.

"Sarangeun amuna hana" (Can everyone love?). Tae Jin-a, *2000 Tae Jin-a* (Daeyeong A/V DYCD-1108), 2000.

"Scarborough Fair/Canticle." Simon and Garfunkel, *Parsley, Sage, Rosemary, and Thyme* (Columbia Records CS 9363), 1966.

"Seukabeuro ui chueok" (Memories of Scarborough). Ddua e Mua, *Hit Album Vol. 1* (Grand Records GH00004), 1970.

"Shina no yoru "(China nights). Watanabe Hamako (Nihon Columbia 30051), 1938.

"Soshyû yakyoku" (Suzhou nocturne). Yamaguchi Yoshiko (Nihon Columbia JL-31), 1953.

"Ue wo muite arukô" (Let's look up and walk). Sakamoto Kyû (Toshiba JP-5083), 1961.

"Ulgin wae ureo" (Crying, why cry). Na Hun-a, *1982 Vol. 3* (Daeyang Eumhyang TYL-1006), 1982.

"Ureora gitajura" (Cry, guitar string). Son Inho, *Son Inho and others, Uleora gitajul-a* (Oasis OL 10417), 1960.

"Uska Dara (a Turkish Tale)." Eartha Kitt (Nihon Victor S-107), 1953.

"Usukudara, Turko tan" (Uska Dara, a Turkish tale). Eri Chiemi (King Records CL-160), 1954.

INDEX

collaboration with Japanese colonial authority, 25
"comfort women" as victims of colonial, sexual, and other sorts of exploitation, 28
conscription campaigns during Asia-Pacific War, 80
critical reexamination of Japanese colonial era discouraged under authoritarianism, 8
feminism, and issues of race and colonialism, 28
Gwangbokjeol (Independence Day), 28, 96, 97
"liberation songs" (*haebang-ga*), 45
and moral authority for South Korean dictatorships, 25
song as part of practice of domination, 75, 76
wounds of colonial era, 25
See also post-colonial Korea
"comfort station," Japanese euphemism for military sex camp, 34
"comfort women" (*ianfu*), 7, 8
archetypal, 10, 27, 28, 52, 59, 95–97, 108
as composite of colonial, sexual, and other sorts of exploitation, 28
cost to patrons, 148
diet, 150
movement. *See* activism and "comfort women" movement
number of, 7, 156n10
number of survivors, 156n1
resulting health issues
hearing loss, xiii, 34, 53, 145, 149, 152
lymphogranuloma inguinale, 168n8
singing with and for soldiers, 15, 75, 76, 100
suicides, 8
"comfort women grandmothers"
archetypal, 10, 27, 28, 52, 59, 95–97, 108
double-consciousness, 86
social tendency to ignore songs and stories of elderly women, 63
stipends for survivors, 16
Tribute to wianbu halmeoni (Tribute to comfort women grandmothers), 92, 93

vague statement of apology by Japanese, 7, 18. *See also* activism and "comfort women" movement, aging
conscription campaigns during Asia-Pacific War, 80
contraception, 148, 149
cosmopolitanism. *See* Bae Chunhui
"courtesan tourism" (*gisaeng gwan-gwang*) industry in South Korea, 116
crying
in song, 67, 74, 8–7, 90, 101, 102, songs as, 27
transformation into laughter, 63
"Crying, Why Cry?" ("Ulgin wae ureo"), 102
cultural nonlistening, 11
"culture life" (*bunka seikatsu*) in Japan, 118

daejung gayo (mass/popular song), 78
dancing, with Mun Pilgi, 68
deafness of Pak Duri, 34, 37, 145, 149, 152
death
apprehension and defetishization of, 43, 49, 50, 53
death and mortality themes in song, 49, 51
of Mun Pilgi, 71, 103
of Pak Duri, 65
Pak Duri's wish for, 65
DeNora, Tia, 155n3, 157n4
Deokgyeong Kang. *See Kang Deokgyeong*
diet. *See* food
directness about sex. *See* bawdiness
double-consciousness, 86
Dragged Away (*Kkeullyeogam*), painting by Kim Sundeok, 93
dreams
Bae Chunhui's dream visit by Shakyamuni, 124
iljang chunmong (one night's spring dream), 47
Mun Pilgi's nightmares, 71, 74, 75
Pak Duri's nightmares, 35
drinking houses (*suljip*), 71, 84, 107, 124, 125
Du Bois, W.E.B., 162n19
Duri Pak. *See Pak Duri*

Eckert, Carter, 157n12
English subtitles in *The Murmuring*, 60, 61

enka, 78, 119, 122
  origin of, 161n8
  similarities and differences between
    Korean teuroteu and Japanese
    enka, 123
  teuroteu, enka-style balladry coming to be
    known as, 79
Everland theme park, 138–140
everyday speech and testimony
    (jeung-eon), 55

Feld, Stephen, 166n35
female professional entertainers (gisaeng),
    43, 44, 46, 130, 164n10, 164 n11
feminism, and issues of race and
    colonialism, 28
film trilogy by Byun Young-joo, 46, 50, 55,
    60–63, 65, 73, 158n14
first lines of songs vs. titles of songs, 46, 47,
    99, 130
Fiumara, Gemma, 11
Flam, Gila, 15
folk music, 42–44
  flexibility of folk song medium, 40, 83
  modern popularization of some
    repertoires, 43
  sinminyo (new folk song), 128, 132
  sorikkun (itinerant male professional
    folksingers), 44
  standardization of folk songs, 44, 45
  as tool of emotional transformation, 41
food
  eating at the House of Sharing, 28, 29,
    31, 109
  eating wild greens to survive, 145
  hunger of women in sex camps, 107, 150
  inside of pine tree as food, 3, 4, 67
  intimate experience, eating as, 25
forced military service and labor during
    Asia-Pacific War, 80
foreign language ability, 39, 108, 113, 117,
    134, 135, 150
Fox, Aaron, 48
friendships
  Kim Sundeok and Pak Duri, 64
  Mun Pilgi and Bae Chunhui, 100, 125
  during internment at sex camp, 150
Fujiko, as Pak Duri's Japanese name, 149

gaeryang hanbok (modernized Korean
    clothing), 130, 135

geori (section of shaman ceremony), 42
ghosts, visitation by, 35, 64
Gilroy, Paul, 162n19
gisaeng (female professional entertainers),
    43, 46, 116, 130
gisaeng gwan-gwang ("courtesan tourism")
    industry in South Korea, 116,
gochu (hot pepper), Korean slang for male
    sex organ, 92
gohyang (hometown)
  characterization of in song, 6, 84, 86–7
  displacement from, 80
  longing for, 6, 79, 125,
  return to, 70, 124, 151
grandmother (halmeoni), 17, 20. See also
    "comfort women grandmothers"
gunka (military songs), 112, 122
Gwangbokjeol (Independence Day), 28,
    96, 97
gwangdae (itinerant male entertainers),
    42, 43
gwangdaesin, 42
Gyeongancheon (river), 20

Habitual Sadness. See Najeun moksori 2
haebang-ga ("liberation songs"), 45
halmeoni (grandmother), 17, 20. See also
    "comfort women grandmothers"
han, 26, 27, 96
  defined, 26, 157n9
Han Dosun, 29, 125
Han, Hongkoo, 25
Han River, 20
Hanguk jeongshindae munje daechaek
    hyobuihoe. See Korean Council for
    Women Drafted for Military Sexual
    Slavery by Japan
Hannerz, Ulf, 120
Hendrix, Jimi, 93
Herman, Judith, 52, 53, 75, 160n42
High Plains Drifter, 122
historic background of Japanese popular
    music, 78, 79, 117–119
historic background of Korean popular
    music, 78–81
hometown (gohyang). See gohyang
hope
  and han, 27
  "Huimang ui norae" ("Songs of hope"), 63
  "Song of Hope" ("Huimang-ga"), 142
  threshold of despair and, 65

hot pepper (*gochu*), Korean slang for male
  sex organ, 92
hourglass drum. *See janggo*
House of Sharing (Nanum ui jip), 3, 16,
  21–26
  Bae Chunhui at, 100, 125, 132
  as center of activism, 22
  history of, 21
  Mun Pilgi's move to, 71
  Pak Duri's move to, 35, 152
  photographs, 22–24, 42
  source of name, 25
Howard, Keith, 158*n*12
humor and laughter, 32, 33, 38–40, 49, 51,
  53, 65
  bringing listeners together, 39, 40, 49,
    51, 77
  life raft on sea of hardship and sorrow, 6
  suffering turned into laughter, 53
  three-part pattern of vitality, death, and
    laughter, 51
  as trope in song, 74
hunger
  inside of pine tree as food, 3, 4, 67
  suffered by Bae Chunhui, 107, 150
  suffered by Pak Duri, 150
Hwang Geumju, 17, 19, 20, 157*n*7
hyeongnim, 157*n*2
Hyon Kiron, 157*n*12

ianfu. See "comfort women"
Ilja ne maeum (My heart, the number one),
  painting by Mun Pilgi, 87, 88
iljang chunmong (one night's spring
  dream), 47
ilpyeon dansim (singleness of heart/mind),
  87, 104
Im Oksang, 24
improvisation, 40, 44, 45, 157*n*7
Independence Day (*Gwangbokjeol*), 28,
  96, 97
industrialization of folk songs, 44, 45
innocence
  Ppae-atgin sunjeong (Stolen innocence)
    painting by Kang Deokgyeong,
    91–93
  in Mun Pilgi's song world, 90, 91
Isakovsky, Mikhail, 112
isolation, 8, 10, 53, 73
  of traumatic experience, 76
  of the wanderer, 85

itinerant male entertainers (*gwangdae*),
  42, 43
itinerant male professional folksingers
  (*sorikkun*), 44
Ivy, Marylin, 162*n*18

janggo (Korean hourglass drum), 116, 124,
  125, 128, 130, 135
  photograph, 66
Japan
  allied occupation, cabaret scene during,
    114, 115
  allied occupation, sex industry during,
    114, 115
  Bae Chunhui's life in Japan. *See* Bae
    Chunhui
  budan seiji (Japanese military government
    policy in colonial Korea), 79
  "culture life" (*bunka seikatsu*)
    in Japan, 118
  denial of official system of military sexual
    slavery, 35
  historic background of Japanese popular
    music, 78, 79, 117–119
  increased importation of South Korean
    popular films, music, and
    television, 123
  Japanese colonial period (1910–1945).
    See colonialism
  Korean residents in, 107, 108, 114–117,
    120–124, 128, 129
  popularity of Korean music in, 118, 122,
    135, 136
  reparations and apology to women, 17, 18,
    63, 65, 97, 126, 153
  responsibility for wartime crimes, 36
  revision of ideas of "Japanese music" and
    Japanese cultural history, 12
  Western songs in Japanese music,
    117–119
  Women's Volunteer Labor Corps, 163*n*25
  See also colonialism, popular music
Japanese language
  Pak Duri's testimony regarding, 150
  transliterations, xvii
Japanese-occupied Shanghai, 6, 114, 119
Jeju Island Uprising, 129
Jeong Hunhui, 133
Jeong Jae-eun, 89
jeongshindae ("volunteer corps"), 163*n*25
jeung-eon, (testimony), 55. *See also* testimony

mantras sung by Mun Pilgi, 87
marginalization, 10, 74, 104. *See also* isolation, loneliness, outsider experience
melisma, defined, 159*n*17
memories. *See* remembering
metaphor
   to evade censors, 80
   love as metaphor for domination, 119
   nation as female, 25
   technique of layering, displacing, and concealing meaning, 41
military conscription campaigns during Asia-Pacific War, 80
military songs (*gunka*), 112, 122
missionaries, effect on popular music, 78
moral authority
   national, colonial wounds as source of, 25, 27, 95, 96
   survivors' senses of, 27
mudang, 42
Mun Pilgi, 3, 4, 17, 67–104, 143
   activism and participation in "comfort women" movement, 71, 72, 91, 97
   and archetypal "comfort woman grandmother," 95–97
   Bae Chunhui, friendship with, 100, 125
   cassette listening, 4, 72, 73
   childhood, 68, 69
   dancing with, 68
   death of, 71, 103
   education, desire for, 69, 70, 81
   grandson of sister, raised by Mun Pilgi, 71
   innocence in song world, 91
   My Heart, the Number One (*Ilja ne maeum*), painting by Mun Pilgi, 88, 89
   nightmares, 71, 74, 75
   "number eighteen" (*sipbalbeon*) showpiece songs, 82, 83, 89, 103
   onomatopoeic expression, 74
   paintings by, 87, 88
   parents of, 68, 69, 73, 81, 82
   photographs of, 19, 22, 69, 72, 98, 104
   public attention, 91, 97
   quiet of social repression and traumatic experience, 74
   recruitment to Japanese sexual slavery, 70
   self-purification, 83, 87, 88, 90, 96, 103
   soldiers, singing with and for, 75, 76, 100

solitude and loneliness, 71, 73, 74, 77
   and quiet, 4, 74
song as tactic of recovery, 75
   escape from isolation of traumatic experience and toward social and personal coherence, 76, 77
   reworking lyrics, 77, 82, 83
   reworking melodies, 83
   sociality of sound and music, 75
song party on bus, 67, 68, 77, 97–99
song world
   change in, 89
   innocence in song world, 91
   suljip (drinking houses), work in, 71, 84
   television viewing, 4, 73, 75, 76, 89
   testimony, 91, 98
   and *teuroteu*, 68, 73–76, 84–90, 93, 96–102
   as wanderer, 71, 84–86, 89
The Murmuring. See Najeun moksori
My Heart, the Number One (*Ilja ne maeum*), painting by Mun Pilgi, 88, 89

Na Hun-a, 102, 127
Na Un-gyu, 118
Najeun moksori (*The Murmuring*), 59, 62, 65
   English subtitles in *Najeun moksori*, providing example of containment of song play, 60, 61
   irony of film title, 160*n*32
   as part of film trilogy by Byun Young-joo, 50, 55, 60–63, 65
Najeun moksori 2 (*Habitual Sadness*), 50, 62
   as part of film trilogy by Byun Young-joo, 50, 55, 60–63, 65
nanum (sharing), in Korean culture, 25, 26
Nanum ui chukje, 157*n*8
Nanum ui jip. *See* House of Sharing
narrativization process in traumatic recovery, 52
nationalism, 25–28
   fickleness of national interest in "comfort women issue," 97
   national woundedness, 25, 27, 28, 52, 62
   patriarchal nationalism, interest in sexual exploitation issues, 28
   peak surrounding *Gwangbokjeol* (Independence Day), 28, 96, 97
   practical applications of women's suffering to nationalist causes, 27

spoken expressions of suffering in contrast to humorous transformations of suffering in song play, 59, 63

sung eloquence, transferability to speech, 69

in testimony (*jeung-eon*), 55

explosion of song out of talk, 46, 47, 49

expressive life normalized to meet social expectations, 61

friendships during internment at sex camp, 150

ghosts, visitation by, 64

headaches, 152

House of Sharing, move to, 35, 152

humor and laughter, 32, 33, 38–40, 49, 51, 53, 65

    bringing listeners together in laughter, 39, 40, 49, 51

    suffering turned into laughter, 53

    three-part pattern of vitality, death, and laughter, 51

interview by Byun Young-joo, 55

testimony, 55, 56, 64, 145–53

language, choice of, 47, 48, 51, 56

"liberation" from sex camp, 34, 151

loneliness

    at the House of Sharing, 125

    pattern of being left behind, 33

    transformed into companionship, 4, 53, 74

    as trope in song and talk, 4, 53, 73

marriage and husband, 34, 55, 64, 151, 152

medical examination, 149

nightmares, 35, 64

"number eighteen" (*sipbalbeon*) showpiece song, 38

parents and siblings, 145, 146, 151

    letters to parents, 150

patrons at sex camp, description of, 147, 148

philosophical expression in song, 43, 47

photographs, 32, 36, 42, 57

playing tricks, 33

power and domination, reversing relations of, 51, 52, 54

public expectations

    expressive life normalized to meet social expectations, 61

"normal forming" of text to create political message, 61

publicity in later life, 54, 58, 59, 63, 64

recruitment by Japanese, 33, 146, 152

refrain, "*a-ni nojineun mot harira*," 42

refrain of "I suffered," 55, 56

reparations from Japanese government, desire for, 153

    legal action, 36, 37

sexuality, 40, 41, 52, 53

in Shōka (Changhua), 146–148, 152

silence, propriety pressuring silence about experiences, 41, 59

simultaneous celebration of life and apprehension of death, 43

smoking and drinking habits, 31, 34, 35, 37, 50, 148, 152, 153

"song play," 40–42, 59–64

song world of, 49, 53–56, 59–64

    platform for expression of joy, fear, and philosophy of life, 47

    power and domination, reversing relations of, 51, 52, 54

    recording of, 63

    spoken expressions of suffering in contrast to humorous transformations of suffering in song play, 59, 63

spiritual advisor, Kim Sundeok, 68

style, 39, 40, 47, 56

taboo subjects, 49, 54

    bawdiness, 5, 49–53, 61, 64

    English subtitles in *The Murmuring*, providing example of containment of song play, 60, 61

in Taiwan, 146–148, 152

testimony regarding enslavement, 145–153

    beatings, 149, 152

    clothing and makeup, 148

    contraception, 148, 149

    cost to soldiers, 148

    deception of parents, 151

    diet, 150

    eloquence in, 55, 56, 64

    Fujiko as Japanese name, 149

    hunger, 150

    interview by Byun Young-joo, 55

    Japanese language requirement, 150

    parents, letters to, 150

    punishment, 149, 150, 152

of national solidarity and moral
authority, 27
sex and entertainment industry, 8, 18,
84, 116
wounds of colonial era, 25, 27, 28,
52, 62
Ppae-atgin sunjeong (*Stolen innocence*),
painting by Kang Deokgyeong,
91–93, 95
Project on Disney, 167n44
public expectations
breaking unspoken rules, 40
expressive life normalized to meet, 61
pressure to reawaken or perform
woundedness, 27
speaking competency, 58
public secrets, 9, 10
punishment suffered by Pak Duri, 149,
150, 152

question and answer in song, 48
quiet, 4, 73, 74, 77. *See also* silence
Quine, Willard Van Orman, 138

radio and recording
boundary of live and recorded sound, 74
cassette exchange, 135
effect on popular music and cultural
circulation, 43, 44, 78, 79, 118
learning songs from cassettes, 73, 117, 125
listening to, xi, 4, 72, 73
rebirth in song, 94, 95
recruitment to sex camps
Bae Chunhui, 107
Mun Pilgi, 70
Pak Duri, 33, 146, 152
remembering
integration of traumatic memories, 75–77
repressed memories, 27
singing to remember, 9
reparations and apology by Japanese
government, 17, 18, 63, 65, 97,
126, 153
legal action, 36, 37
revision of reductive categories of "Korean
music" and "Korean experience," 12
reworking lyrics, 39, 40, 45, 77, 82, 83
reworking melodies, 39, 40, 83
Ri Kôran (Li Xianglan), 119–121
rock/*teuroteu* fusion, 124
Ruslanova, Lidiya, 112

Sand, Jordan, 164n13
Scarry, Elaine, 54
Secret Garden, 6, 126
Seol Undo, 89
sexuality
bawdiness, 5, 49–53, 61, 64
expressed in song, 40, 41
sexlessness of archetypal "comfort woman
grandmother," 40, 52, 53
sexually transmitted diseases, 149
shamanism
and "Ballad of the Traveling Entertainer,"
42, 43
majority of shamans as women, 158n8
shamanist expressions in song, 42, 43, 49
sharing (*nanum*), in Korean culture, 25, 26
Shina no yoru (China nights) film, 119
Shôka (Changhua), 146–148, 152
showpiece songs. *See* "number eighteen"
songs
silence
about experiences, 41
"listening silences," 11
See also quiet
Sim Subong, 125, 132
sinminyo (new folk song), 118, 128, 132
sipbalbeon. See "number eighteen" songs
society and social issues
aging, social tendency to ignore songs and
stories of elderly women, 63
marginalization, 10, 74, 104
outsider experience, 8, 10, 85, 89, 104,
121, 122, 133
song as escape from isolation of
traumatic experience, 76, 77. *See also*
loneliness
morality, social order and, 46
nonlistening, 11
quiet of social repression and traumatic
experience, 74
rebirth of person as capable subject and
social actor, recovery from trauma
requiring, 75
solidarity forged through song, 9
sound and music, sociality of, 75
"speed personality" society in modern
Korea, 20
traumatic memory, asocial nature of, 75
soldiers, singing with and for, 15, 75, 76, 100
Son Inho, 84, 90, 101
Son Panim, 59

titles of songs *vs.* first lines of songs, 46

Tokushu ian shisetsu kyōkai ("Special Comfort Facility Association"), 164*n*8

tong-gita (acoustic guitar) music, 161*n*12

transliterations of Korean and Japanese languages, xvii

transnational revision of reductive categories of "Korean music" and "Korean experience," 12

traumatic experience
  asocial nature of traumatic memory, 75
  coherence, trauma recovery requiring integration of memories, 75–77
  difficulty of approaching solely through language, 7
  escape from isolation of traumatic experience, 76, 77
  and *han*, 27
  inchoate nature of traumatic memories, 75, 76
  making sense of, 27, 50
  music's participation in, 15
  narrativization process in traumatic recovery, 52, 75
  recovery, stages, 52, 53

traveling entertainers, 42–44, 158*n*10
  "Ballad of the Traveling Entertainer," 31, 39, 41–48, 50, 56, 59, 60, 62, 143
  deified itinerant outcast traveling entertainers, 42
  gwangdae (itinerant male entertainers), 42, 43

The Tree of Aizen (*Aizen Katsura*), 100

tribute projects to "comfort women", 92, 93

True Stories of the Korean Comfort Women, 15

trust issues, 33, 36, 37, 61, 107, 108, 111

Turner, Victor, 158*n*13

Unblossomed Flower (*Motdapin kkot*), painting by Kim Sundeok, 23, 93, 95, 157*n*8

Unblossomed Flower (*Motdapin kkot*) statue, 23, 24, 93

"unspeakable" experiences, 9. *See also* taboo subjects

victims seeking kinds of power denied them by torturers, 54

voices, language and meaning valued over, 11

"volunteer corps" (*jeongshindae*), 163*n*25

wanderer, Mun Pilgi as, 71, 84–86, 89

Wang Luobin, 121, 133

Wednesday demonstrations, xiv, 16–20
  directions to, 16
  Bae Chunhui's participation in, 17, 19, 105, 108, 117
  Mun Pilgi's participation in, 17, 19, 71, 97
  Pak Duri's participation in, 17, 37
  Singing on the way to, 28

wianbu. See "comfort women"

Woman of the Earth, 24

woundedness ideology, 25, 27, 28, 52, 58, 61, 62, 64, 65, 94–96, 108
  providing receptive audience to acknowledge and validate experiences, 58

Yajima Tsukasa, 71, 133, 135

Yamaguchi Yoshiko (Ri Kōran), 119

Yano, Christine, 164*n*18

Yi Eunhye, 94

Yi Jaeho, 81, 84, 166*n*28

Yi Mija, 89

Yi Nan-yeong, 80

Yi Okseon, 21, 29, 38, 128, 132, 133, 157*n*8, 161*n*11

Yi Sanghun, 91, 92, 95, 96

Yi Yongnyeo, 130

Yi Yongsu, 19, 77, 78

Yoshimi Yoshiyaki, 156*n*10

Yu Inhyeok, 17

Yun Mee-hyang, 19, 28, 67, 163*n*29

Yun Yeongseok, 23

yunnori (stick-throwing game), 130